SpringerBriefs in Energy

SpringerBriefs in Energy presents concise summaries of cutting-edge research and practical applications in all aspects of Energy. Featuring compact volumes of 50 to 125 pages, the series covers a range of content from professional to academic. Typical topics might include:

- A snapshot of a hot or emerging topic
- A contextual literature review
- A timely report of state-of-the art analytical techniques
- An in-depth case study
- A presentation of core concepts that students must understand in order to make independent contributions.

Briefs allow authors to present their ideas and readers to absorb them with minimal time investment.

Briefs will be published as part of Springer's eBook collection, with millions of users worldwide. In addition, Briefs will be available for individual print and electronic purchase. Briefs are characterized by fast, global electronic dissemination, standard publishing contracts, easy-to-use manuscript preparation and formatting guidelines, and expedited production schedules. We aim for publication 8–12 weeks after acceptance.

Both solicited and unsolicited manuscripts are considered for publication in this series. Briefs can also arise from the scale up of a planned chapter. Instead of simply contributing to an edited volume, the author gets an authored book with the space necessary to provide more data, fundamentals and background on the subject, methodology, future outlook, etc.

SpringerBriefs in Energy contains a distinct subseries focusing on Energy Analysis and edited by Charles Hall, State University of New York. Books for this subseries will emphasize quantitative accounting of energy use and availability, including the potential and limitations of new technologies in terms of energy returned on energy invested.

More information about this series at http://www.springer.com/series/8903

Bruno Michoud · Manfred Hafner

Financing Clean Energy Access in Sub-Saharan Africa

Risk Mitigation Strategies and Innovative Financing Structures

Bruno Michoud
Fondazione Eni Enrico Mattei
Milan, Italy

Manfred Hafner
Fondazione Eni Enrico Mattei
Milan, Italy

SciencesPo—Paris School of
International Affairs
Paris, France

Johns Hopkins University—School of
Advanced International Studies
(SAIS-Europe)
Bologna, Italy

ISSN 2191-5520 ISSN 2191-5539 (electronic)
SpringerBriefs in Energy
ISBN 978-3-030-75828-8 ISBN 978-3-030-75829-5 (eBook)
https://doi.org/10.1007/978-3-030-75829-5

© The Author(s) 2021. This book is an open access publication.
Open Access This book is licensed under the terms of the Creative Commons Attribution 4.0 International License (http://creativecommons.org/licenses/by/4.0/), which permits use, sharing, adaptation, distribution and reproduction in any medium or format, as long as you give appropriate credit to the original author(s) and the source, provide a link to the Creative Commons license and indicate if changes were made.

The images or other third party material in this book are included in the book's Creative Commons license, unless indicated otherwise in a credit line to the material. If material is not included in the book's Creative Commons license and your intended use is not permitted by statutory regulation or exceeds the permitted use, you will need to obtain permission directly from the copyright holder.

The use of general descriptive names, registered names, trademarks, service marks, etc. in this publication does not imply, even in the absence of a specific statement, that such names are exempt from the relevant protective laws and regulations and therefore free for general use.

The publisher, the authors and the editors are safe to assume that the advice and information in this book are believed to be true and accurate at the date of publication. Neither the publisher nor the authors or the editors give a warranty, expressed or implied, with respect to the material contained herein or for any errors or omissions that may have been made. The publisher remains neutral with regard to jurisdictional claims in published maps and institutional affiliations.

This Springer imprint is published by the registered company Springer Nature Switzerland AG
The registered company address is: Gewerbestrasse 11, 6330 Cham, Switzerland

Foreword

With some of the lowest energy access rates in the world, most of sub-Saharan Africa suffers from extreme energy poverty. The potential for clean energy access in sub-Saharan Africa is, however, mindboggling. After all, most of its countries are located on the solar belt. In fact, given its high solar irradiation, solar belt countries could not only provide affordable clean energy for everyone, everywhere in Sub-Saharan Africa, but also potentially power large parts of the world. Its potential, however, remains largely unrealised.

Given the potential of sub-Saharan Africa to power vast parts of the world, a global rather than local solution to finance clean energy access is needed. A 2019 Boston Consulting Group (BCG) study indicated that there is ample capital available, globally, to finance clean energy access projects. With more than $200 trillion of global accumulated wealth, access to finance should not be a problem. While the local risks (i.e. economic and financial factors, overall country situation, the business environment and environmental and social considerations) as categorised by the authors need to be addressed, global access to financing needs to be channelled to the region.

Oil and gas companies are navigating their own energy transition, and Shell, Total, BP and ENI have made commitments to become net-zero emission companies by 2050 or earlier. The market capitalisation of renewable energy companies, such as Enel, Iberdrola, Nextera and Orsted, has equalled or surpassed that of the oil and gas companies, including the mighty Exxon Mobil Corporation. By making them part of the solution, sub-Saharan Africa could secure its own clean energy access, while selling surplus renewable energy on international markets. After all, international energy companies bring the following to the table:

- Access to financing: International companies can tap into capital markets to raise equity financing.
- Project structuring: Projects can be constructed as public–private partnerships, which have the advantage over publicly funded projects that they are risk incentivised. The involvement of the public sector ensures that local bureaucratic barriers are addressed in a timely manner.

- Access to technology: International companies have access to technology that may not be locally available. The creation of joint ventures with local partners would combine state-of-the-art access to technology with local entrepreneurship and low labour costs.
- Project execution: International companies often have excellent track records in project execution and deliver projects on time and at cost.
- Involvement of multilateral banks: International companies have experience working with multilateral banks. Involvement of these would further risk incentivise the local government and potentially reduce the cost of capital.

The combination of addressing the local risks with global access to financing will allow sub-Saharan Africa to address its clean energy challenges, while becoming part of a global solution to accelerate the sustainable energy transition.

The authors of the book *Financing Clean Energy Access in Sub-Saharan Africa: Risk Mitigation Strategies and Innovative Financing Structures* make a compelling case of how to overcome the investment barriers to address clean energy access challenges.

Prof. Alexander Van de Putte
IE Business School, Madrid, Spain

Astana International Financial Centre,
Nur-Sultan, Kazakhstan

Acknowledgements

Support from the Fondazione Eni Enrico Mattei (FEEM) in realising this book and financing its open access is gratefully acknowledged. Founded 1989, FEEM is a non-profit, policy-oriented and international research centre and think tank producing high-quality, scientifically sound, innovative and interdisciplinary applied research on sustainable development. It contributes to the quality of decision-making in the public and private spheres through analytical studies, policy advice, scientific dissemination and high-level education. Thanks to its international network, FEEM integrates its research and dissemination activities with those of the best academic institutions and think tanks around the world. It applies its methodology to a wide range of issues, including energy scenarios, infrastructures, financing, market analyses and socio-economic impacts of energy policies. This innovative and interdisciplinary approach puts together the major factors driving the change in global energy dynamics (i.e. technological, economic, financial, geopolitical, institutional and sociological aspects).

The authors are particularly thankful to Simone Tagliapietra, Senior Researcher at FEEM, for his valuable comments all along the elaboration of this book.

Milan, Italy
March 2021

Bruno Michoud
Manfred Hafner

Contents

1	**Introduction**		1
	References		6
2	**Energy Access in Sub-Saharan Africa: General Context**		7
	2.1	The Importance of Energy	8
		2.1.1 The Root Causes of Energy Poverty	10
		2.1.2 Energy, Welfare and Economic Development	11
		2.1.3 Climate Change and Price Volatility	14
		2.1.4 Health and Gender Considerations	15
	2.2	The Financing Gaps	15
	2.3	Current Investment Trends	17
		2.3.1 Electricity Access	18
		2.3.2 Clean Cooking	21
	References		25
3	**Risk Analysis and Mitigation Strategy Identification**		27
	3.1	Investment Opportunities in the Clean Energy Sector	28
		3.1.1 Stand-Alone Systems	28
		3.1.2 Mini-Grids	29
		3.1.3 Medium- and Large-Scale Power Generation Plants	30
		3.1.4 National Grid	31
		3.1.5 Clean Cooking Systems	32
	3.2	Identification of Core Stakeholders	33
		3.2.1 Capital Providers	33
	3.3	Identification of Investment Risks	42
		3.3.1 Investment Risks	42
		3.3.2 Risk Management as a Dynamic and Context-Dependent Process	42
		3.3.3 Risk Definition	43
		3.3.4 Risks Associated with Investment Opportunities	48

	3.4	De-risking Strategies and Risk Mitigation Actions	50
		3.4.1 Four Different Spheres of Interest	51
		3.4.2 Risk Mitigation Strategy Identification	51
	References		53
4	**Public Policies and Initiatives in the Energy Sector**		**57**
	4.1	The Importance of Energy Policies	58
	4.2	National Energy Planning	59
	4.3	Public Sector Initiatives	60
		4.3.1 Governance and Management Practices	60
		4.3.2 Market Information	61
		4.3.3 Standards of Quality	61
		4.3.4 Administrative Procedures	62
		4.3.5 Pipeline Facilities	64
		4.3.6 Capacity Building	64
		4.3.7 Awareness Campaigns	65
		4.3.8 Rural Energy Agencies	67
		4.3.9 Grid Arrival and Access to the National Grid	67
	4.4	Utility Reform	68
	4.5	Tariff Setting	70
		4.5.1 Mini-Grids	70
		4.5.2 National Grid	73
	4.6	International Cooperation and Partnerships	74
		4.6.1 Regional Power Pools	75
	4.7	Fiscal Incentives	76
	4.8	Subsidies	76
		4.8.1 Subsidies in the Clean Energy Sector	77
		4.8.2 Subsidy Reform	78
	4.9	Priority Sector Lending	79
	4.10	Obstacles and Opportunities for a Fast and Comprehensive Implementation—The Political Economy of Policy Implementation	79
	References		81
5	**Direct and Indirect Investments in the Energy Sector**		**83**
	5.1	The Role of Public Finance	84
	5.2	Traditional and Alternative Financial Instruments	84
		5.2.1 Grants	85
		5.2.2 Debt-Like Instruments	86
		5.2.3 Equity-Like Investments	88
	5.3	Special-Purpose Investment Vehicles	88
	5.4	Alternative Financial Structures	89
		5.4.1 Blended Finance	89
		5.4.2 Crowdfunding Platforms	91
		5.4.3 Structured Finance	93

Contents

		5.4.4	Financial Structures for Large and Complex Energy Projects	97
	References			100
6	**Capital Markets for the Financing of Clean Energy Access in Sub-Saharan Africa**			**103**
	6.1	Green Bonds		104
		6.1.1	Other Financing Opportunities in the Bond Markets	107
	6.2	A Price on Carbon: Carbon Pricing and Carbon Finance as Sources of Capital		108
		6.2.1	Clean Development Mechanism (CDM)	110
		6.2.2	Voluntary Carbon Markets (VCMs)	111
		6.2.3	Carbon Market Shortcomings	111
	6.3	The Financial Sector and Capital Markets in Africa		112
		6.3.1	The Development of Capital Markets	113
		6.3.2	African Banking Systems	116
	References			117
7	**Risk Mitigation Instruments Targeting Specific Investment Risks**			**119**
	7.1	Guarantee Instruments and Insurance		119
		7.1.1	Guarantees Issued by Governments	120
		7.1.2	Political Risk Guarantees and Insurance	121
		7.1.3	Credit Risk Guarantees	121
	7.2	Currency Risk Mitigation		121
	7.3	Liquidity Risk Mitigation		124
		7.3.1	Public External Liquidity Facilities	124
		7.3.2	Liquidity Guarantees	124
		7.3.3	Internal Liquidity Facilities	125
	References			125
8	**Business Model Adaptation**			**127**
	8.1	Strategies for Risk Transfer		128
	8.2	Strategies for Risk Avoidance and Compensation		129
		8.2.1	Customer Risk in the Off-Grid and Clean Cooking Sectors	129
		8.2.2	Power Utilities and Low-Income Households	131
		8.2.3	Political Risk	133
		8.2.4	Strategic Partnerships	133
		8.2.5	Operational Risk	134
		8.2.6	Social Acceptance Risk	135
	8.3	External Consulting		135
	References			136

9	**The Role of Multilateral Agencies and Development Banks**		137
	9.1	Capacity Building, Technical Assistance and Advisory Services	138
		9.1.1 Public Sector	138
		9.1.2 Project Developers	139
		9.1.3 Financial Institutions and Capital Providers	139
	9.2	Direct Investments	139
	9.3	Mobilisation Tools	140
	9.4	Stakeholder Engagement and Management	141
	9.5	Business Model Evolution	142
	References		143
10	**Conclusions and Policy Recommendations**		145
	10.1	Creating an Enabling Investment and Business Environment	146
	10.2	Improvement of Risk-Reward Profiles of Investment Opportunities	148
	10.3	Deployment of Mechanisms Aimed at Catalysing Private Capital	149
11	**Further Areas of Work**		151
12	**Annex**		153
	12.1	Annex 1: Definition of the Tiers of the Multitier Framework (MTF) Initiative	153
	12.2	Annex 2: Population With Access to Electricity and Clean Cooking In African Countries	154
	12.3	Annex 3: Risks Associated With Investment Opportunities and Stakeholders	156
	12.4	Annex 4: De-risking Matrix	186
	12.5	Annex 5: Carbon Tax and Emission Trading Systems (ETS)	196
	12.6	Annex 6: MSCI Market Classification Framework and Requirements	196
	References		197

About the Authors

Bruno Michoud is a Senior Researcher in the "Geopolitics and Energy Transition" (formerly "Future Energy") research programme at the Fondazione Eni Enrico Mattei (FEEM), where he deals with sustainable finance and carries out applied research on climate policies and actions emanating from the public and private spheres aimed at leveraging private capital to reshape the global energy landscape. He has almost a decade of operational experience in sustainable finance and impact investing in Africa, Latin America and Europe. Along his professional path, he has accompanied social and environmental entities in activities related to financing strategies, business development, risk management and fund-raising processes. Moreover, he designed and managed an innovative financial vehicle targeting impact-driven enterprises and has collaborated with several investment funds, financial institutions, private companies and government entities. He holds a M.Sc. in Green Management, Energy and Corporate Social Responsibility from Bocconi University (Milan, Italy), a M.Sc. in Socio-economics from the University of Geneva and a B.Sc. in Economics from HEC Lausanne (University of Lausanne), Switzerland.

Manfred Hafner is Programme Director of the "Geopolitics and Energy Transition" (formerly "Future Energy") research programme at the Fondazione Eni Enrico Mattei (FEEM). He is Professor of International Energy Studies, teaching at The Johns Hopkins University—School of Advanced International Studies (SAIS Europe) and at SciencesPo—Paris School of International Affairs (PSIA). He also teaches in many Executive Education masters and MBA courses worldwide. He has more than 30 years of experience in consulting on international energy issues for governments, international organisations and industry. He is/was Member of several high-level intergovernmental energy cooperation networks and councils. He has a long track record of interdisciplinary research coordination. He has published extensively, including on sub-Saharan Africa energy access challenges. He holds several master's degrees: in engineering from the Technical University of Munich (Germany); in economics and business from the IFP-School, the University of Paris-2 Pantheon-Assas and the University of Bourgogne (France); and in energy economics and policy from the University of Pennsylvania (US). He obtained his Ph.D. in Energy Studies with "summa cum laude" at Mines-ParisTech (Ecole des Mines de Paris).

Chapter 1
Introduction

Notwithstanding the ample and critical challenge regarding clean energy access globally, the African continent is the region with the highest number of people facing this issue worldwide. According to recent estimates, in sub-Saharan Africa, close to 580 million persons lack access to electricity (IEA, 2020) and over 900 million cook with inefficient and polluting stoves (WHO, 2020), representing, respectively, 52 and 85% of the subcontinent's 1.1 billion inhabitants.

This situation inhibits socio-economic development in the region and prevents populations from prospering. In addition, this painful statement is in stark contrast to the large availability of energy resources across the continent.

Providing reliable access to energy will unlock substantial benefits and improve living conditions of sub-Saharan African citizens. Moreover, it will allow the development of the economic and industrial sectors as well as reinforce the competitiveness of the whole region. In addition, the utilisation of clean and renewable energy resources will lessen the dependence on fossil fuels and contribute to global climate change mitigation efforts.

Technical solutions exist to reach the first target of Sustainable Development Goal 7 (SDG 7.1.1), namely ensuring by 2030 universal access to affordable, reliable and modern energy services. However, significant additional investments in low-carbon technologies are required in order to achieve access to clean energy for all. In sub-Saharan Africa, around $350 and $23 billion are needed for the power and clean cooking sectors, respectively (Corfee-Morlot et al., 2018).

Given the limited public resources and in order to avoid unsustainable debt to gross domestic product (GDP) ratios, most of the investment needed has to come from the private sector. Indeed, public finance alone will not be able to bridge this funding gap. However, the public sphere has a vital role to play in catalysing private investments in clean energy access initiatives. For its part, the private sector may bring not only capital but also a broad range of skills as well as innovative mechanisms to foster the allocation of funds into this pressing development challenge. Therefore, both are crucial and need to be complementary.

Private capital providers tend to limit investments or cover risk premiums due to higher perceived risks in the region, thus reducing the availability of affordable capital for clean energy-related projects. Indeed, the cost of financing is still relatively high in sub-Saharan Africa, despite ongoing reliability improvement and decreasing technological costs in the energy sector. Therefore, many project developers and companies face important difficulties in accessing the necessary capital to build and scale up innovative business models.

In this context, this book has the objective to contribute to the scientific literature related to sustainable development and the future of energy in the region. The general purpose is to support the achievement of an enabling investment climate in sub-Saharan Africa, with a particular focus on the energy sector. More specifically, the present book aims at analysing how to (i) enhance capital allocation in projects and organisations that foster clean energy access in the region, (ii) mobilise private capital at scale and (iii) decrease the cost of financing through risk mitigation strategies.

To that end, this publication adopts a comprehensive approach, encompassing economic, financial, political, environmental and social perspectives. Moreover, this book aspires to go beyond traditional initiatives and presents innovative solutions to approach the financing of universal clean energy access in sub-Saharan Africa. In addition, it seeks to adapt to the various specificities and remain consistent with the cultural and socio-economic contexts of the African continent.

Mainly because of the negative consequences generated by a lack of access to clean energy on socio-economic development and environmental concerns, this particular topic has been widely discussed by several research centres, think tanks and academics, providing a solid basis for the elaboration of the present book. Most of this work has focused on one specific aspect or technology associated with clean energy access in emerging countries. On top of that, emphasis is usually put on actions available to the public sphere, with the objective of creating enabling investment environments and attracting private capital at scale. However, little work has been done on potential initiatives that private actors can undertake.

This book concentrates on a specific geographical zone, sub-Saharan Africa, which is the world region where energy poverty is the most severe. Moreover, it aims at highlighting specific initiatives and actions available to the public and private spheres, at an international, regional and domestic level. It provides a holistic view of the opportunities and challenges related to the financing of clean energy projects and companies in sub-Saharan Africa, encompassing different technologies adapted to energy needs in urban and rural areas.

The book aims to be accessible to a wide readership of both academics and professionals working in the energy industry, the financial sector and the political sphere, as well as to general readers interested in the ongoing debate about energy, sustainable development and finance. Moreover, it has the objective to provide a solid basis for further analysis regarding the financing of clean energy access initiatives in specific contexts and for research projects in both academic institutions and think tanks. More specifically, the book targets project developers, policymakers, regulators, public and private financial institutions, asset managers, development agencies and researchers.

In addition, the present book provides a fervent call to action in order to elaborate inclusive and sustainable energy pathways in sub-Saharan African countries. It not only outlines the barriers, but also presents solutions available to public agencies, professionals active in the energy industry and various financial institutions (public and private) in order to mitigate and decrease the risk perception of different capital providers, as well as redirect financial flows towards access to clean energy.

Considering the vast subjects covered in this book, we included small introductory boxes at the beginning of each chapter in order to guide the reader through the various topics explored. Those boxes have the objective to introduce the overall content of each section, indicate which readers are particularly targeted and explain the reasons behind the integration of the aspects described as well as their importance for the overall theme.

The first part of this book (Chaps. 1–3) has the objective to provide an overall context around the energy access challenge in sub-Saharan Africa and its financing. The second part (Chaps. 4–9) aims at exploring public and private risk mitigation strategies and innovative investment schemes, as well as specific barriers hindering their use and implementation. Finally, the book ends with conclusions and targeted policy recommendations intended to enhance the financing of clean energy access across the region (Chap. 10).

More precisely, after the present Chap. 1 (**Introduction**), the book consists of the following chapters, which are briefly presented hereafter.

Chapter 2 (**Energy access in sub-Saharan Africa: general context**) starts by exploring the opportunities and challenges related to energy in sub-Saharan Africa. It then presents the investment trends and the financing gaps associated with the power and clean cooking sectors in the subcontinent.

Chapter 3 (**Risk analysis and mitigation strategy identification**) aims at describing different investment opportunities in the clean energy sector. It also provides a mapping of the barriers hindering their financing in the region. The investment risks are classified into four distinct categories: (i) economic and financial factors, (ii) the overall country situation, (iii) the business environment and (iv) environmental and social considerations. Furthermore, this part also presents core stakeholders which, through action or inaction, may influence the risk perception of potential capital providers.

Once obstacles to financing are properly identified, actions may be undertaken to improve the risk-reward profiles of investment opportunities. With appropriate mechanisms and facilities in place, investments in clean energy access activities can be scaled up. Therefore, the second part of the book exposes various instruments and strategies aimed at mitigating risks for potential capital providers. They are divided into four different spheres of interest: (i) public policies and initiatives, (ii) public financial and fiscal mechanisms, (iii) private financial structures and schemes and (iv) private initiatives.

The selection of a tailored and cost-effective set of tools and actions strongly depends on the context in which it is implemented, including the resources available and the maturity level of markets. This book does not focus on particular countries, but rather aims to give an overview of the mechanisms available to public and private players, allowing to leverage affordable capital for clean energy access initiatives.

To that end, public policies and initiatives, as well as specific reforms associated with the energy sector, are explored (Chap. 4: **Public policies and initiatives in the energy sector**). This section includes an analysis of the necessary adaptations to sub-Saharan African contexts, the challenges associated with the introduction of public actions, as well as particular measures aimed at preventing policy implementation gaps.

Moreover, emphasis is placed on alternative and innovative financing instruments and schemes tailored to the specific needs of the clean energy sector (Chap. 5: **Direct and indirect investments in the energy sector**), as well as on solutions aimed at improving and stabilising the overall investment climate.

In addition, this book focuses on the development and strengthening of local capital markets (Chap. 6: **Capital markets for the financing of clean energy access in sub-Saharan Africa**), as several schemes presented here are highly dependent to the well-functioning of the financial sector, including secondary and derivative markets. Accordingly, the complementarity with the banking sector is presented, and approaches aimed at transforming underdeveloped capital markets in the region are explored. Furthermore, opportunities in the bond markets and in carbon finance are covered, encompassing an overview of concerns that may potentially hinder their use in the subcontinent.

Chapter 7 (**Risk mitigation instruments targeting specific investment risks**) focuses on guarantee instruments and insurance, as well as on their availability in the clean energy sector. Moreover, this section addresses the currency and liquidity risks, considering the complexities of sub-Saharan African contexts and the energy sector.

Initiatives and actions at the disposal of project developers and managers are presented in Chap. 8 (**Business model adaptation**), with a particular focus on strategies for risk transfer, avoidance and compensation. Furthermore, solutions are explored to support internal risk management processes and business management in the energy sector.

Additionally, an entire section (Chap. 9: **The role of multilateral agencies and development banks**) concentrates on multilateral agencies and development banks, focusing on their role in the financing of clean energy access in sub-Saharan Africa. Through their particular relationships with national governments and their local expertise, those institutions are highly important and uniquely positioned to tackle this development issue. Moreover, they have a wide set of tools at their disposal in order to improve the risk-return profiles of investment opportunities in the clean energy sector. Thus, it is appropriate to require that their limited resources are used effectively to crowd in private capital. This chapter ends with a proposition of business model evolution for development agencies, including an emphasis on mobilisation tools, capacity building programs and stakeholder engagement.

Finally, the last section (Chap. 10: **Conclusions and policy recommendations**) focuses on policy recommendations for the public sphere, involving national and local governments as well as international public institutions. Three core areas considered

1 Introduction

as necessary to pave the way for private players are presented: (i) the creation of an enabling business and investment environment, (ii) the improvement of risk-reward profiles of investment opportunities in the clean energy sector and (iii) public strategies aimed at catalysing private capital.

The analysis of this book focuses on two important domains: the power and cooking sectors. They indeed strongly affect socio-economic conditions, human well-being and the environment.

Within the power sector, the present publication includes investment opportunities in decentralised systems, power generation plants, as well as national electricity grids, while relying on the multitier framework[1] (MTF) initiative to assess electricity access.

The energy resources considered for electricity generation are solar PV, wind, hydro and natural gas. The latter is not a renewable energy resource, and its utilisation emits non-negligible greenhouse gases (GHG) into this atmosphere. However, given the scale of the energy access challenge in sub-Saharan Africa, natural gas, when locally available, represents a cleaner option to generate power compared to coal or oil.

Nuclear energy is not included in this book as the analysis of the associated risks is very specific. Considering their particular features, the implementation of nuclear power plants should be preceded by the disclosure of all relevant information and the consultation of civil society.

Regarding clean cooking, the emphasis is put on liquified petroleum gas (LPG), improved biomass cookstoves, electrical cooking systems and biogas digesters. Solutions using piped natural gas have been disregarded for the purpose of this analysis, first because of lack of pipelines across Africa, second since new installations in the continent would require to cover long distances and third as low levels of demand associated with cooking do generally not justify such scheme.

Even though they can influence the financing of clean energy access in sub-Saharan Africa, geopolitical considerations, including international treaties, cross-border laws and trade relations among countries, are not covered in this book. In addition, this book concentrates on public policies emanating from sub-Saharan countries and international public organisations, but not on the ones coming from other countries.

This is the third open access book in the *Springer Briefs in Energy* series produced recently by researchers of the Fondazione Eni Enrico Mattei to address issues related to energy access in sub-Saharan Africa. The first book *"Energy in Africa: Challenges and Opportunities"* (Hafner et al., 2018) addresses energy challenges (including energy access) on the African continent (and the Sub-Saharan region in

---

[1]Launched in June 2015 by the Energy Sector Management Assistance Program (a global knowledge and technical assistance program administered by the World Bank), the MTF initiative is an innovative tool aimed at measuring energy access and providing valuable data and analytics. It uses a multidimensional approach, acknowledging the necessity to go beyond traditional binary variables (access or not) and considering other factors, such as reliability and affordability, to assess the service levels experienced by end-users.

For a complete definition of each tier associated with access to household electricity supply and clean cooking solutions, please refer to Annex 12.1.

particular) and proposes pathways for an accelerated energy transition. The second book *"Renewables for Energy Access and Sustainable Development in East Africa"* (Hafner et al., 2019) presents a modelling framework for least cost 100% electrification scenarios by 2030 in East Africa, investigates the role of renewable energy and provides policy-relevant inputs for the achievement of a cost-effective electrification process in the region. Both books also address some key barriers related to the investments required to upscale Africa's energy systems, and they elaborate general policy recommendations targeted at international cooperation and development institutions, local policymakers and private stakeholders in the region. The present book focuses much more deeply and comprehensively on the huge challenge related to financing clean energy access in sub-Saharan Africa, by analysing holistically and in-depth investment risk mitigation strategies and proposing innovative financing structures. It also provides ample policy recommendations.

References

Corfee-Morlot, J., Parks, P., Ogunleye, J. & Ayeni, F. (2018). *Achieving clean energy access in sub-Saharan Africa. A case study for the OECD, UN Environment Programme. "World Bank project: Financing climate Futures: Rethinking Infrastructure"*. https://doi.org/10.1787/9789264308114-en.

Hafner, M., Tagliapietra, S., & De Strasser, L. (2018). *Energy in Africa: Challenges and opportunities*. Springer.

Hafner, M., Tagliapietra, S., Falchetta, G., & Occhiali, G. (2019). *Renewables for energy access and sustainable development in East Africa*. Springer.

IEA (2020). *SDG7: Data and projections*. Paris: International Energy Agency. https://www.iea.org/reports/sdg7-data-and-projections.

WHO (2020). *Access to clean fuels and technologies for cooking (% of population—sub-Saharan Africa)*. Database from WHO Global Household Energy Database, World Bank Group, Sustainable Energy for All. Retrieved October 5, 2020, from https://data.worldbank.org/indicator/EG.CFT.ACCS.ZS?locations=ZG.

Open Access This chapter is licensed under the terms of the Creative Commons Attribution 4.0 International License (http://creativecommons.org/licenses/by/4.0/), which permits use, sharing, adaptation, distribution and reproduction in any medium or format, as long as you give appropriate credit to the original author(s) and the source, provide a link to the Creative Commons license and indicate if changes were made.

The images or other third party material in this chapter are included in the chapter's Creative Commons license, unless indicated otherwise in a credit line to the material. If material is not included in the chapter's Creative Commons license and your intended use is not permitted by statutory regulation or exceeds the permitted use, you will need to obtain permission directly from the copyright holder.

Chapter 2
Energy Access in Sub-Saharan Africa: General Context

> *The objective of this chapter is to provide the reader with an overall view of the current situation regarding clean energy access in sub-Saharan Africa, as well as to compare it with other developing and emerging economies. It focuses on the role played by energy in our daily lives and the financing gaps in the power and clean cooking sectors in the subcontinent. This section aims at setting the scene and giving more information about the dramatic energy challenges the region is currently facing.*
>
> *The chapter starts by presenting the importance of energy access for living conditions, socioeconomic development as well as economic and industrial sectors, considering the various sub-Saharan African contexts and complexities such as low population density and poverty. In addition, it explains what are the root causes of energy poverty, as well as the negative social and environmental consequences generated by a lack of access to clean energy.*
>
> *The second part of the present chapter focuses on the financing of clean energy access in the region. It aims at presenting key numbers, including the financing gaps associated with access to modern energy solutions and a comparison with current investment trends in the power and clean cooking sectors across the subcontinent. On top of that, it explores the involvement of key stakeholders in the financing of the access to clean energy in the region, encompassing public and private capital providers, both at domestic and international level.*

Energy is a key economic factor worldwide and plays an important role in many aspects of our daily lives. Nowadays, energy is consumed in a broad range of end-use sectors, including industry, transport, residential and services, and Africa is no exception.

However, energy access remains a major challenge for the African continent (Fig. 2.1). According to recent estimates, out of a total population of 1.1 billion in sub-Saharan Africa, close to 580 million people (52%) lack access to electricity and

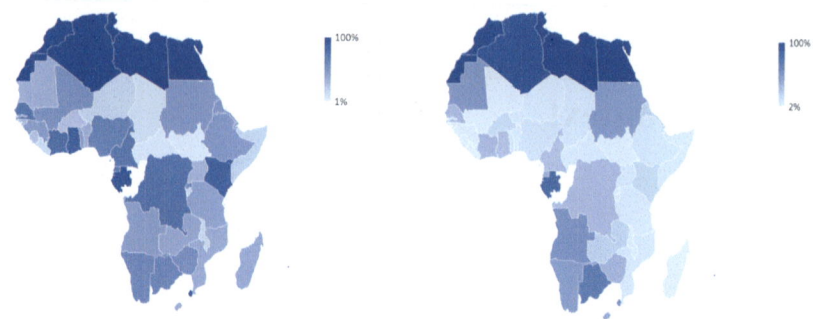

Fig. 2.1 Energy access in Africa, population with access to electricity in 2019 (left) and with access to clean cooking in 2018 (right) (Numbers for each African country are available in Annex 12.2). *Source* Authors' elaboration, based on IEA (2020a)

over 900 million (85%) cook with inefficient and polluting stoves (IEA, 2020a). This current status is in stark contrast to the large availability of clean energy resources in the region. Apart from the negative consequences on the populations and the environment, said situation deprives many African citizens of an essential input for the enhancement of socioeconomic conditions and a necessary prerequisite for poverty alleviation. Similarly, it impacts several development indicators related to health, education, food security and gender equality.

Even though efforts to promote access to clean energy are gaining momentum in Africa, they barely outpaced population growth. Indeed, cities are rapidly growing with insufficient urban planning, while rural zones are scattered over vast areas with little or no infrastructural connection.

Africa is currently the region with the fastest-growing population worldwide. With half of global demographic growth expected to occur in the continent in the next decades (UN, 2019a), it is estimated that around 530 million African inhabitants will still lack electricity and 1 billion won't have access to clean cooking systems[1] in 2030 (IEA, 2019). Under these circumstances, achieving universal access to clean energy in the region becomes a real race against time. Moreover, historical data show that progress regarding energy access has been made mainly in other parts of the globe (see Tables 2.1 and 2.2 for detailed numbers by region).

2.1 The Importance of Energy

Energy consumption constantly influences our wellbeing and living conditions. It also benefits vital domains of the economy and presents interesting opportunities in many industries, such as health, agriculture and telecommunications to name a

---

[1] This book considers four different options for clean cooking: (i) electrical cooking systems, (ii) LPG tanks, (iii) improved cookstoves for biomass combustion and (iv) biogas digesters.

2.1 The Importance of Energy

Table 2.1 Electricity access by region[a],[b]

Electricity access, summary by region

	Proportion of the population with access to electricity							Population without access (million)
	National					Urban	Rural	
	2000 (%)	2005 (%)	2010 (%)	2015 (%)	2019 (%)	2019 (%)	2019 (%)	2019
WORLD	73	77	80	85	90	96	85	771
Africa	36	40	44	49	56	81	37	579
North Africa	91	97	> 99	> 99	> 99	> 99	> 99	< 1
Sub-Saharan Africa	24	28	33	40	48	76	29	578
Developing Asia	67	74	79	87	96	99	94	155
China	99	> 99	> 99	> 99	> 99	> 99	> 99	< 1
India	43	58	68	79	> 99	> 99	> 99	6
Indonesia	53	56	67	88	> 99	> 99	99	2
Other Southeast Asia	65	75	79	85	91	98	85	36
Other Developing Asia	38	46	58	73	79	88	74	112
Central and South America	87	91	94	96	97	99	87	16
Middle East	91	90	91	92	92	98	77	19

[a]For detailed numbers about African countries and electricity access, please see Annex 12.2
[b]Other Southeast Asia countries are: Brunei, Cambodia, Laos, Malaysia, Myanmar, Philippines, Singapore, Thailand and Vietnam
Other Developing Asia countries are: Bangladesh, DPR Korea, Mongolia, Nepal, Pakistan and Sri Lanka

few. Simultaneously, it seriously impacts the climate and the planet we are living in. Therefore, energy is of utmost importance for the society as a whole.

In sub-Saharan African, lack of access to clean energy is a significant threat for its inhabitants and its economic and industrial sectors. Energy poverty implies that the region struggles to meet its development objectives. It should thus remain of paramount concern for future global prospects, especially in the context of a growing population.

By being at the core of a strategy that facilitates and extends opportunities as well as fosters socioeconomic prosperity, clean energy access may raise hopes for hundreds of millions of people across the region. Indeed, ensuring universal access to affordable, reliable and modern energy services (Sustainable Development Goal 7) is an essential requisite to create a brighter future, avoid extreme inconveniences and achieve many other objectives set by the United Nations.

Table 2.2 Access to clean cooking by region[a,b]

Access to clean cooking, summary by region

	Proportion of the population with access to clean cooking					Population without access (million)	Population relying on traditional use of biomass (million)
	2000 (%)	2005 (%)	2010 (%)	2015 (%)	2018 (%)	2018	2018
WORLD	52	55	58	63	65	2651	2374
Developing Countries	37	41	45	53	56	2651	2374
Africa	23	25	26	28	29	910	853
North Africa	87	93	96	98	98	4	4
Sub-Saharan Africa	10	11	13	15	17	905	848
Developing Asia	33	37	43	53	57	1674	1460
China	47	51	55	67	72	399	242
India	22	28	34	44	49	688	681
Indonesia	12	18	40	68	68	85	55
Other Southeast Asia	36	42	48	54	58	164	163
Other Developing Asia	22	26	27	33	35	337	318
Central and South America	78	82	85	88	89	57	53
Middle East	84	91	95	96	96	10	9

Source IEA (2020a)
[a]For detailed numbers about African countries and electricity access, please see Annex 12.2
[b]Other Southeast Asia countries are: Brunei, Cambodia, Laos, Malaysia, Myanmar, Philippines, Singapore, Thailand and Vietnam
Other Developing Asia countries are: Bangladesh, DPR Korea, Mongolia, Nepal, Pakistan and Sri Lanka

2.1.1 The Root Causes of Energy Poverty

Lack of access to energy arises from different factors, even though energy poverty is mostly related to economic issues in sub-Saharan Africa. This document focuses on various solutions to address the diverse barriers hindering clean energy access in the region, using a holistic approach to tackle all the root causes associated with this challenge.

2.1 The Importance of Energy

First, lack of access to energy may be attributed to physical considerations. Indeed, some individuals live in remote locations where commercial energy provisioning and utilisation are complex. Second, unreliable infrastructures combined with supply shortage do not fully satisfy energy demand and prevent proper domestic and productive uses. According to the World Bank, sub-Saharan African countries have power outages ranging from 50 to 4600 h per year,[2] causing frequent disruptions for households and firms (WB, 2016). Finally, financial constraints represent a major hurdle to overcome, as many African citizens face difficulties in covering energy-related costs, either upfront and/or consumption costs.

2.1.2 Energy, Welfare and Economic Development

Energy is used for domestic and community needs (i.e. lightening, cooking, water supply, heating, cooling, food conservation), as well as for business purposes and income generating activities. It is a powerful tool to escape persistent poverty. Indeed, the positive relationship between energy consumption and gross domestic product (GDP) per capita[3] indicates that energy poverty is an important barrier to socioeconomic development (Fig. 2.2). Even though Africa has experienced notable economic

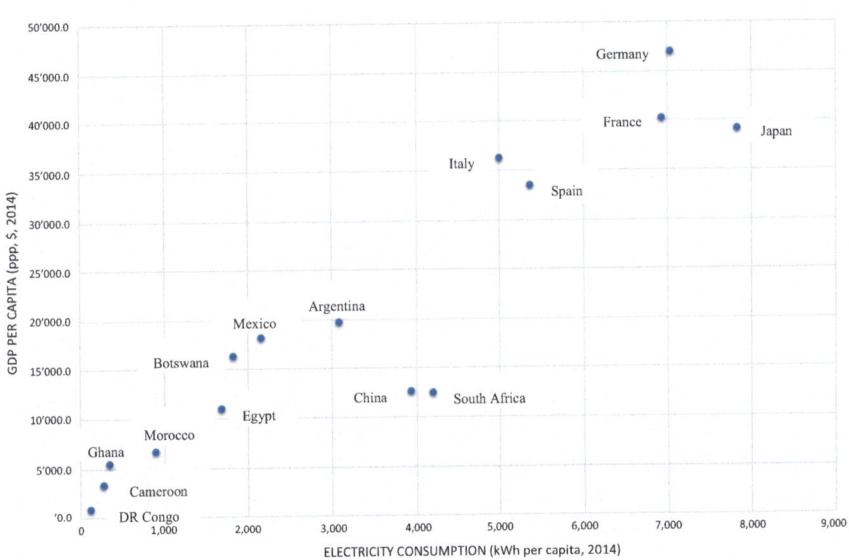

Fig. 2.2 Relationship between electricity consumption per capita and GDP per capita (PPP), 2014. *Source* Authors' elaboration, based on IEA (2014)

---

[2]For detailed numbers about sub-Saharan African countries, see Table 2.4.

[3]Some exceptions exist, mainly in countries with rich natural-resource endowments. However, social and economic inequalities remain often an important issue in those territories.

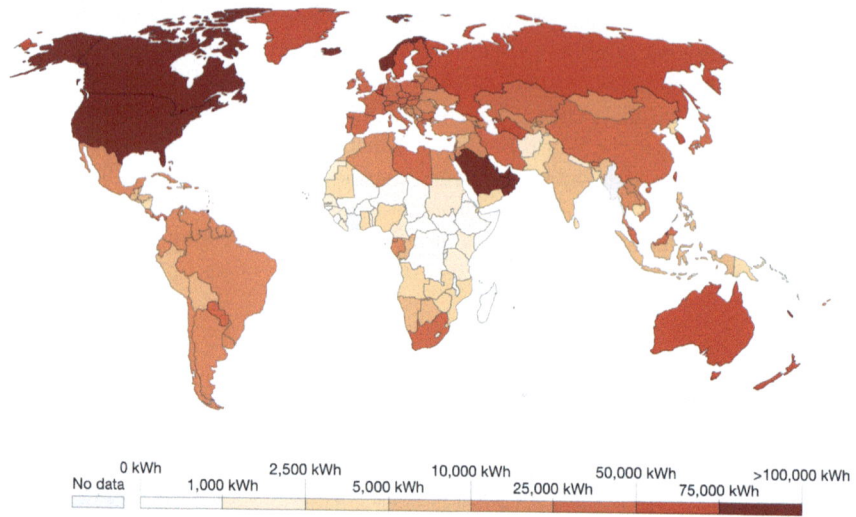

Fig. 2.3 Energy demand (Energy demand refers here to primary energy, namely the energy input before the transformation to forms of energy for end-uses such as electricity or petroleum products for transport and other uses) per capita, 2019. *Source* Our World in Data (based on BP and Shift Data Portal), 2019

growth over the last decades, poverty levels are still extremely high, especially in sub-Saharan Africa (AfDB, 2020). The region's gross domestic product (GDP) is equivalent to 11.3% of the European Union's GDP, even though its population is 2.5 times bigger (WB, 2019b). Accordingly, energy consumption per capita is very low across the region (Fig. 2.3).

Furthermore, Africa is characterised by a low population density, with many rural settings deprived of access to energy. Populations living in those zones are generally poor and face major hindrances in developing income generating activities. Currently, only 30% of the sub-Saharan African inhabitants living outside urban centres have access to electricity (Table 2.3) (SEforAll, 2020). The vast majority cook with inefficient systems relying on unmanaged and unsustainable biomass sources, causing indoor pollution and forest degradation (IEA, 2020a). Therefore, decentralised solutions as well as grid expansion (where technically feasible and economically rational) may bring considerable benefits and opportunities for rural dwellers to thrive.

Moreover, energy access and energy security are also important for Africa's industrial and economic sectors. Indeed, chronic power shortages and frequent blackouts enforce many enterprises to have recourse to backup power, incurring significant additional operational costs (Table 2.4). In Nigeria, the estimated loss for the national economy caused by inadequate electricity supply is estimated to exceed $28 billion per year, equivalent to 2% of its GDP (WB, 2020). Poor system reliability combined with high electricity tariffs in certain countries hamper economic and industrial development (AfDB, 2013). Hence, reliable and affordable energy for shops, plants and factories would provide the basis for transformative change for the whole region.

2.1 The Importance of Energy

Table 2.3 Electricity access—comparison between urban and rural areas, 2019[a]

Region	Proportion of the population with access to electricity in urban areas (%)	Proportion of the population with access to electricity in rural areas (%)
Africa	81	37
Sub-Saharan Africa	76	29
Central Africa	44	6
East Africa	79	35
West Africa	87	28
Southern Africa (except South Africa)	67	20

Source Authors' elaboration, based on SEforAll (2020)
[a]Numbers for each African country are available in Annex 12.2

Table 2.4 Average outage hours (per year), 2014

Country	Average outage hours per year	Installed capacity of the national grid (GW)	Backup generator availability (% of grid capacity) (%)
Angola	760	1.7	8
Cameroon	790	1.6	1
Côte d'Ivoire	230	1.8	6
DR Congo	830	2.6	46
Ethiopia	570	2.4	1
Ghana	790	2.8	12
Kenya	420	2.2	7
Mozambique	80	2.6	1
Niger	1400	0.18	20
Nigeria	4600	10.5	22
Senegal	130	0.96	1
South Africa	50	46	2.5
Tanzania	670	1.2	12
Zambia	180	2.3	3
Zimbabwe	280	2.1	5

Source Authors' elaboration, based on Farquharson et al. (2018)

It may reinforce productivity and competitiveness, boost the continent's industrialisation, expand service markets and potentially create decent jobs for many African citizens.

2.1.3 Climate Change and Price Volatility

As previously mentioned, lack of access to energy hinders sub-Saharan Africa's socioeconomic prosperity and should thus be a priority concern. Yet, depending on how efforts are underway, universal energy access could result in another negative implication for the region and the planet as a whole. Indeed, climate change is a reality and will increase over time. Its impacts could even undermine development efforts. Even though Africa is a minor emitter of greenhouse gases (GHG) at a global level,[4] the continent remains in the front line of the consequences of a changing climate and air pollution (IEA, 2019), besides potentially incurring important expenses (Beat, 2019).

Some countries could be tempted to extract and use their ample fossil fuel endowments, thus not focusing their efforts on cleaner energy sources to meet their needs despite the huge potential of the continent. A substantial part of Africa's energy mix currently relies on fossil fuels (Fig. 2.4). In addition, the massive use of biomass across the region, often coming from unsustainable sources, causes environmental degradation and destruction of vital natural areas, as many African households depend on this resource notably for cooking purposes (IRENA et al., 2018).

While proving significant incomes to exporting countries, the current fossil fuel dependency exposes African economies to price volatility and the unpredictability of global energy markets. Accordingly, such a situation may result in high costs to ensure energy security for the entire population.

Primary energy supply varies across the continent and related challenges and opportunities widely differ. However, the region's natural resources coupled with

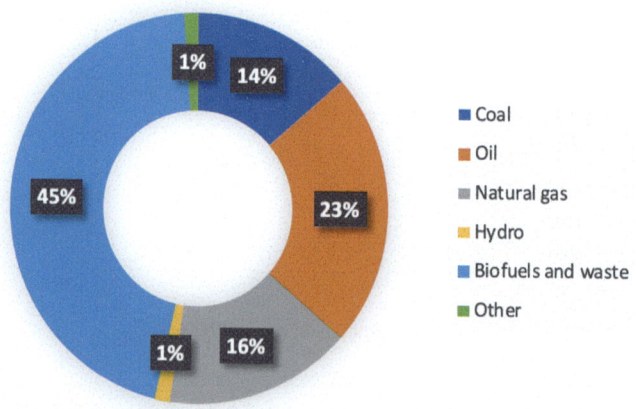

Fig. 2.4 Total primary energy supply by fuel in Africa, 2018. *Source* Authors' elaboration, based on IEA (2020b)

---

[4] Around 2% of cumulative energy-related CO_2 emissions globally.

technology improvements offer the possibility to develop low-carbon-intensive economic and industrial models. Providing universal energy access is crucial to allow every African to strive, yet environmental concerns need to be taken in consideration to limit the impacts on climate change, provide relief to deforestation and protect the continent's natural environment. For this reason, the use of clean energy resources in a responsible manner must be a key component of the overall action plan for the continent's energy transition, as it can significantly contribute to global climate change mitigation efforts.

2.1.4 Health and Gender Considerations

In addition to the socioeconomic and environmental considerations raised by clean energy access, health as well as gender concerns linked to the consequences of energy consumption must also be underlined (Hafner et al., 2018).

Even though the quantification of repercussions on people's health may be challenging, premature death caused by outdoor air pollution are estimated at 780,000 per year in the African continent (Bourzac, 2019). Should this trend continue in the years to come, it would lead the region to an important health crisis. On top of that, indoor air pollution coming from inefficient cooking facilities is responsible for the death of close to 490,000 persons each year in sub-Saharan Africa, with women and children being particularly impacted because of longer exposure (IEA, 2020a).

Furthermore, women and girls are frequently negatively affected by activities related to fuel gathering. Apart from the above-mentioned health concerns, they have to face the dangers posed by less secure environments when collecting fuelwood (WB, 2019a). Simultaneously, those time-consuming tasks make school enrolment very difficult and limit other productive activities, consequently constraining the building of a brighter future for women.

Moreover, energy plays a vital role in the health industry. Providing access to electricity to health centres is crucial, as it is used to power medical devices as well as for vaccine and medicine storage. An on-gong reliable and stable electricity supply is therefore critical to offer high-quality medical services in rural and urban areas.

2.2 The Financing Gaps

Technical solutions exist to achieve the first target of Sustainable Development Goal 7 (SDG 7.1.1) in sub-Saharan Africa, namely ensuring by 2030 universal access to affordable, reliable and modern energy services (UN, 2015). In addition, there is a massive abundance of clean energy resources across the region. However, substantial additional investments in low-carbon technologies compared to current and planned funding will be required to achieve access to clean energy for all in the continent.

Despite increasing international financial flows to developing countries in support of clean and renewable energy development, higher levels of ambition are needed (UN, 2019b). Indeed, universal electrification of sub-Saharan Africa needs an estimated $27 billion per year (2018–2030), which represents at least double the current levels of financing (Corfee-Morlot et al., 2018). The financing gap is also considerable for clean cooking, being valued at $1.8 billion per year by 2030 (ibid.). Compared to the $28 million dedicated to this sector in 2017, investments will need to increase significantly to allow the provision of clean cooking systems to every African household by 2030.

Public finance alone will not be able to bridge this funding gap (Natural Resources Defence Council et al., 2016). First because of limited financial resources and second to avoid increasing and unsustainable debt to gross domestic product (GDP) ratios. Therefore, private financing is absolutely necessary to reach this crucial objective.

The overall $350 and $23 billion (total estimated financing needs of sub-Saharan Africa for the 2018–2030 period) needed to finance, respectively, universal provision of low-carbon power and clean cooking systems in sub-Saharan Africa seems enormous. Yet when compared with the global wealth estimated at $360 trillion at the end of 2019 (CS, 2019), it shows that there is no shortage of capital, but rather a necessity to crowd in private investments, by creating enabling business climates and attractive investment opportunities. Financing energy access in sub-Saharan Africa should represent an exciting market opportunity for global investors, allowing them to advance sustainability objectives and changing the lives of millions while potentially generating attractive financial returns.

As presented in Table 2.5, total investment needs in both sectors, electricity and clean cooking, appear to be within reach. When reported to an average investment need per capita, considering the entire population or people without access to energy, the amount seems realistic. Similarly, the total investment needs represented as a percentage of gross domestic product (GDP) reinforce the impression that the financing gaps can be bridged, in case proper actions are taken as well as close and solidary collaboration prevails.

Table 2.5 Sub-Saharan African funding needs for universal access to energy in perspective

	Electricity	Clean cooking
Total investment needs, 2018–2030, billion (US $)	350	23
Average investment needs per year, billion (US $)	27	1.8
Average investment needs per year, $ per capita (entire population)	$25.05	$1.67
Average investment per year, $ per capita (population without access)	$46.55	$2.00
Investment as a share of PPP GDP in 2018 (sub-Saharan Africa, %)	0.65%	0.04%

Source Authors' elaboration, based on WB (2019b), Hafner et al. (2019)

2.2 The Financing Gaps

However, the African continent is currently receiving less attention than other emerging and developing economies regarding clean energy investments. As an example, between 2009 and 2018, only 2% of the global new installed power generation capacity using renewable energies were located in Africa (Res4Africa, 2020), while the continent is home to around 17% of the world population (UN, 2019a).

Consequently, only 48% of the African citizens have access to electricity (WHO, 2020) and 15% cook with clean systems (IEA, 2020a). Moreover, considering the evolution observed over the last years, the sub-Saharan region is not on track to achieve universal energy access by 2030 (ibid).

This alarming situation may come from the predominant perception that most African countries are difficult and risky environments for businesses and investments. Therefore, capital providers tend to be reticent to invest in the continent. Accordingly, the next chapter of the present book aims at analysing the risk environment associated with the region and clean energy initiatives.

2.3 Current Investment Trends

Before exploring investment opportunities and barriers to financing in clean energy access in sub-Saharan Africa, it is useful to provide an overview of current investment trends focusing on energy poverty at a global level.

This subsection emphasises on finance commitments in the clean cooking and electricity[5] sectors in the twenty countries with the largest share of the population without energy access worldwide (high impact countries—HICs[6]), covering 70% and 87% of the total population without access to power and clean cooking systems, respectively (SEforAll, 2019).

This general overview is broad as data collection regarding financing flows is usually challenging. In particular, the coverage of domestic finance (mainly private investments) and carbon finance is limited as this information may sometimes be confidential. Nevertheless, it intends to identify sources of capital and financial actors currently involved in the energy poverty issue, as well as geographic concentration and technological focuses.

---

[5] It includes renewable energy resources, fossil fuels, transmission and distribution, energy efficiency as well as market support.

[6] Regarding electricity access, those countries are Afghanistan, Angola, Bangladesh, Burkina Faso, DR Congo, Ethiopia, India, Kenya, DPR Korea, Madagascar, Malawi, Mozambique, Myanmar, Niger, Nigeria, the Philippines, Sudan, Tanzania, Uganda and Yemen.

For the access to clean cooking solutions, the concerned countries are Afghanistan, Bangladesh, China, DR Congo, Ethiopia, India, Indonesia, Kenya, DPR Korea, Madagascar, Mozambique, Myanmar, Nepal, Nigeria, Pakistan, the Philippines, Sudan, Tanzania, Uganda and Vietnam.

2.3.1 Electricity Access

Even though average annual investments targeting the electricity sector are on the rise in the above-mentioned high impact countries (HICs), they are still short compared to the estimated needs. Indeed, they increased from around $30 billion in 2015 and 2016 to $36 billion in 2017 (Fig. 2.5), while $51 billion are required each year until 2030 (SEforAll, 2019). In addition, emphasis is generally put on urban and peri-urban areas, while remote and rural communities are less represented in most territories.

In the electricity sector, sources of financing (Fig. 2.6) are mostly international and public, with public export credit agencies from China (mainly) and India playing a big role especially in large power generation projects (SEforAll, 2019). However, financial commitments of certain industrialised countries have recently decreased, in particular in Japan and the USA (ibid).

Development finance institutions (DFIs), national and multilateral, are another important component of public money, devoting around 60% of their investing activities in the power sector to transmission and distribution, and 20% to on-grid renewable energy resources (ibid). Off-grid solutions, namely stand-alone and mini-grid systems, reach so far only 2% of finance commitments of DFIs (ibid).

Regarding private investments, project developers represent an important source of capital in the power sector, meaning that private external financing was still low in 2017. Furthermore, domestic private finance is significantly present only in few countries (Nigeria, Uganda, India, Bangladesh and the Philippines), partly explained by more enabling policy and regulatory frameworks (ibid).

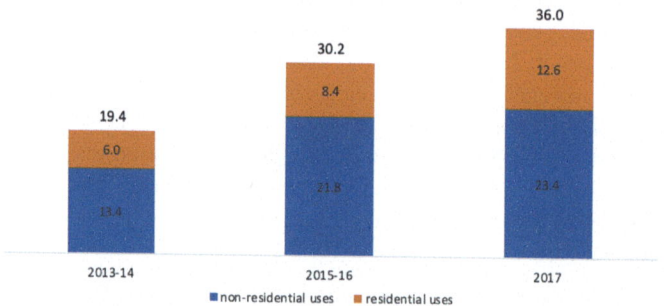

Fig. 2.5 Total yearly committed finance for the electricity sector across the 20 HICs[7], USD billion/year. *Source* Authors' elaboration, based on SEforAll (2019)

---

[7] Regarding electricity access, those countries are Afghanistan, Angola, Bangladesh, Burkina Faso, DR Congo, Ethiopia, India, Kenya, DPR Korea, Madagascar, Malawi, Mozambique, Myanmar, Niger, Nigeria, the Philippines, Sudan, Tanzania, Uganda and Yemen. For the access to clean cooking solutions, the concerned countries are Afghanistan, Bangladesh, China, DR Congo, Ethiopia, India, Indonesia, Kenya, DPR Korea, Madagascar, Mozambique, Myanmar, Nepal, Nigeria, Pakistan, the Philippines, Sudan, Tanzania, Uganda and Vietnam.

2.3 Current Investment Trends

India and Bangladesh accounted for around two-thirds of total committed financing in the electricity sector in 2017, while Nigeria was also a main recipient thanks to a $5 billion hydro-power plant financed by the Ex-Im Bank of China, the Chinese public export credit agency (SEforAll, 2019). Other sub-Saharan African countries received less attention, even though the share of their populations without access to electricity is significantly high (Fig. 2.7).

In 2017, around $20 billion was targeting privately owned initiatives across the 20 HICs, while publicly managed ones accounted for nearly $12 billion and public–private partnerships $4 billion (ibid).

In 2017, more than 60% of total committed financing was targeting grid-connected renewable energy resources, mostly solar PV (around 45%) due mainly to decreased technological costs, effective supply chains and manufacturing processes, as well as

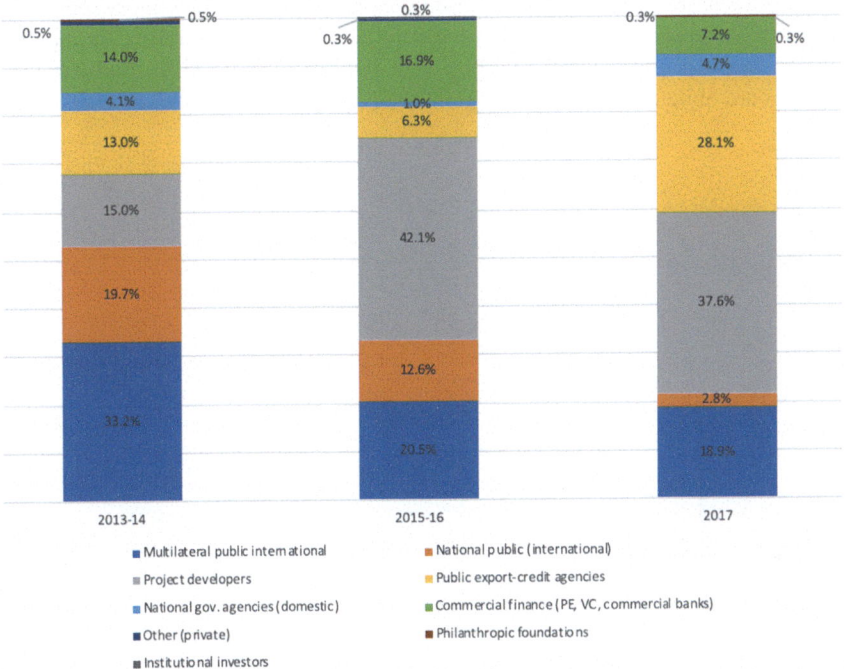

Fig. 2.6 Sources of finance for the electricity sector across the 20 HICs[8], share. *Source* Authors' elaboration, based on SEforAll (2019)

---

[8] Regarding electricity access, those countries are Afghanistan, Angola, Bangladesh, Burkina Faso, DR Congo, Ethiopia, India, Kenya, DPR Korea, Madagascar, Malawi, Mozambique, Myanmar, Niger, Nigeria, the Philippines, Sudan, Tanzania, Uganda and Yemen. For the access to clean cooking solutions, the concerned countries are Afghanistan, Bangladesh, China, DR Congo, Ethiopia, India, Indonesia, Kenya, DPR Korea, Madagascar, Mozambique, Myanmar, Nepal, Nigeria, Pakistan, the Philippines, Sudan, Tanzania, Uganda and Vietnam.

public tendering procedures (Fig. 2.8) (SEforAll, 2019). Nevertheless, around 30% of grid-connected energy investments was dedicated to fossil fuels, with coal being strongly represented (ibid).

Investments in off-grid solutions stagnated between 2013 and 2017 and focused mostly on stand-alone systems and some East African countries (Kenya, Uganda and Tanzania), using predominantly international financing sources (public and private) (ibid). According to recent estimates, close to 75% of all off-grid energy financing between January 2019 and August 2020 was committed to only three international companies, meaning that local solar entrepreneurs are still barely considered and are thus a negligible market factor (GOGLA, 2020). Hence, it remains clear that the industry has failed to build and establish a viable SME sector, important for the development of sustainable economies and to lessen unfavourable market concentration.

Even though investments in transmission and distribution of electricity increased in the selected countries, it declined by $400 million in sub-Saharan Africa compared to 2015 and 2016, and reached $1.1 billion in 2017 (SEforAll, 2019). Furthermore, final uses are quite different in the region compared to other frontier markets, with

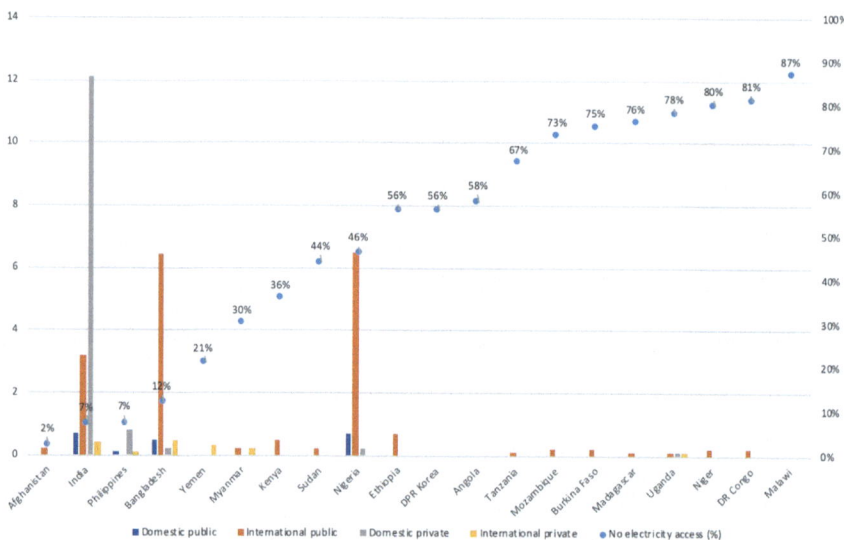

Fig. 2.7 Destination of finance for the electricity sector across the 20 HICs[9] in 2017, USD billion. *Source* Authors' elaboration, based on SEforAll (2019)

---

[9]Regarding electricity access, those countries are Afghanistan, Angola, Bangladesh, Burkina Faso, DR Congo, Ethiopia, India, Kenya, DPR Korea, Madagascar, Malawi, Mozambique, Myanmar, Niger, Nigeria, the Philippines, Sudan, Tanzania, Uganda and Yemen. For the access to clean cooking solutions, the concerned countries are Afghanistan, Bangladesh, China, DR Congo, Ethiopia, India, Indonesia, Kenya, DPR Korea, Madagascar, Mozambique, Myanmar, Nepal, Nigeria, Pakistan, the Philippines, Sudan, Tanzania, Uganda and Vietnam.

2.3 Current Investment Trends

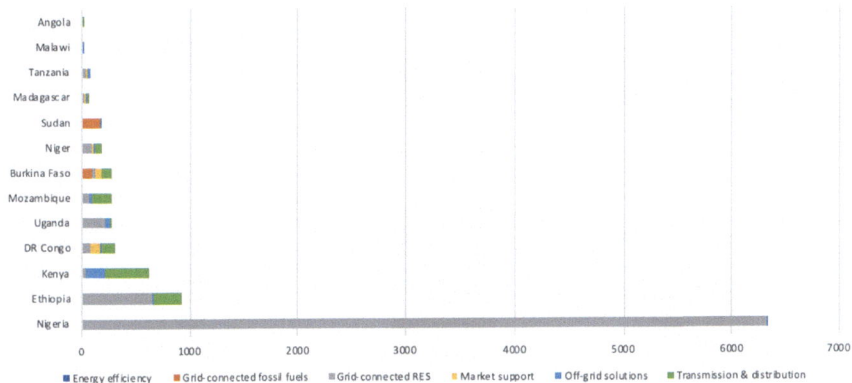

Fig. 2.8 Sub-sectors financed in the electricity sector in Africa in 2017, USD million. *Source* Authors' elaboration, based on SEforAll (2019)

a significant part of investment activities focusing off-grid solutions, driven by a massive utilisation of mobile money and pay-as-you-go (PAYGO) systems (ibid).

Finally, around 1% of total finance committed in 2017 was for capacity building programs, technical assistance and institutional support (i.e. energy reforms, policies and regulations) (SEforAll, 2019). The absolute number has declined to $350 million, from $870 million on annual average in 2015 and 2016 (ibid).

Regarding on-grid systems, the majority (around 65%) of investments targeted commercial and industrial uses, as well as public institutions (schools and hospitals) and community activities such as street lighting in 2017 (SEforAll, 2019). The rest focused on the residential sector. This trend is reversed when looking at off-grid systems, with 87% of financing dedicated to residential uses. Finally, investors are generally favouring Tiers 3 and 4[10] access when providing electricity to households (ibid).

2.3.2 Clean Cooking

Financial commitments for residential clean cooking systems significantly decreased from $117 million on annual average in 2015 and 2016 to $32 million in 2017 (SEforAll, 2019). This decline can be explained in part by large projects located in China and financed by the World Bank in 2015. Nevertheless, financing has been historically low in this sector, causing a continued and serious gap for this pressing development concern (Fig. 2.9).

---

[10] For a complete definition of Tiers, please refer to Annex 12.1.

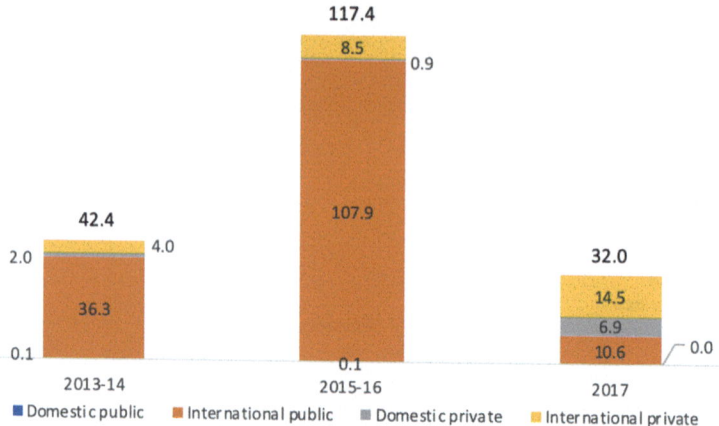

Fig. 2.9 Sources of finance for residential clean cooking systems across the 20 HICs[11], USD million/year. *Source* Authors' elaboration, based on SEforAll (2019)

Until 2016, investments were mainly coming from international public sources, including national governments, DFIs and climate funds (SEforAll, 2019). This trend changed in 2017, with financing emanating mostly from commercially oriented actors such as private equity funds, venture capitalists and institutional investors, as well as philanthropic foundations (ibid). It is interesting to note that international and domestic private capital providers are increasingly demonstrating appetite for clean cooking business models (Fig. 2.10).

Sub-Saharan Africa is the main recipient (86%) of committed financial flows associated with clean cooking solutions, with Kenya accounting for around 65% of total commitments thanks to a favouring investment climate (Fig. 2.11) (SEforAll, 2019).

---

[11] Regarding electricity access, those countries are Afghanistan, Angola, Bangladesh, Burkina Faso, DR Congo, Ethiopia, India, Kenya, DPR Korea, Madagascar, Malawi, Mozambique, Myanmar, Niger, Nigeria, the Philippines, Sudan, Tanzania, Uganda and Yemen. For the access to clean cooking solutions, the concerned countries are Afghanistan, Bangladesh, China, DR Congo, Ethiopia, India, Indonesia, Kenya, DPR Korea, Madagascar, Mozambique, Myanmar, Nepal, Nigeria, Pakistan, the Philippines, Sudan, Tanzania, Uganda and Vietnam.

2.3 Current Investment Trends

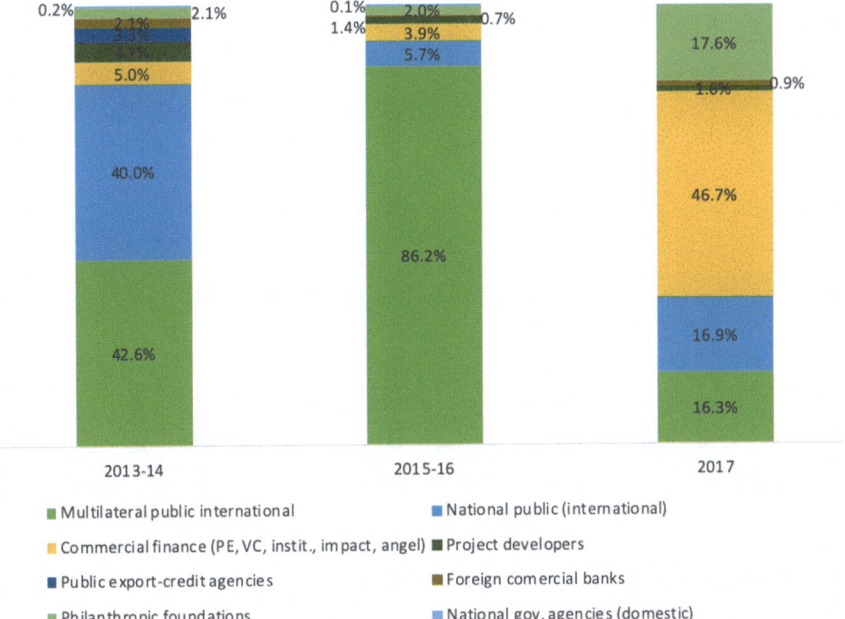

Fig. 2.10 Sources of finance for the clean cooking sector across the 20 HICs[12], share. *Source* Authors' elaboration, based on SEforAll (2019)

Regarding technological focus and end-uses, committed financing is mostly targeting improved cookstoves for biomass combustion and biogas digesters, providing clean cooking systems mainly to the residential sector (Fig. 2.12).

---

[12] Regarding electricity access, those countries are Afghanistan, Angola, Bangladesh, Burkina Faso, DR Congo, Ethiopia, India, Kenya, DPR Korea, Madagascar, Malawi, Mozambique, Myanmar, Niger, Nigeria, the Philippines, Sudan, Tanzania, Uganda and Yemen. For the access to clean cooking solutions, the concerned countries are Afghanistan, Bangladesh, China, DR Congo, Ethiopia, India, Indonesia, Kenya, DPR Korea, Madagascar, Mozambique, Myanmar, Nepal, Nigeria, Pakistan, the Philippines, Sudan, Tanzania, Uganda and Vietnam.

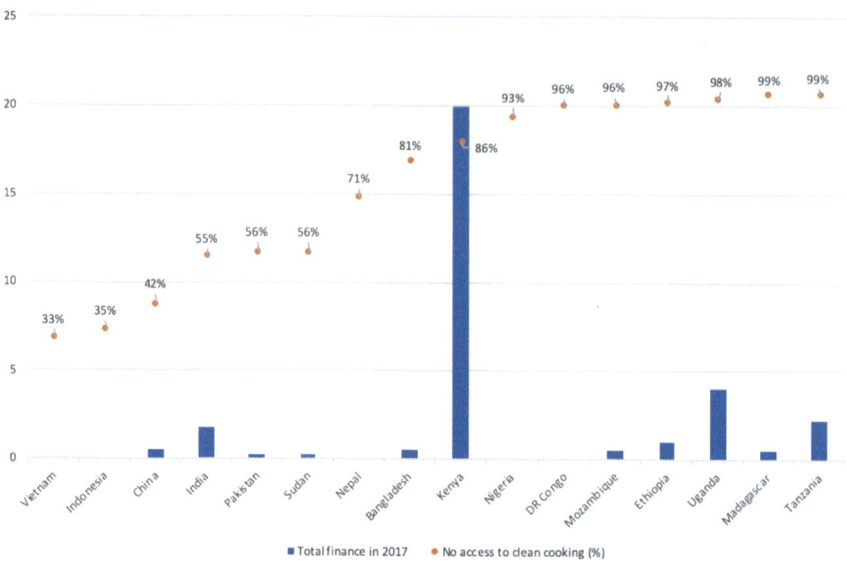

Fig. 2.11 Distribution of finance for the clean cooking sector across the 20 HICs in 2017, USD million. *Source* Authors' elaboration, based on SEforAll (2019)

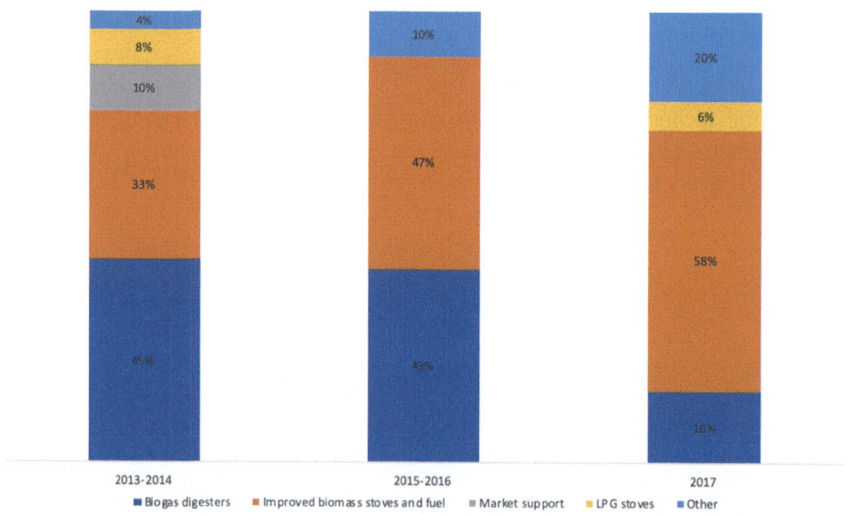

Fig. 2.12 Committed finance in the clean cooking sector, by end-uses (2017), share. *Source* Authors' elaboration, based on SEforAll (2019)

References

AfDB (2013). *The high cost of electricity generation in Africa*. African Development Bank, February 18, 2013.

AfDB (2020). *African economic outlook 2020: Developing Africa's workforce for the future*. African Development Bank.

Beat, S. (2019). *Africa must become more resilient to climate risk. Here's how*. World Economic Forum on Africa, August 28, 2019.

Bourzac, K. (2019). *Air pollution kills 780,000 people in Africa each year*. Chemical & Engineering News, April 23, 2019.

Corfee-Morlot, J., Parks, P., Ogunleye, J. & Ayeni, F. (2018). Achieving clean energy access in sub-Saharan Africa. A case study for the OECD, UN Environment Programme. World Bank project: "Financing Climate Futures: Rethinking Infrastructure". https://doi.org/10.1787/9789264308114-en.

CS (2019). *Global wealth report 2019*. Credit Suisse Research Institute.

Farquharson, D., Jaramillo, P., & Samaras, C. (2018). Sustainability implications of electricity outages in Sub-Saharan Africa. *Nature Sustainability, 1*, 589–598. https://doi.org/10.1038/s41893-018-0151-8

GOGLA (2020). *Off-grid solar investment trends: Key takeaways from the GOGLA deals database 2019 to August 2020*, October, 2020.

Hafner, M., Tagliapietra, S., De Strasser L. (2018). *Energy in Africa: Challenges and opportunities*. Springer.

Hafner, M., Tagliapietra, S., Falchetta, G., Occhiali, G. (2019). *Renewables for energy access and sustainable development in East Africa*. Springer.

IEA (2014). *Electric power consumption (kWh per capita)*. Database from IEA Statistics, International Energy Agency. Retrieved November 2, 2020, from https://data.worldbank.org/indicator/EG.USE.ELEC.KH.PC.

IEA (2019). *Africa energy outlook 2019*. Paris: International Energy Agency. www.iea.org/reports/africa-energy-outlook-2019.

IEA (2020a). *SDG7: Data and projections*. Paris: International Energy Agency. https://www.iea.org/reports/sdg7-data-and-projections.

IEA (2020b). *World energy balances: Overview*. Paris: IEA. https://www.iea.org/reports/world-energy-balances-overview.

IRENA, IEA and REN21 (2018). Renewable energy policies in a time of transition. IRENA, OECD/IEA and REN21.

Natural Resources Defence Council, Coalition for Green Capital, Climate Finance Advisors (2016). *Green & resilience banks: How the green investment bank model can play a role in scaling up climate finance in emerging markets*, November 2016.

Res4Africa (2020). *Why did only 2% of RE addition in the last decade occur in Africa?* Webinar given by Res4Africa, July 8, 2020.

SEforAll (2019). *Energizing finance 2019: understanding the landscape 2019*. Sustainable Energy for All. Climate Policy Initiative. www.seforall.org/data-and-evidence/energizing-finance-series/energizing-finance-2019.

SEforAll (2020). *Access to electricity (% of population)*. Database from the SE4ALL Global Tracking Framework, World Bank Group, International Energy Agency, Energy Sector Management Assistance Program. Retrieved September 27, 2020, from https://data.worldbank.org/indicator/EG.ELC.ACCS.ZS?end=2018&locations=IN&start=1990&view=chart.

UN (2015). *Resolution adopted by the general assembly on 25 September 2015. Transforming our world: The 2030 agenda for sustainable development*. New York: United Nations.

UN (2019a). *World population prospects 2019*. United Nations, Department of Economic and Social Affairs, Population Dynamics. Retrieved October 3, 2020, from https://population.un.org/wpp/.

UN (2019b). *Special edition: Progress towards the sustainable development goals.* Report of the Secretary-General. New York: United Nations, Economic and Social Council. https://undocs.org/E/2019/68.

WB (2016). *Enterprise survey.* World Bank Group. http://enterprisesurveys.org.

WB (2019a). *Clean cooking: Why it matters.* The World Bank. Published November 4, 2019. Retrieved August 3, 2020, from https://www.worldbank.org/en/news/feature/2019/11/04/why-clean-cooking-matters.

WB (2019b). GDP (current US $), World Bank National Accounts Data. Retrieved November 5, 2020, from https://data.worldbank.org/indicator/NY.GDP.MKTP.CD?name_desc=false.

WB (2020). *Nigeria to keep the lights on and power its economy.* World Bank Group, Press Release, June 23, 2020. Retrieved October 1, 2020, from https://www.worldbank.org/en/news/press-release/2020/06/23/nigeria-to-keep-the-lights-on-and-power-its-economy.

WHO (2020). *Access to clean fuels and technologies for cooking (% of population—sub-Saharan Africa).* Database from WHO Global Household Energy database, World Bank Group, Sustainable Energy for All. Retrieved October 5, 2020, from https://data.worldbank.org/indicator/EG.CFT.ACCS.ZS?locations=ZG.

Open Access This chapter is licensed under the terms of the Creative Commons Attribution 4.0 International License (http://creativecommons.org/licenses/by/4.0/), which permits use, sharing, adaptation, distribution and reproduction in any medium or format, as long as you give appropriate credit to the original author(s) and the source, provide a link to the Creative Commons license and indicate if changes were made.

The images or other third party material in this chapter are included in the chapter's Creative Commons license, unless indicated otherwise in a credit line to the material. If material is not included in the chapter's Creative Commons license and your intended use is not permitted by statutory regulation or exceeds the permitted use, you will need to obtain permission directly from the copyright holder.

Chapter 3
Risk Analysis and Mitigation Strategy Identification

> *Before exploring risk mitigation solutions available to public and private actors, this chapter first focuses on the identification and definition of investment risks associated with clean energy access solutions in sub-Saharan Africa. It provides the reader with a comprehensive understanding of the hurdles linked to clean energy access financing across the region.*
>
> *It starts by presenting the different investment opportunities considered in this book, namely stand-alone solar systems, mini-grids, power generation plants, national grids and clean cooking systems. Moreover, it identifies core stakeholders, both public and private, that may significantly influence risk perception of potential funders. On top of that, a particular emphasis is put on capital providers, with the aim of presenting their key features, including the types of financial instruments and schemes usually used. It has the objective to provide the reader with a comprehensive overview of investors potentially active in the region for investments related to clean energy access.*
>
> *The second part of the present chapter focuses on the definition of the investment risks, encompassing economic and financial factors, the overall country situation, the business environment, and social and environmental considerations. Furthermore, these investment barriers are linked to each investment opportunity. Finally, risk mitigation strategies are identified as well as associated with the targeted risks, in order to provide a common basis before describing each de-risking solutions in the following chapters.*

Risks act as barriers to investments as they increase the probability of occurrence of a negative event, affecting business activities and financial returns. It is therefore important to release a comprehensive mapping of investment risks as well as understand their root causes. This involves three core tasks:

i. Description of investment opportunities able to promote clean energy access in sub-Saharan Africa
ii. Identification of core stakeholders directly and indirectly involved in the clean energy sector
iii. Identification of investment risks behind the selected investment opportunities

3.1 Investment Opportunities in the Clean Energy Sector

Energy access can be addressed by different production means (e.g. stand-alone systems, mini-grids, extension of the grid, etc.) depending on site-specific elements like the expected demand, the resource base, the comparative costs of different equipment and the distance to the grid. Site-specific least-cost electrification solutions can be modelled (Hafner et al., 2019).

This subsection provides a definition of every solution chosen for the scope of this book, having the potential to enhance the access to clean energy in both urban and rural areas across sub-Saharan Africa. This will allow an understanding of the risks associated as well as the drivers behind those investment opportunities. The risks are presented in detail in the following subsection.

3.1.1 Stand-Alone Systems

Stand-alone systems are designed for persons living beyond the reach of the grid or with unreliable power supply. These solutions enable different domestic and productive energy uses (Tier 1 and above[1]), from lighting and phone charging to the provision of power for household appliances and micro-, small- and medium-scale businesses (i.e. refrigeration, irrigation, agro-processing). Stand-alone solutions can operate with or without storage capacity and may possibly combine solar power with another energy resource (hybrid solutions).

During the last two decades, many aspects of this sector have undergone profound changes and business models have deeply evolved. Innovations continue to this day, enabling products and services to be customised to energy consumption and financial affordability of targeted customers (GOGLA, 2020). Energy solutions are now proposed in various formats, ranging from service-based, pay-as-you-go (PAYGO) and leasing models to the sales of devices through single or multiple payments. In addition, mobile money and consumer finance becoming incrementally more available have been instrumental in supporting sales growth (Persistent Energy Capital et al., n.d.).

Nowadays, the sector is mainly vertically integrated even though specialisation has started to emerge. Companies are operating in a highly dynamic and increasingly

---

[1] For a complete definition of Tiers, please refer to Annex 1.

competitive market. Some of them are beginning to diversify their product range, pairing the provision of energy devices with the selling of other products.

Stand-alone systems can be installed rapidly, and their payback periods are relatively short. In addition, they represent a cost-effective option in many situations thanks to an increasing reliability and decreasing costs of technologies (IRENA, 2015). The sector is usually lowly correlated with the global economy and less dependent to specific regulations like tariff setting and permitting. Consequently, they are seen as a powerful solution in the quest for universal access to clean energy.

The addressable market is potentially huge, encompassing rural and peri-urban zones, without grid connection or with low reliability of supply. Some companies have reached a significant size and are now serving an important number of households, located in different geographical areas, with distinct demographic and socioeconomic profiles, thus enabling customer portfolio diversification.

Over the last decade, unit economics have improved significantly in the sector. However, most of the companies active in the sub-Saharan region have not achieved profitability yet. The main reasons are the elevated costs related to hardware development as well as expensive and possibly complex last-mile distribution. In addition, stand-alone systems are capital-intensive businesses since they usually hold substantial inventories and client receivables. And the working capital needs increase with the customer portfolio.

To date, investments have been largely concentrated in few companies and in countries presenting stable macroeconomic situations (Acumen, 2018). By 2030, stand-alone systems might represent the least-cost electrification option for nearly 25% of the continent population (IEA, 2019).

3.1.2 Mini-Grids

Mini-grids are schemes consisting of small-scale decentralised systems providing power into a network which supplies a limited number of customers. Most of the time, they are employed in relatively remote zones, as they can operate in isolation from national grids. The energy resources considered here are solar PV, wind or hydro, as well as hybrid solutions.

By offering a significant and stable source of power (Tier 1–5[2]), mini-grids have the potential to support local economic development, enabling access to electricity for households, micro- to medium-scale enterprises as well as anchor consumers (e.g. health centres, telecom towers, schools).

Unlike stand-alone systems, mini-grids are not retail businesses and rather act as small-scale utilities. They have characteristics close to an infrastructure investment and high sensitivity to financing costs. Moreover, they face significant upfront costs as well as specific regulations regarding licensing, permitting and in some cases tariff setting. However, the construction period is shorter than medium- and large-scale

---

[2] For a complete definition of Tiers, please refer to Annex 1.

power generation plants, as project developers try to adapt the installed capacity to the community served.

The ownership and operational structures of mini-grids can vary significantly. This is an important aspect since it may strongly impact the management and operations, as well as the risks associated with this investment opportunity. The owners and operators can be either a private, public or community-based entity.

As stand-alone systems, mini-grids have witnessed a decrease in costs of technologies and an improved reliability. They also target rural and peri-urban areas and consequently operate in an important addressable market. However, they require concentrated settlements to power a certain number of customers in order to become financially viable. In addition, when managing a single mini-grid, economies of scale and diversification opportunities are low. Nevertheless, project developers generally operate a portfolio of mini-grids, allowing to serve heterogeneous communities.

In some countries across Africa, governmental entities are considering mini-grids as a crucial part of their energy roadmap and are increasingly favouring their development. According to the International Energy Agency, mini-grids will provide access to electricity to over 30% of the continent's inhabitants by 2030 (IEA, 2019).

3.1.3 Medium- and Large-Scale Power Generation Plants

Concerning power supplied in centralised systems or for significant electricity needs, this book considers generation plants with an installed capacity of 50 MW and above, that are usually but not necessarily connected to the national grid. The book focuses on decarbonised and low-carbon energy resources, including solar PV, wind, hydro and natural gas. Similar to other regions around the globe, power demand is growing in Africa, leading governments to increase the supply in their territories. Combining this with environmental considerations and the energy access challenge, renewable and low-carbon resources are regarded as interesting options for power generation in the region.

Like the two investment opportunities presented previously, power generation plants benefit from an increasing reliability as well as decreasing costs of technologies (Boston University et al., 2020). In addition, they are characterised by capital intensity,[3] the need for long-term financing due to long payback periods and a high sensitivity to financing costs (Waissbein et al., 2013).

Over the last years, the African continent has started to witness vertical disintegration and the privatization of power generation in several countries. One of the objectives behind those initiatives was to encourage the presence of private players and the involvement of strategic actors, in order to improve efficiency within the sector and crowd in private capital (REW, 2019). Accordingly, many medium- and

---

[3] Renewables energy resources have a higher capital intensity (high investment costs and low operational ones) than natural gas.

large-scale power generation plants across the continent are built and managed in the form of independent power producers (IPPs).

Several innovative financial mechanisms and tariff schemes aimed at reinforcing the competitiveness and attractiveness of renewable energy resources for power generation have been introduced during the last decades. Those opportunities as well as their availability and implementation in sub-Saharan Africa are analysed further in this book.

3.1.4 National Grid

National grids transmit and distribute the power generated in dedicated plants. For the scope of this document, two different types of investment opportunities are considered: (i) upgrade and reliability improvement, (ii) grid expansion. They are grouped under the same category as they present some similar risk features.

Vertical disintegration of the power sector has emerged in several African countries (Attia, 2019). However, apart from few exceptions, distribution and transmission infrastructures have traditionally been publicly owned and operated (Pudney, 2018). Less than 20% of sub-Saharan countries allow the participation of private actors in this part of the power supply chain (Res4Africa, 2020). Accordingly, short political cycles may challenge public commitment to long-term transmission and distribution projects.

Investment sizes are relatively less substantial compared to power generation plants. Nevertheless, frequent financial difficulties faced by many African electricity utilities as well as low financial returns commonly associated with transmission and distribution prevent the realisation of the required investments for maintenance, upgrade and expansion. Consequently, energy infrastructures in the region are usually ageing, facing reliability issues and significant line loss rates, thus partly explaining the relatively high electricity tariffs charged in several sub-Saharan countries (Attia and Shirley, 2018). Moreover, electricity grids are generally not adapted to the integration of renewable energy resources and frequently deprived of technical innovations of a modern power system, supporting supply and demand management (i.e. smart grid technologies).

In addition, several locations in the region are not connected to national networks yet, whereas projects dedicated to grid expansion can be complementary to decentralised solutions and enhance access to electricity in many areas. However, grid extension is often technically complex. Furthermore, few African power utilities are tasked with a universal service mandate. This combined with cost-recovery issues and poorly maintained assets leave millions of potential customers unconnected, including 110 million living beneath existing grid infrastructure in sub-Saharan Africa alone (ibid.).

In order to provide universal and high-quality service to end-consumers as well as meet existing and future power demand, substantial investments are urgently needed to close the power infrastructure gap across the region. Grid extension and densification will be, according to the International Energy Agency, the most effective solutions for nearly 45% of the population gaining access to reliable electricity supply by 2030 (IEA, 2019).

3.1.5 Clean Cooking Systems

This book considers four different options for clean cooking: (i) electrical cooking systems, (ii) LPG tanks, (iii) improved cookstoves for biomass combustion and (iv) biogas digesters. The first listed solution is strongly linked to electrification. The last three may entail not only the selling of cookstoves, but also the production and distribution of their respective fuels, which adds complexity for business models proposing those devices. Biomass combustion is widely used in Africa, sometimes causing forest degradation and health issues. Here, the book focuses on improved solutions avoiding indoor pollution and consuming biomass coming from sustainable harvesting of fuelwood. Cooking solutions using piped natural gas are not considered in the present book because of lack of pipelines across the continent. Moreover, the construction of a gas pipeline network in a near future is unlikely due to the necessity to cover long distances and—most importantly—the weak financial viability owing to low energy demand levels associated with cooking.

Just like for stand-alone systems, clean cooking companies are retail businesses selling assets with relatively short installation time and payback periods. The four clean cooking solutions presented above are grouped into a single category since broadly speaking they present similar risk features, apart from the above-mentioned complexities linked to fuel supply and distribution. At the same time, those business models can capture deeper commercial opportunities provided by recurring revenue streams associated with fuel selling activities.

Over the last decades, the sector has been constantly innovating and adapting to customers' needs, gaining increasing attention especially in East Africa. However, clean cooking is often seen as a second level priority in many emerging and developing markets despite its huge social and environmental benefits (Bhalla, 2019). Accordingly, the level of funding dedicated to this sector is still relatively low, mainly due to a lack of supporting policies targeting the industry compared to other development sectors.

Even though the addressable market is significant, massive deployment is also constrained by a lack of awareness concerning health and environmental issues linked to cooking in many African countries. The difficulty to change customers' behaviour makes clean devices often seen as an unnecessary expense among communities, preferring to rely on traditional systems and using energy resources that are sometimes available for free (i.e. fuelwood).

To date, clean cooking companies have faced challenges in setting affordable pricing while presenting attractive risk-return profiles to investors. Nevertheless, financially viable enterprises are starting to emerge and raise the interest of the public and private spheres (Clean Cooking Alliance, 2019). In addition, clean cooking

3.1 Investment Opportunities in the Clean Energy Sector

companies benefit from the increasing availability of mobile money and consumer finance across the continent.

Like for stand-alone systems, investments in clean cooking companies are skewed towards a selected few enterprises having reached a significant size and active in countries presenting a stable macroeconomic situation (Acumen, 2018).

3.2 Identification of Core Stakeholders

The identification of relevant stakeholders, directly and indirectly involved in the financing of clean energy access in sub-Saharan Africa, is a necessary step to properly analyse the barriers related to each investment opportunity considered in this book. This mapping helps determine groups of entities whose behaviour, through action or inaction, can potentially influence investors' risk perception, thereby affecting capital allocation and the cost of financing. Therefore, it is crucial to define their role in order to describe strategic investment pathways towards universal clean energy access in the region, without leaving certain hurdles unaddressed.

It is also important to connect each barrier to investment with groups of stakeholders able to mitigate or overcome it, thus reinforcing the understanding of the overall investment environment. Equally important, it avoids an overlapping of risk categories and increases the likelihood of developing and implementing successful de-risking strategies and risk mitigation actions.

Table 3.1 presents the groups of stakeholders considered in this book.

3.2.1 Capital Providers

This subsection provides a mapping and description of the capital providers, domestic and international, considered in this book. It aims at presenting what are the sources of funding available, the financial instruments and mechanisms commonly used as well as some key characteristics. There are categorised as follows: domestic public sources, domestic private sources, international public sources, international private sources.

3.2.1.1 The Role of Financing

As reported previously, additional investments are urgently required to ensure universal access to clean energy in sub-Saharan Africa. Potential sources of capital come from heterogenous actors with different utility functions. They include development and climate finance, concessional and patient capital, grants and commercially oriented financing. Each capital provider has its own risk appetite as well as specific focuses on different sectors and development stages. Accordingly, it is necessary

Table 3.1 Core stakeholders

Stakeholder group	Description
Public authorities	Public bodies, local and national, that establish country's objectives, policies and regulations, as well as energy targets. This category encompasses policymakers, public administrators, regulators, legislators and ministers
Power utility companies and grid operators	Organisations, usually state-owned companies, responsible for the transmission and distribution of electricity as well as in charge of grid operation. Power utilities are also electricity purchaser and off-taker from the perspective of power generators
Public development and financial institutions, multilateral agencies	National, bi- and multilateral institutions created by a single state or a group of countries, providing professional services, including financial ones, aimed at addressing social and environmental challenges
Project developers and operators	Entrepreneurs and persons involved in the development and management of clean energy-related projects, investing time (and usually money) as well as bringing specific skills and expertise
Investors and capital providers	Domestic and international capital providers, individuals or institutions, using different financial instruments and schemes, ranging from traditional to alternative ones. For more details, see the next subsection dedicated to this group of stakeholders
Supply chain and business partners	Players, including intermediaries, active in the supply chain of the power and clean cooking sectors (upstream and downstream), as well as other actors involved directly or indirectly in energy access (i.e. microfinance institutions)
End-consumers, end-users	Customers and communities using energy services and products
Civil society	General public and non-governmental organisations (NGOs) representing the voice of the civil society

Source Authors' elaboration, based on IRENA et al. (2018), UNDP and ETH Zurich (2018), Waissbein et al. (2013)

to align financing needs, risk-reward profiles and risk tolerance levels in order to catalyse the required redirection of finance and effectively mobilise or blend those sources of capital.

Investments in clean energy access span multiple asset classes, ranging from equity and fixed income to real estate and commodities (Donovan, 2015). Consequently, the clean energy sector is not an asset class by itself, but rather a sub-category within a variety of distinct asset classes, helping positioning it within the universe of investment opportunities available to different capital providers. Therefore, the sector has the potential to attract various investors, coming from the public and private spheres.

As previously reported, public funds alone will not be sufficient to bridge the funding gap related to clean energy access in the sub-Saharan region. However, the public sector has a key role to play in creating of an enabling investment climate and attracting private capital. Policymakers and public financial institutions should make an effective use of their limited resources, directing them where most needed and addressing specific constraints faced by private actors.

Similarly, the private sector is also crucial. Apart from capital, it may bring innovative financing schemes and mechanisms. Moreover, private players can add new and valuable skills to the table and create competitive frameworks. Therefore, the public and private spheres are both necessary and must complement each other in order to maximise efficiency in tackling the clean energy access challenge across sub-Saharan Africa.

3.2.1.2 Public Actors

Public actors have traditionally focused on direct investments, using mainly equity financing, lending (concessional or not) and grants, targeting public and private entities. However, recent years have seen an increasing emphasis on the use of mobilisation tools (i.e. public-backed investments, liquidity facilities, derivatives instruments), as well as on the funding of specific programs and policies aimed at crowding in private capital (IRENA, 2016).

Table 3.2 presents public capital providers considered in this book along with some key features.

3.2.1.3 Private Actors

Over the years, the private sector has accumulated significant experience in using different types of financial instruments, structures and mechanisms, providing constant innovation and adapting to specific needs of various industries, including the energy sector.

Table 3.3 presents private capital providers considered in this book along with some key features.

Table 3.2 Public capital providers

Description	Main features	Location	Financial instruments and schemes[a]	Examples
National government agencies	Public financial resources coming from tax revenues, national budgets, public financial institutions, sovereign wealth funds and public pension funds	Domestic	Grant Debt Green bonds Equity Specialised investment vehicles Blended finance Guarantees and insurance Subsidies	National Development Bank of Zimbabwe, Agaciro Development Fund (Rwanda), Bayelsa Development and Investment Corporation (Nigeria), Equatorial Guinea Fund for Future Generation, Bank Windhoek Retirement Fund (Namibia), Caisse Nationale de Prévoyance Sociale (Côte d'Ivoire), Libyan Investment Authority, Algeria Revenue Regulation Fund, Government Employees Pension Fund (South Africa)
International financial institutions, development finance institutions (DFIs) and multilateral agencies	Regional, bi- or multilateral agencies, using raised capital or acting on behalf of donors	International	Grant Debt A/B syndicated loans Equity Specialised investment vehicles Blended finance Credit lines Guarantees and insurance Liquidity facilities Derivative instruments	African Development Bank (AfDB), Development Bank of Southern Africa (DBSA), Islamic Development Bank (IsDB), New Development Bank (NDB), World Bank, European Bank for Reconstruction and Development (EBRD), European Investment Bank (EIB)

(continued)

Table 3.2 (continued)

Description	Main features	Location	Financial instruments and schemes[a]	Examples
Public financial agencies and national development institutions	Sovereign wealth funds and national development agencies	International	Grant Debt A/B syndicated loans Blended finance Liquidity facilities	Department for International Development (DFID), China Investment Corp., China Exim Bank (CHEXIM), Gesellschaft für Internationale Zusammenarbeit (GIZ), Agence Française de Développement (AFD), Norway Government Pension Funds
Climate finance institutions	International climate funds and intermediary institutions aimed at channelling public funds to climate-related projects	International	Grant Debt Equity Blended finance Guarantees Credit lines Derivative instruments	Global Environment Facilities (GEF), Green Climate Fund (GCF), Climate Investment Funds (CIFs)

(continued)

Table 3.2 (continued)

Description	Main features	Location	Financial instruments and schemes[a]	Examples
Public export credit agencies	Public organisations supporting corporations doing business in developing and emerging markets	Domestic/international	Debt Guarantee instruments (mainly targeting political and commercial risks)	Nigerian Export–Import Bank, Export Credit Guarantee Corporation of Zimbabwe (ECGI), Multilateral Investment Guarantee Agency (MIGA), Compagnie Française d'Assurance pour le Commerce Extérieur—Coface (France), Euler Hermes Kreditversicherung (Germany), Servizi Assicurativi del Commercio Estero—SACE (Italy)

Source Authors' elaboration, based on GCF (2013), Hafner et al. (2020), WEF (2019)
[a]Here, the financial instruments and schemes commonly used are listed, without excluding possible exceptions

3.2 Identification of Core Stakeholders

Table 3.3 Private capital providers

Description	Main features	Location	Financial instruments and schemes[a]	Examples
Local banks	Private commercial, investment and development banks, providing local currency financing but usually constrained by their balance sheet sizes, prudential ratios and liquidity costs	Domestic	Debt Syndicated loan Equity	Eritrean Investment and Development Bank, Ecobank Nigeria Plc, Nedbank
Private institutional investors	Large-scale and long-term-oriented investors, which pool capital to purchase securities, real estate properties or investment assets They can potentially play a major role in the financing of clean energy access, having large assets under management (AUM) In addition, they have an appetite for responsible investments due to their fiduciary duties, even though their primary objective is to ensure expenditures (pensions, annuities, insurance)	Domestic/international	Debt Syndicated loan Equity	Private insurance companies and pension funds
Foreign banks	Private and commercially oriented banks, investing not only locally but also aboard	International	Debt Syndicated loan Equity	Credit Suisse, BNP Paribas, UniCredit

(continued)

Table 3.3 (continued)

Description	Main features	Location	Financial instruments and schemes[a]	Examples
Investment funds, venture capitalists (VC), private equity investors, non-bank financial institutions (NBFI) and asset managers[b]	Collective investment schemes used to invest directly in clean energy initiatives or through financial intermediaries	Domestic/international	Debt Equity Derivatives	Investment Fund Africa (IFA), Energy Capital Partners, Simmons Energy, BlackRock
Impact investors	Investors looking for financial returns along with positive social and environmental impacts	International	Debt Equity Alternative financial instruments	Acumen, Bamboo Capital Partners, ResponsAbility Investments, Symbiotics, OikoCredit, Triodos Bank, The Ecosystem Integrity Fund
Philanthropic foundations, endowments, trusts	Non-governmental organisations and corporations, using capital provided by donors or philanthropic arms for social and environmental purposes	International	Grant Debt	Open Society Foundations, philanthropic arm of big corporations[c]
Strategic partners, enterprises and corporations	Private utilities, energy companies and big corporations investing in energy-related projects	Domestic/international	Debt Equity	ENI, Enel Green Power, Facebook, Google, Microsoft
Private export guarantee agencies	Private organisations supporting corporations doing business in developing and emerging markets	International	Debt Guarantees	Foreign Trade and Investment Promotion Scheme (AGA, Germany)

(continued)

3.2 Identification of Core Stakeholders

Table 3.3 (continued)

Description	Main features	Location	Financial instruments and schemes[a]	Examples
Crowdfunding and P2P lending platforms	Clustering of a large number of investors (usually investing small amounts of capital) to finance businesses through digital platforms that bring the supply and demand of capital together	Domestic/international	Grant Debt Equity	Energise Africa, M-Change, Crowd Power
Angel investors	Individuals investing at the earliest development stages of a business	Domestic/international	Equity Alternative financial instruments	–
Project developers/entrepreneurs	Persons and private entities starting and managing a project or a business in the clean energy sector	Domestic/international	Equity Shareholder loans	Sonnedix, African Clean Energy, Juneme

Source Authors' elaboration, based on AfDB (2013), IRENA (2016), UN (2019)

[a] Here, the financial instruments and schemes commonly used are listed, without excluding possible exceptions

[b] This category also encompasses family offices and high-net-worth individuals

[c] As an example, *Energias de Portugal* provided grants for mini-grid deployment in Mozambique

3.3 Identification of Investment Risks

3.3.1 Investment Risks

From a capital provider perspective, investments risks are often defined as the occurrence probability of an event implying negative consequences on expected financial returns. They are caused by uncertainties, human behaviour and/or unpredictable events related to complex situations.

Investment risks and expected returns are strongly linked. Indeed, investors adjust their requested financial returns considering the risks taken. Accordingly, the perceived risks in an investment environment should be reflected in the cost of financing. In addition, if the risks perceived are considered as too elevated in a given situation, some capital providers can even decide not to invest, thus reducing the supply of capital in a specific market or for a particular sector.

Certain risks are directly associated with the technical characteristics and financial structures of the selected investment opportunities. Others echo broader concerns in particular macroeconomic contexts and may vary greatly from one place to another. Generally speaking, developing and emerging countries tend to have higher financing costs, reflecting a number of actual and perceived risks (UNDP and ETH Zurich, 2018). As many clean energy initiatives are highly sensitive to the cost of financing, the later can thus negatively affect their financial viability.

3.3.2 Risk Management as a Dynamic and Context-Dependent Process

Nowadays, socioeconomic status, geopolitical balances and political situations are constantly and rapidly evolving. For this reason, a risk management framework cannot be static. Conditions change overtime, bringing out new risks and affecting the identified ones, thus constraining regular iterations and ongoing monitoring.

In order to attract private investments at scale and decrease the cost of financing, a thorough understanding of all the risks involved is required to properly address them and create interesting risk-return profiles adapted to the heterogeneity of capital providers. To do so, the first step consists of building a comprehensive list of risks for each selected investment opportunity, providing an overview of the risk environment (**risk identification**). Equally important is the assessment of the identified risks, particularly their probability of occurrence and loss potential (**risk evaluation**). The mapping of all involved risks, their description and a grasp of their different levels of importance will ease the elaboration of de-risking strategies and risk mitigation actions (**risk treatment**) (Alliance for Rural Electrification et al., 2015). This last step also includes an effectiveness assessment of those initiatives through cost–benefit analysis.

3.3 Identification of Investment Risks

The present book focuses on identifying risks associated with clean energy initiatives as well as presenting strategies emanating from public and private players to mitigate them. Risk evaluation and the selection of an adequate set of tools to address specific investment barriers should be context-dependent and reflect specific socioeconomic and cultural factors. Therefore, those last two steps of the risk management process are outside the scope of this book.

3.3.3 Risk Definition

This book classifies the investment risks into the following four areas: (i) economic and financial factors, (ii) overall country situation, (iii) business environment and (iv) environmental and social considerations.

This subsection aims at defining every risk category to facilitate their allocation to investment opportunities, link them with relevant groups of stakeholders and identify adequate de-risking and risk mitigation strategies.

3.3.3.1 Economic and Financial Factors

a. Currency risk

Also referred to as the exchange rate risk, the currency risk arises from unpredictable change in the value of one currency relative to another, thus affecting assets, liabilities and cash-flows over time.

More specifically for the sub-Saharan African energy sector, investors are exposed to the currency risk when investing in hard currencies[4] (thus requiring associated payments in those legal tenders), whereas investees generate revenues and carry out commercial transactions in local currencies.

In addition, some countries have poor currency convertibility, meaning the swap of the domestic currency for another can be limited. A difficult economic and political situation within a country may lead to low currency convertibility and thus create an additional risk for investors.

b. Liquidity risk

In a context of debt-like instruments, the liquidity risk refers to the inability of a borrower to fulfil its financial obligations when due, without selling less-liquid assets at a discount price. For equity investors, an illiquid market offering few or no exit opportunities inhibits the generation of part or the entirety of financial returns. The

---

[4] Hard currencies are issued by nations seen as politically and economically stable. They are considered as highly liquid and benefit from the confidence of international investors and businesses. Broadly speaking, they include the US dollar, the European euro, the Japanese yen, the British pound, the Swiss franc, the Canadian dollar and the Australian dollar.

liquidity risk also includes refinancing, namely the incapacity to replace a financial obligation with a new injection of capital, ideally at a lower cost.

The liquidity risk can stem from internal factors linked to the investees (i.e. cash-flow issues, low credit rating) or external ones associated with the market environment, ranging from little or no availability of capital to limited access to affordable financing options. In addition, certain investment opportunities considered here have long payback periods, high upfront costs and/or low expected financial returns. Those inherent characteristics require specific financial terms and instruments as well as adequate ticket sizes, not necessarily available in every capital market in sub-Saharan Africa.

The reduced availability of tailored and affordable financing may in part be explained by the limited experience of certain capital providers with regard to some financial structures and/or the clean energy sector. The latter has a relatively low track record as far as finance is concerned compared with the fossil fuel industry. Accordingly, many potential sources of capital lack familiarity with certain specificities of the associated investment opportunities. Moreover, several local capital markets across the African continent are currently under-developed, thus restricting market participants from accessing specific financial schemes and cheaper capital.[5]

c. Other financial and economic risks

The potential change in global interest rates is another risk that may affect financial investments, most directly the value of bonds and other fixed-income securities.

Furthermore, inflation can undermine an expected financial return through a decline in purchasing power (all other things being equal). It may create a significant gap between nominal and real returns of financial investments.

Those two risks as well as the currency risk are not directly linked to the clean energy sector, but rather to macroeconomic considerations.

3.3.3.2 Overall Country Situation

a. Political, legal and regulatory risk

Also known as the country risk, this category is broad and encompasses instability arising from changes in governing bodies, legislative resolutions within a country or a region, as well as lack of public commitment. Political volatility can potentially alter expected outcomes, annihilate financial investments or even remove the possibility to withdraw capital from a financial operation. Furthermore, government interferences, bureaucratic hurdles and administrative delays are important features that may impede the implementation of a project and increase the associated costs. Considering the extensiveness and potential impact of this risk category, mitigation without external support is usually complicated.

---

[5] See Chap. 6 dealing with capital market development for more detail.

3.3 Identification of Investment Risks

Businesses, industries and the overall economy can be strongly disrupted by uncertainties concerning political decisions and legal frameworks, in particular changes in regulations, fiscal regimes, labour laws and public spending. Some private actors may even witness asset expropriation, leading to the impossibility to conduct operations. In addition, geopolitical considerations, together with political turmoil, conflicts and international disputes might impact the envisaged transactions and the expected outcomes.

Equally important, problems of corruption can hinder the uptake of clean energy solutions and the entrance of private market participants. It may for instance affect public commitment, procurement processes and project assignation. Moreover, market distortion created by public policies (i.e. fossil fuel subsidies) impacts the competitiveness of clean energy solutions. Similarly, complex procedures and time-consuming processes raise transaction costs and may hamper the development of the sector.

Certain investment opportunities in the clean energy sector are deeply concerned by the country risk. For example, the development and operations of power generation plants and mini-grids strongly depend on specific political decisions such as tariff setting, licensing, permitting, land concessions and grid access. Likewise, grid arrival represents an important risk for the mini-grid sector and is considered as a political one since grid expansion is usually part of electrification roadmaps defined by public authorities.

Finally, the overall context can affect financial investments aimed at fostering the access to clean energy in sub-Saharan Africa. Indeed, the state of infrastructures represents a major challenge for power generation plants, since the deployment of renewable energies induce an upgrade or expansion of the national grid to manage intermittency and ensure connection with the transmission lines. Likewise, other factors, like mobile money penetration, need to be supported by public authorities in order to achieve their initial objectives as well as support the use of clean energy products and services.

b. Lack of investment-ready projects

As previously mentioned, there is no capital shortage at a global level. However, capital providers may face challenges in finding high-quality projects that are ready to be financed. This may happen for projects or companies at different development stages.

It is mainly attributed to a lack of common understanding between project developers and capital providers. This gap may come from different factors such as lack of capabilities to develop and present a bankable project, inappropriate risk allocation, as well as weak feasibility studies and business plans (McKinsey, 2020). Accordingly, it hinders financial closure, letting financing needs unmet and available capital not directed towards the clean energy sector.

3.3.3.3 Business Environment

a. Customer risk

In this present context, customer risk is related to unpredictable consumption, low energy demand as well as non-payments by end-users.

In developing and emerging economies, lack of information is frequent regarding socioeconomic situations and energy demand. Therefore, it adds uncertainty and blurs the assessment of the addressable market. Particularly in the power sector, a lower than expected electricity consumption can endanger the economic situation of a company.

In addition, the demand of energy may be particularly low in certain areas of the African continent, especially in rural zones where markets are small and dispersed, making financial viability difficult to reach and reducing commercial appeal of investment opportunities.

Finally, non-payments by customers can occur in two distinct situations. First because of financial constraints, as some consumers do not own and earn the necessary financial resources to cover energy-related costs. Second, unwillingness to pay due to a lack of satisfaction regarding a product or a service may also lead to non-payment, thus negatively affecting the financial viability of a project or a company.

b. Operational risk

It refers to internal procedures, workforce and systems, as opposed to systemic risks that concern an entire industry, country or region. Operational risk focuses on the manner things are executed and managed within a specific organisation. This risk category may be caused by a lack of skilled personnel, technical issues or fraud, which leads to system and operation failure. Likewise, an improper management of external stakeholders can strongly affect the conduct of a business and its functioning.

The clean energy sector presents particular features that increase the operational risk. For instance, power generation plants face specific risks associated with system interconnection. Similarly, the decommissioning of power generation plants as well as the management of energy assets when they reach the end-of-their life cycle are important factors to consider for project developers and investors. Finally, the operational risk also comprises the complexity of specific activities linked to the off-grid and cleans cooking sectors such as distribution and after-sales services.[6]

c. Counterparty risk

It refers to the likelihood that a business partner or a component of the value chain defaults on its obligation. For instance, limited financial capacities of power off-takers add significant risk for investors and may prevent the ability to secure adequate

---

[6]For stand-alone systems, limited product range is also considered as a risk. Indeed, certain enterprises have started to pair the selling of power devices with other products to mitigate this risk.

3.3 Identification of Investment Risks

guarantees and collaterals for project developers. It is often cited as the most pressing deterrent to power generation plants financing (Boston University et al., 2020).

This risk category is also linked to technical malfunctions, defects or failures of a system, thus posing a risk that assets do not perform according to expectations. Furthermore, delays during the precompletion phase (construction and development risk associated with greenfield projects) or while operations are ongoing can be caused by business partners and may thus entail cost overruns.

Moreover, the absence of clear and detailed information coming for a third party may affect investment decisions. Unreliable data related to specific markets, grid infrastructures or energy demand may engender the development of an inadequate business model. Furthermore, a rushed feasibility study may cause lower revenues than expected[7] when solar, hydro and wind energies are used.

In addition, certain investment opportunities considered here may face important issues linked to fuel supply[8] when biomass or natural gas are used as energy resources. Two distinct situations can arise: lack of resource availability implying the impossibility to use energy devices; an unexpected increase in prices resulting in higher operational or utilisation costs.

d. Competitive risk

It corresponds to a decrease of market shares due to competitive forces, leading to a decline in revenues. In addition, an energy device may become obsolete because of technological evolution, affecting its competitiveness.

Apart for direct competitors active in the same industry and with an equivalent geographical focus, any available alternatives directly compete with a product or a service as well. For instance, the abundance of coal in certain regions and its historical legacy may make the move to cleaner energy resources long and complex.

3.3.3.4 Environmental and Social Considerations

a. Climate risk

Climate conditions are a risk caused by external environmental influences, which may affect the development and operations of activities in the clean energy sector. Indeed, an environmental disaster can be devastating. Similarly, climate change may strongly impact the general performance of a project.

For example, a crippling drought strongly decreases the performance or even stops the operations of a hydro power plant. Energy scarcity is equally valid for devices using biomass as energy resource. Likewise, floods could make roads impassable, preventing distribution and maintenance activities. Moreover, weather events, like cloud coverage, alter the outcome of a solar energy system.

---

[7] For instance, an over-estimation of solar radiation will cause lower revenues than expected.

[8] It can also be seen as an operational risk in the case a company is vertically integrated and manages its own fuel supply.

Energy infrastructures are also exposed to the impacts of climate change, potentially causing system breakdowns, supply disruptions and power losses. Finally, pollution coming from the use of natural gas is also included in this category.

b. Social acceptance risk

Potential social barriers to the implementation of clean energy solutions can be very challenging to overcome and must be properly thought out in advance. The ability to ensure that a project is well embedded in a specific sociocultural context is crucial in order to avoid a certain number of issues. Otherwise, the probability of project delay or even failure is high.

In the energy sector, a first obstacle is public unacceptance. The latter can stem from a misperception of the long-term effectiveness of clean energy solutions when compared to traditional ones already in place. Moreover, low awareness of potential co-benefits in the use of clean energy products and services can lead to strong opposition movements and a limited interest of the private and public sectors. Similarly, the not-in-my-backyard (NIMBY) syndrome, based on the potential economic, social and/or environmental impacts a project can provoke, may cause delays and even the cancellation of a project proposal, thereby incurring additional costs.

Additionally, some groups have vested interests in maintaining the status quo. As a matter of fact, players and countries involve in the fossil fuel industry might have little incentives to promote clean energy solutions. Certain sectors, such as coal in South Africa, might fear job losses. Therefore, actors active in this industry may oppose the deployment of cleaner energy solutions, seen as a direct threat for their business activities and employment situations.

Finally, certain energy resources like hydropower and biomass are not exclusively used for energy purposes. Their exploitation can therefore enter in competition with other utilisations and generate conflicts between involved parties.

The above-described situations can have a strong impact on the deployment of certain businesses and affect the security of sites of operation. They may lead to vandalism, physical damages as well as theft of valuable material and system components. Furthermore, when a local community does not accept the implementation of a project, illegal connections[9] are more frequent.

Table 3.4 sums up the different risks previously explained.

3.3.4 Risks Associated with Investment Opportunities

Depending on the contexts and business models considered, certain investment risks identified in Sect. 3.3 might not be relevant. However, the intention of this book is to encompass several barriers present in sub-Saharan Africa in order to propose pertinent de-risking actions and risk mitigation mechanisms.

---

[9]Illegal connections may also be linked to other factors such as financial affordability.

3.3 Identification of Investment Risks

Table 3.4 Investment risks

Risk group	Risk category	Sub-category
Economic and financial	Currency risk	Exchange rate
		Currency convertibility
	Liquidity risk	Default/bankruptcy
		Access to affordable capital
		Refinancing risk
		Lack of exit strategies
	Inflation	–
	Interest rate	–
Overall country situation	Political, legal and regulatory risk	Policies and regulations
		Political turmoil and instability
		Bad governance, corruption, lack of political commitment
		Bureaucratic hurdles
		Market distortion
		State of the infrastructures
		International disputes
		Grid arrival and access
	Lack of investment-ready projects	–
Business environment	Customer risk	Lack of information
		Low demand
		Affordability/viability gap
		Willingness to pay
	Operational risk	Internal operations
		Workforce
		Stakeholder management
		Complex business model
		System interconnection
		Decommissioning
		End-of-life cycle management
	Counterparty risk	Breach of contract
		Unreliable data
		Delays and bad performance, technological risk
	Competitive risk	Direct competition
		Alternatives
		Technological evolution

(continued)

Table 3.4 (continued)

Risk group	Risk category	Sub-category
Social and environmental considerations	Climate risk	Climate conditions
		Resource scarcity
		Pollution (natural gas)
	Social acceptance risk	Social opposition and vested interest
		Lack of awareness
		Resource competition
		Vandalism and resistance
		Illegal connections

Source Authors' elaboration

Annex 3 presents each investment opportunity considered in this document, together with their associated investment risks as well as corresponding stakeholders that may influence each risk category.[10]

Many investment risks are common to all clean energy solutions and business models explored in this book. However, some differences exist. For instance, the grid arrival is considered for mini-grids but not for solar home systems or clean cooking. Likewise, system interconnection is related to power generation plants and national grids.

3.4 De-risking Strategies and Risk Mitigation Actions

After a comprehensive mapping of the investment barriers, the identification of core stakeholders able to influence each risk category and the description of potential sources of capital, this section presents risk mitigation strategies emanating from public and private actors. They focus on both country-level and project-related concerns, and have the objective to address the identified investment hurdles, ensure enabling business climates and/or reinforce the competitiveness of clean energy initiatives.

As reported earlier, investment risks are strongly linked with the availability of capital and the cost of financing. In order to increase the funding flows towards clean energy activities, risk-reward profiles need to be more attractive for capital providers. Two different but not mutually exclusive solutions are conceivable: (i) decrease the perceived risks and/or (ii) increase the potential financial returns. If feasible, the combination of both is even better to create commercially enticing investment opportunities.

---

[10] Further explanations about actions aimed at decreasing investment risks are given in the following sections.

3.4 De-risking Strategies and Risk Mitigation Actions

Additionally, this section presents specific strategies aimed at aligning the supply and demand of capital. As a matter of fact, some clean energy-related projects present specific features that do not necessarily fit with traditional approaches of financing. Therefore, some mechanisms need to be developed and implemented to match the needs of all stakeholders.

While a wide range of risk mitigation and de-risking strategies are available, the selection of an effective and efficient mix of tools is very challenging and would differ from one country to another and from one project to another. As previously mentioned, it should reflect socioeconomic profiles, cultural factors, energy demand levels, current access status and national endowments. In addition, institutional, technical and human abilities, as well as resource availability need to be considered.

As this section does not focus on a specific geographical area, it presents public and private schemes and mechanisms without assessing their cost-effectiveness and efficiency in concrete situations.

3.4.1 Four Different Spheres of Interest

This book considers de-risking strategies and risk mitigation actions in four distinct areas:

A. **Public policies and initiatives**: they focus on specific risks and aspire to mitigate or remove the root causes of the targeted barriers. The latter are not only linked to the deployment of clean energy solutions, but also to particular concerns faced by capital providers at a country level.
B. **Public financial and fiscal mechanisms**: this category encompasses the transfer of risks from the private to the public sector as well as direct financial incentives to compensate for residual investment barriers, without attempting to address a specific hurdle.
C. **Private financial structures and mechanisms**: in this area, the emphasis is placed on private financial schemes aimed at fostering the allocation of capital in the clean energy sector.
D. **Private initiatives**: they include specific actions undertaken by project developers and managers to reduce risk perception of potential capital providers. They usually target specific risks associated with their business models.

Figure 3.1 shows a visual representation of the classification of risk mitigation and de-risking actions.

3.4.2 Risk Mitigation Strategy Identification

The following table summarises risk mitigations actions within their respective categories. In addition, Annex 4 links those schemes with the identified investment

Fig. 3.1 Risk classification. *Source* Authors' elaboration

barriers presented in the previous section. The next chapters provide a description and deeper analysis of each instrument and scheme reported in Table 3.5.

Table 3.5 Risk mitigation strategies

Public	Policies and initiatives	Energy strategy and planning
		Governance and management practices
		Market information
		Standards of quality
		Standardisation/streamlined regulations and requirements
		Land rights and concessions
		Pipeline facilities
		Technical assistance and capacity building
		Awareness campaign
		Rural energy agencies
		Grid arrival and grid access provisions
		Utility and subsidy reforms
		Tariff setting
		International cooperation and partnerships
		Regional power pools
		Fiscal incentives
		Priority sector lending
	Financial structures and mechanisms	Direct public investments/special-purpose investment vehicles
		Alternative financial instruments and schemes[a]
		Subsidies
		Credit lines/on-lending structures

(continued)

Table 3.5 (continued)

Private	Financial structures and mechanisms	Guarantees and insurance[b]
		Hard currency PPAs
		Concessional finance and patient capital
		Alternative financial instruments and schemes[c]
		Structured finance
		Project finance
		Loan syndication
		Green bonds
		Carbon finance
		Guarantees and insurance
		Derivative and hedging instruments
	Initiatives	Internal liquidity facilities
		Flexible payment methods
		Payment default management
		Stakeholder engagement and market knowledge
		Strategic agreements, M&A and investors
		Good governance, internal procedures and staff training
		External consulting and technical assistance

Source Authors' elaboration
[a]Including blended finance
[b]Including currency risk guarantee funds, public external liquidity facilities, liquidity guarantees, third-party collaterisation
[c]Including crowdfunding platforms

References

Acumen (2018). *Accelerating energy access: The role of patient capital*. Acumen.
AfDB (2013). *African development bank: Initiative for risk mitigation. Needs assessment for risk mitigation in Africa: Demands and solutions*. African Development Bank, March 2013.
Alliance for Rural Electrification, Hochschule New-Ulm University of Applied Science, Institute id-eee, Deutsche Gesellschaft für Internationale Zusammenarbeit (2015). *Risk management for mini-grids: A new approach to guide mini-grid deployment*, January 2015.
Attia, B. (2019). *Big solar bankability & utility performance can benefit from power pools*. Energy for Growth Hub, September 2019.
Attia, B., Shirley, R. (2018). *Distributed models for grid extension could save African utilities billions of dollars*. Green Tech Media, June 2018.
Bhalla, N. (2019). *Dirty fuels kill millions as investment in clean cooking runs short*.Thomson Reuters Foundation, November 22, 2019.
Boston University, University of Pretoria, The Southern Africa Development Community Development Finance Resource Center, The Development Bank of Southern Africa (2020). *Expanding*

renewable energy for access and development: The role of development finance institutions in Southern Africa. Boston: Global Development Policy Center, Boston University.

Clean Cooking Alliance (2019). *2019 clean cooking industry snapshot*. Clean Cooking Alliance.

Donovan, C. (2015). *Introduction to renewable energy finance*. Imperial College Business School, August, 2015. https://doi.org/10.1142/9781783267774_0001.

GCF (2013). *Business model framework: Financial instruments*. Green Climate Fund, GCF/B.04/06, June 10, 2013, Songdo, Republic of Korea.

GOGLA, Lighting Global, Energy Sector Management Assistance Program (2020). *Off-grid solar market trends report 2020: Report summary*. February, 2020.

Hafner, M., Tagliapietra, S., Falchetta, G., Occhiali, G. (2019). *Renewables for energy access and sustainable development in East Africa*, Springer.

IEA (2019). *Africa energy outlook 2019*. International Energy Agency, Paris. www.iea.org/reports/africa-energy-outlook-2019.

IRENA (2015). *Africa 2030: Roadmap for a renewable energy future*. IRENA, Abu Dhabi. www.irena.org/remap

IRENA (2016). *Unlocking renewable energy investment: The role of risk mitigation and structured finance*. IRENA, Abu Dhabi, 2016.

IRENA, IEA and REN21 (2018). *Renewable energy policies in a time of transition*. IRENA, OECD/IEA and REN21.

McKinsey (2020). *Solving Africa's infrastructure paradox*. Electric Power & Natural Gas, March, 2020, McKinsey & Company.

Persistent Energy Capital, Shell Foundation (n.d.). *Bridging the gap to commercial success for energy access businesses*. Retrieved from https://shellfoundation.org/app/uploads/2018/10/Shell-Foundation_Persistent_PAYGO-Learning.pdf.

Pudney, D. (2018). *Benefits of privatising the electrical distribution sector*. EE Publishers, March 29, 2018.

REW (2019). *The failure of privatization in the energy sector and why today's consumers are reclaiming power*. Renewable Energy World, June, 2019.

Res4Africa (2020). *Scaling up Africa's renewable power: The need for de-risking investments and the case for RenewAfrica*. Res4Africa Foundation, July 2020.

UN (2019). *From philanthropy to profit: How clean energy is Kickstarting sustainable development in East Africa*. United Nations news, May 21, 2019, Retrieved October 17, 2020, from https://news.un.org/en/story/2019/05/1039551.

UNDP & ETH Zurich (2018). *Derisking renewable energy investment: Off-grid electrification*. New York, Zurich, Switzerland: United Nations Development Programme, ETH Zurich, and Energy Politics Group.

WEF (2019). *From funding to financing: Transforming SDG finance for country success*. World Economic Forum, April, 2019.

Waissbein, O., Glemarec, Y., Bayraktar, H., Schmidt, T.S. (2013). *Derisking renewable energy investment. A framework to support policymakers in selecting public instruments to promote renewable energy investment in developing countries*. New York, NY: United Nations Development Programme.

Open Access This chapter is licensed under the terms of the Creative Commons Attribution 4.0 International License (http://creativecommons.org/licenses/by/4.0/), which permits use, sharing, adaptation, distribution and reproduction in any medium or format, as long as you give appropriate credit to the original author(s) and the source, provide a link to the Creative Commons license and indicate if changes were made.

The images or other third party material in this chapter are included in the chapter's Creative Commons license, unless indicated otherwise in a credit line to the material. If material is not included in the chapter's Creative Commons license and your intended use is not permitted by statutory regulation or exceeds the permitted use, you will need to obtain permission directly from the copyright holder.

Chapter 4
Public Policies and Initiatives in the Energy Sector

This chapter focuses on the public sector and the tools at its disposal to decrease the risk perception in the clean energy sector in sub-Saharan Africa, encompassing policies, regulations and specific initiatives. It particularly targets policy-makers across the region, as well as development institutions supporting government agencies.

It presents various initiatives that can be undertaken by public authorities with the objective of improving the overall context as well as providing clarity and direction for project developers and capital providers. It ranges from national energy planning, governance and administrative procedures, to international cooperation and rural agencies.

Moreover, emphasis is put on the role of power utility companies and the necessary reforms that may foster clean energy access for populations. In addition, the chapter focuses on schemes and mechanisms that can strengthen the competitivity and attractiveness of clean energy access solutions, including fiscal incentives, tariff setting, subsidies and priority sector lending.

Finally, this section ends with a presentation of the potential obstacles to the implementation of the public policies and initiatives previously described, and explores some lines of thought to mitigate them.

In industrialised as well as developing economies, private capital is predominantly commercially oriented, meaning that investors seek to cover their costs and receive financial returns corresponding to the risks taken. In many sectors, financing needs are fulfilled following this principle, and public resources and actions are therefore not necessary. However, issues of under-investment and slow dissemination are acute for clean energy initiatives located in sub-Saharan Africa. Accordingly, the public sector can act as a catalyst through appropriate policies, mechanisms and initiatives, in order to create a propitious investment climate and mobilise private capital at scale for clean energy access.

Over the years, energy policies have expanded across all regions of the globe due to different factors, including the drive towards decarbonization, the implementation of intermittent renewable energies and cross-border power markets (Pérez-Arriaga, 2017). Similarly, several public initiatives aimed at supporting the deployment and encouraging the financing of clean energy access solutions have emerged across the African continent. Even though they are not necessarily sufficient by themselves, those public actions are essential and represent a first step towards the building of an enabling investment environment.

The role of the public sector is complex and requires long-term political commitment, leadership as well as effective planning to drive forward a process of reforms and ensure adequate resource allocation. Regarding the clean energy sector, the current landscape usually tends to be fragmented and let often some barriers unaddressed (Res4Africa, 2020). In particular, deployed instruments and mechanisms frequently cover only certain phases of project life cycles, generally early development stages, and focus mainly on medium- and large power generation plants. Thus, there is a need to fill this gap and advance a comprehensive and end-to-end strategy able to tackle the clean energy access challenge in the region.

4.1 The Importance of Energy Policies

Capital providers and project developers, commercially oriented or not, preferentially allocate their resources towards countries that present a stable and auspicious business environment (Concern Worldwide, 2020). The principle is equally valid for the energy sector. Comprehensible roadmaps and sound policies are thus necessary to reduce risk perception, provide valuable insights and clarity to key stakeholders as well as tailored incentives which correct market failures.

Energy policies seek to back political commitment and advance national goals. Their general objective is to create a favourable and predictable legislative and regulatory framework, as well as provide adequate incentives to support the development of the sector, including the access to clean energy. They are part of a global strategy aimed at tackling either project-specific and country-level concerns faced by stakeholders and overcoming barriers related to different areas of the energy industry (i.e. resources, distribution, consumption, access, etc.). They shall create confidence as well as stimulate growth and competitiveness of dedicated initiatives. Energy policies are therefore particularly important in sub-Saharan African contexts, usually perceived as risky environments.

To achieve those objectives, energy policies may include different elements, ranging from national planning and capacity building to sector-specific, cross-cutting and finance policies. They should reflect socioeconomic and cultural conditions, be inclusive and customised to local circumstances (i.e. energy needs, resource potential, affordability, etc.). Indeed, each country has its own specific environment, and thus, a one-size-fits-all solution will not necessarily lead to the expected outcomes.

Finally, this approach has to be dynamic to allow a reflection of the evolution of the society and the business environment, as well as consider implementation challenges. Moreover, the presence of credible institutions that have the necessary autonomy to implement and enforce regulation as well as establish clear procedures is another indispensable element to build a reliable and stable policy framework.

4.2 National Energy Planning

The very first step to ensure the proper development of adequate energy policies is the elaboration of a national energy master plan. The latter has to be adapted to the overall context as well as maturity of the targeted markets. It acts as an aspirational guidance, demonstrating political commitment and providing critical signals to relevant stakeholders. It aims at informing and communicating the overall energy objectives of a particular country and describing the global strategy to reach them within an appropriate timeframe. Therefore, it has to be publicly available, clear and transparent, as well as reliable and coherent. In addition, it should specify the energy resources and technologies expected to be used in order to meet national goals, giving project developers and capital providers key information about the different opportunities within the state.

The design of a national energy strategy requires a holistic approach, encompassing economic, environmental, social, political and technical aspects. Therefore, it should go beyond the single energy sector and also reflect related factors such as the interrelationship between affordability, quality of supply and accessibility as well as the sustainability of technology and resource options. Moreover, energy planning has to be dynamic, thus responding to demographic considerations and energy demand forecasting. It might also indicate the financial resources needed to achieve the expected results.

Traditionally, many national energy strategies across sub-Saharan Africa have focused on centralised power networks and the share of renewable energy resources within their respective territories. Nevertheless, off-grid systems as well as clean cooking solutions are fundamental parts of national development and energy access objectives. They must be included in national energy master plans to inform project developers and capital providers about government's intentions and opportunities within those sectors. Furthermore, rural settings, where a substantial percentage of the populations live without access to clean energy, are often not included in national energy roadmaps. Indeed, less than 30% of sub-Saharan African countries have stated specific rural electrification objectives (Attia and Shirley, 2018).

Once the national energy plan is clearly settled, the main challenge consists in translating the overall strategy into concrete actions as well as legally binding policies and regulations. Moreover, a public entity needs to be in charge of tracking and monitoring energy data and statistics and integrates the required changes to achieve national targets in due time if necessary.

4.3 Public Sector Initiatives

In addition to national energy strategies, public authorities can put in place targeted initiatives that address specific barriers hindering the financing of clean energy initiatives in their country. They may focus on project-related risks as well as country-level concerns.

4.3.1 Governance and Management Practices

According to the Corruption Perceptions Index, sub-Saharan Africa is the world lowest-scoring region, which draws a bleak picture of the overall situation (Transparency International, 2020). Indeed, there is an urgent need to address governance issues in the continent and removes the undue influence corruption exerts on political systems. In this context, economic development is impeded, democracy is weakened and social divisions as well as inequalities appear.

The current status erodes trust in public entities and reduces the willingness of the civil society and the private sector to respond to specific policies, affecting the expected outcomes of a wide range of public actions depending on behavioural patterns and cooperation.

Sound governance practices are fundamental for citizens, companies and investors, as they foster the creation of an enabling investment and business climate as well as increase efficiency of public institutions. In addition, they may improve the overall performance of state-owned enterprises, including their financial management, thus preventing large economic losses and enhancing their creditworthiness.

Accordingly, many African countries need to restore confidence in government bodies and strengthen public governance to properly respond to economic, social and environmental challenges as well as fulfil energy access objectives. To that end, anti-corruption reforms have to be set up to create accountable and effective institutions. This entails the use of modern tools and management systems as well as dedicated professionals committed to the development of an inclusive economy. Moreover, public finances and activities may be disclosed to increase transparency and provide relevant information to domestic and international stakeholders.

Finally, government resources should be used in a responsible manner in order to address the energy access challenge. National and local authorities have to align their actions with their energy targets and shift away from counterproductive policies such as fossil fuel subsidies.[1]

---

[1] See Sect. 4.8 for more details.

4.3.2 Market Information

In many African countries, relevant information directly or indirectly linked to the energy sector are sometimes unclear and fragmented, making it difficult for project developers and capital providers to understand the challenges and opportunities behind clean energy solutions.

Governments could collect and disclose valuable data such as population density, income levels, energy potential, current state of infrastructures and energy consumption. Similarly, the presence of potential anchor consumers like specific industries or productive loads (i.e. telecom towers, health centres, mines) as well as information about existing and future policies and incentives is valuable insights.

In addition, the monitoring of economic, social and environmental performances of clean energy-related projects may help assess dedicated policies and regulations as well as special-purpose programs. Moreover, it fosters the building of a solid track record, thus raising the interest of potential private investors.

Public authorities need to understand what is the most relevant information for core stakeholders in the clean energy sector as well as develop specific methodologies to collect and share appropriate data, with the objective to increase transparency and engage the necessary players in the continent.

4.3.3 Standards of Quality

Energy assets and devices not only need to be affordable and environmentally friendly. They also have to be reliable and respond to consumers' expectations. Meeting requirements is important to build trust and thereby support the deployment of clean energy solutions. In addition, quality and reliability are becoming key differentiating factors in the energy industry, especially in the off-grid and clean cooking sectors where competition is increasing.

Public authorities can support the selling and use of high-quality products in their own country in different ways:

- Labels and certifications

The adoption of standards and the establishment of quality assurance frameworks for technologies (i.e. labels, certifications, warranties) are interesting tools to increase confidence and protect end-users.

- Fiscal and financial incentives

Moreover, governments can promote certain products and services through the implementation of targeted measures such as tax reduction or exemption for high-quality products, and the prohibition to sell low-quality ones.

Several sub-Saharan African states have implemented policies for products meeting high-quality standards, by reducing or eliminating import tariffs. Furthermore, some African countries like Liberia and Ethiopia provide public financing incentives for quality-verified products (Lighting Africa, 2020a).

- Compliance

Similarly, public entities can ensure compliance with specific rules for equipment to be qualified for utilisation as well as for business partners to carry out activities in their territory. Under those circumstances, governments are supporting the deployment of high-quality solutions and business activities, increasing confidence and decreasing the social acceptance risk.

Those specific regulations can be applied not only at national but also regional level, thus reducing complexity and allowing standardisation in a broader geographic zone. As an example, the Lighting Africa Initiative, an innovation of the World Bank Group, developed a series of quality standards and testing methods for solar devises (ibid.). The latter have been adopted by several African governments and are required by the UNFCCC in order to qualify for carbon finance mechanisms like the Clean Development Mechanism.[2]

4.3.4 Administrative Procedures

Bureaucracy and administrative burden can seriously impede the development and implementation of clean energy access solutions in sub-Saharan Africa. Administrative procedures should be transparent, accessible and, when possible, simplified in order to provide a clear framework to all stakeholders and to increase the efficiency of financial transactions.

4.3.4.1 Standardisation

Standardisation consists in implementing technical standards common to an entire sector, ideally based on a stakeholder consensus. It is already widely used in certain industries, such as banking and insurance. By allowing comparability and reducing complexity, standardisation can facilitate due diligence processes and reduce transaction costs, thus improving attractiveness and accessibility of investment opportunities.

In the clean energy sector, certain documentation relative to public tendering, tariff setting, ownership structures, feasibility studies, performance reporting and impact assessment could be standardised and made publicly available to simplify procedures. Similarly, it may facilitate understanding as well as ease project evaluation and approval.

---

[2] See Sect. 6.2 related to carbon markets for more information 6.2.

In addition, standardisation plays an important role in structured finance. It fosters the aggregation of projects as well as allows securitization, thereby broadening the investor pool for small- and medium-scale initiatives.[3]

Yet, governments should not be tempted by over simplification. As a matter of fact, excessive standardisation may not reflect the different contexts and remove the necessary flexibility to ensure long-term efficiency.

4.3.4.2 Clear and Streamlined Regulatory Requirements

It is possible to reduce undue complexity in the clean energy sector by streamlining regulatory frameworks and diminishing excessive bureaucracy, easing the deployment and administration of clean energy projects and reducing their development costs. Furthermore, it would bring clarity for project developers, investors and public actors.

The quantity of documents required for formal registration and obtaining permits, licenses and concessions is sometimes very constraining in terms of time and costs. Yet, it is part of the development and management of a project or a company. Consequently, those procedures have to be accessible and complemented by general guidelines in order to decrease barriers to market entry and potentially reduce delays. Moreover, the overall process may be carried out in a one-stop-shop aimed at providing administrative support, improving the efficiency and effectiveness of bureaucratic procedures.

As previously mentioned, certain investment opportunities in the clean energy sector are more dependent to regulations and administrative burden than others. By providing provisional concessions and licenses guaranteeing exclusivity for a defined time period, public authorities mitigate project development risks for mini-grids and power generation plants. Similarly, legal requirements in the power industry can be less constraining up to a maximum installed capacity.

As an example, Brazil lessened the costs of rural electrification by establishing specific standards that are less complex and onerous to reach than those in urban zones (Pérez-Arriaga, 2017). In South Africa, the Renewable Energy Independent Power Producer Procurement programme (REIPP) has been designed to stimulate the renewable industry in the country, by standardising and streamlining requirements for bidders (IPP Projects, 2020). The terms, which include tariff setting and socioeconomic objectives, balance national energy objectives with technical and commercial constraints. They aim at ensuring competitiveness, transparency and fairness, as well as providing clarity for potential bidders.

However, it is crucial to reach an adequate trade-off between affordable, accessible exigences and the quality of market participants. By over-streamlining procedures and requirements, the public sector may be subjected to the entrance of less reliable players in the market, negatively altering the perception of the civil society and diminishing the likelihood of reaching energy access objectives.

---

[3] See Sect. 5.4.3 related to structured finance for more information.

4.3.5 Pipeline Facilities

Finding high-quality projects with the required risk-return profiles is often mentioned as an important hurdle for investors. This is partly due to a lack of initiatives that meet investment criteria as well as capacity constraints among project developers. Yet, missing information regarding investment-ready initiatives exacerbates this issue. If pipeline[4] is not evident to investors, they would most likely be reluctant to invest time and money in search of attractive investment opportunities.

To address this specific challenge, pipeline facilities can be created to ease the identification of promising initiatives and advance them towards financial closure. Simultaneously, project developers can realise a mapping of potential sources of capital, domestic and international and enter in contact with regional experts.

The general objective is to increase information and knowledge sharing within a sector, attract adequate investors and bridge the financing gap. By constituting virtual or physical spaces where the supply and demand of capital are brought together, it enhances market transparency and liquidity as well as improves visibility. Those facilities may provide relevant information about projects, potential financing sources and risk mitigation mechanisms, as well as guidelines for regulatory procedures.

IRENA created an online platform named Sustainable Energy Marketplace,[5] aimed at connecting project developers with potential financial and business partners, as well as providing data on markets, specific regulations and relevant incentives. It has the objective to accelerate the energy transition via a facilitated access to funding. This marketplace allows users to search projects by geographical region and investment criteria, thus easing investment screening for capital providers. Similar endeavours could be created in sub-Saharan Africa, with a particular focus on clean energy access solutions.

However, it is important to create high-quality and investment-ready projects before looking for capital, in order to avoid being driven by the supply side. It stimulates the development of attractive value propositions responding to the specific needs and targets of a country, thus spurring a proactive engagement with capital providers by creating a demand for resources. For this reason, the public sphere may also provide technical assistance to develop a strong project pipeline.

4.3.6 Capacity Building

Transforming an idea into a solid and viable business model is not an easy task. It requires specific skills, technical capacities and resources. Entrepreneurs need to be updated on regulations governing their respective areas of activity and act in compliance with local requirements. Moreover, the ability to attract a strong team

---

[4]In finance, the term pipeline is used to describe progress toward a long-term goal that involves a series of discrete stages. In this case, it refers to companies and projects that were flagged by capital providers as potential investment opportunities.

[5]For more information: https://marketplace.irena.org.

and adequate investors depends on the preparation and presentation of high-quality proposals.

Project development programs can support the development of promising initiatives by providing capacity building to project developers and managers, with the aim of maximisation the creation of value and increasing confidence among potential investors. The objective is to strengthen capacities within enterprises and set up investment-ready projects with bright perspectives and sound proposals, able to raise the interest of capital providers. It therefore mitigates the project development and operational risks.

Those specific programs focus on project-level challenges and intend to develop entrepreneurial skills through dedicated workshops. They aim at sharing best practices and providing the necessary tools for different development stages of energy-related initiatives, from project preparation activities to scale-up processes. In addition, it helps project developers understand their market and the context in which they evolve (i.e. site identification, stakeholder management, supply–demand dynamics, policies and regulations, resources availability, technical studies, risks and barriers, supply chain, possible partnerships, social and environmental considerations). Finally, they support the preparation of specific documents required during a fundraising process and provide advisory services regarding financial structuring and due diligence processes.

Project development programs can cover numerous and diverse topics. They should be designed to address specific needs of participants and use local and regional expertise when possible. Some may provide technical assistance along with grant funding for initial activities such as resource assessments, market analysis, technical studies and pilot projects.

Capacity building programs can be conducted directly by government agencies, with the advantages of getting information on the main challenges of the industry, aligning the programs with national objectives and positioning the public sphere as a key knowledge broker. However, the public sector needs resources, experience and skilled workforce to do so. Therefore, multilateral agencies and/or private actors can support the development and management of those initiatives. Either way, they offer the possibility to develop and present high-quality projects, attractive for capital providers.

Several programs have been created to support developers in preparing infrastructure projects, including InfraCo Africa, the World Bank's Global Environmental Facility and the African Capacity Building Foundation (AfDB, 2013). However, few initiatives exist with a particular focus on the off-grid sector and clean cooking companies.

4.3.7 Awareness Campaigns

The general perception of a sector has the potential to strongly influence its growth. If negative, it may become an important barrier that needs to be addressed. Awareness campaigns can target this issue, focusing on different groups of stakeholders, including end-users, policymakers and capital providers.

4.3.7.1 End-Users

Even though proposed alternatives may be economically, socially and environmentally advantageous, it can be very challenging to encourage behavioural change when related to common practices. As previously underlined, resistance to change is particularly high in the clean cooking sector. Moreover, the deployment and financing of energy-related projects might be undermined by social oppositions and disinterest resulting from a lack of information-sharing regarding their existence and potential benefits.

By targeting end-users and local residents, awareness campaigns have the potential to reduce the social acceptance risk. With the objective to provide the necessary information to properly assess the features of a product or a service, they encourage the adoption of clean energy solutions and drive their growth. They also facilitate dialogue among parties to lessen the NIMBY syndrome. To increase their effectiveness, awareness campaigns need to be adapted to their audiences and may be combined with pilot projects and demonstrations.

As an example, Lighting Africa, an initiative of the World Bank Group, started consumer education programs back in 2007 in Ghana and Kenya (Lighting Africa, 2020b). At that time, awareness regarding solar lighting products was very low. Since then, targeted campaigns have been the cornerstone of stand-alone systems sales growth in the continent, underscoring the importance of those programs. The initiative has also developed a series of radio-spots and TV ads, in order to reach remote locations.

4.3.7.2 The Public Sphere

Awareness campaigns can be designed for the public sphere with the aim of increasing political commitment and encouraging the creation of regulatory frameworks supporting the implementation of clean energy solutions.

4.3.7.3 Capital Providers

Awareness campaign may also be directed towards capital providers, especially financial institutions lacking experience in investing in clean energy activities. They aim at raising their interest and strengthening their understanding of the sector, by presenting challenges and opportunities as well as specific policies and regulations directly linked to the industry. Moreover, they have the objective to foster the use of available financial structures and mechanisms aimed at enhancing risk management and facilitating capital allocation.

Effective awareness campaigns require expertise and knowledge of the targeted sector and local context, but financial constraints can be an important issue. Therefore, some governments are sponsored and/or supported by external organisations, such as multilateral agencies and non-governmental organisations, in order to help them achieve the expected outcomes.

4.3.8 Rural Energy Agencies

Rural zones in sub-Saharan Africa are sometimes hard to reach and may receive less attention compared to urban areas. To reverse this trend, improve standards of livings and reduce rural exodus, the creation of decentralised public agencies can facilitate access to electricity and the implementation clean cooking solutions in those settings, as well as foster rural development.

By representing public authorities, rural agencies allow the completion of certain procedures linked to the energy industry. Rural players have directly access to public services, avoiding long response time and reducing transaction costs. In addition, those agencies ease the identification of specific challenges and opportunities as well as the coordination of rural energy strategies thanks to their physical presence.

Rural energy agencies manage licensing, permitting and other regulatory requirements (IRENA, 2016). They are also aimed at providing market indicators (i.e. socioeconomic and demographic data, energy access status, energy consumption and demand, resource availability, etc.) as well as relevant information relative to administrative proceedings (i.e. specific fees, public auctions, administrative procedures, etc.) (ibid.). Furthermore, capacity building programs and pipeline facilities can be directly organised in rural zones, without the need for travelling long distances.

The mandates of rural energy agencies can vary and change over time. Some focus only on the off-grid sector up to a certain amount of installed capacity, while others cover the entire energy industry. In addition, certain rural agencies may also manage financial and fiscal schemes.

In Mali for instance, the Agency for Rural Electrification, AMADER, manages financial incentives and has awarded over $500,000 of subsidies for mini-grid deployment since 2005 (USAID, 2018). Since its creation in 2000, rural electrification in the country has risen from 1% to around 25% in 2018 (SEforAll, 2020).

4.3.9 Grid Arrival and Access to the National Grid

4.3.9.1 Grid Arrival

Grid expansion is part of the solution to tackle energy poverty. However, it represents a major risk for mini-grid developers and investors. Indeed, grid arrival can strongly affect revenue streams and thereby endanger financial viability of mini-grids if not fully amortised. Fixed assets may even become stranded since the national grid is usually a cheaper option for power provision.

Consequently, regulation must address this risk with clarity and define in advance the consequences of a subsequent grid arrival. To that end, different options, not necessarily mutually exclusive, are available to the public sector:

- Grid expansion and electrification plan

First, a comprehensive grid expansion plan and electrification roadmap, including their respective time frames, should be publicly available. It allows to assess the potential of the targeted areas for mini-grids and support dialogue and cooperation between project developers and public authorities.

- Specific licences

Secondly, the government may grant land concessions and licenses, providing mini-grid developers with the confidence that the national grid will not reach those areas during the agreed period.

- Compensation schemes

Thirdly, the definition of legally binding compensation schemes offers project developers and investors a clear vision of the financial repercussions linked to grid arrival. Yet, they must be arranged in advance and based on a comprehensive and predefined calculation methodology (for instance based on depreciation). Those schemes may even include the selling of fixed assets to the distribution company under specific terms.

- Connection to the centralised system

Another possibility is the continuation of operations within the grid service area. This implies technical adherence for interconnection and administration in order to transform a decentralised system into a small power producer and/or distributer for the national power utility.

4.3.9.2 Access to the National Grid

An important factor for power generation plants is to ensure access to the national grid. Therefore, clear regulatory mechanisms aimed at promoting the uptake of clean energy resources in national grids are necessary.

They can take the form of specific concessions or mandated grid accesses, giving power producers using clean energies facilitated access to the main grid. In addition, public authorities may charge reduced transmission fees applied to clean and renewable energy resources.

4.4 Utility Reform

The electricity landscape is evolving, and many African countries will most likely pass from centralised to decentralised systems, causing different challenges and opportunities for power utilities. Disruptive technologies like smart grids and distributed generation, as well as the integration of renewable energy resources, are imposing new thinking and approaches in the sector. Driven by innovations in digitalisation and information systems as well as decreasing technological costs, electricity markets are changing, imposing fundamental transformations in grid structures.

As previously reported, sub-Saharan African energy infrastructures are usually aging and badly maintained. Moreover, they let significant part of the population unconnected, whereas grid expansion remains the most cost-effective solution to achieve universal electrification in many cases. On top of that, the region is witnessing an increase in power demand, potentially implying new installed capacity to be managed by power utilities (IEA, 2019).

Measures aimed at improving governance and management in public power utilities are key to properly face those changes, while ensuring financial viability as well as high-quality and affordable services for customers. The adequate workforce is required to design and implement essential institutional modifications as well as manage the assets and capital necessary to ensure proper operation. Apart from maximising the efficiency of power transmission and distribution within a territory, investors' trust will also be reinforced.

African countries vary widely in their openness to the private sector and independent power producers (Res4Africa, 2020). Private players have entered the power generation market, owning, operating and financing plants in several countries across the continent. Yet, the domination of state-owned utilities with a vertically integrated supply chain is also frequent. Accordingly, the participation of private entities in transmission and distribution has been so far very limited in the region (ibid.). This system lacks the necessary flexibility to facilitate market access to private players and increases the risk of political interference. Moreover, many public utilities show financial difficulties and poor creditworthiness, often due to poor billing and payment collection systems as well as non-cost recovery tariffs. This may in part explain the reluctance of private actors in entering the power supply chain in many sub-Saharan African countries.

The 1990s have seen the implementation of reforms targeting the challenges of the African electricity sector. They aimed at improving operation efficiency, stimulating financial stability of power utilities and attracting private actors (WB, 2019). Broadly speaking, they promoted vertical disintegration,[6] predictable and cost-reflective tariffs and a market open to private players in order to increase competition and foster innovation. Moreover, they included the establishment of independent regulators, avoiding potential influences from the public sphere and interferences with political processes. If successful, this approach should enhance resource efficiency, meet energy needs at least cost and catalyse private capital.

Those points may still be relevant today and have proven successful in countries presenting specific prerequisites: high electrification levels, well-functioning operations and stable political frameworks (IISD, 2019). However, they have not been sufficient to achieve clean energy access objectives and attract the private sector in

---

[6] A vertical disintegration of the power market consists of separating generation, transmission, distribution and sales activities.

many others, especially sub-Sahara African countries. Furthermore, certain countries in the developing world have adopted reforms selectively, resulting in hybrid models including elements of a market-oriented economy coexisting with a continued state dominance (ibid.).

Accordingly, complementary policies are needed, tailored to each country context, designed for particular political realities and guided by specific objectives. Here again, there is no one-size-fits-all solution applicable throughout the region, but rather a pluralism and complementarity of context-based approaches, that need to consider social, environmental and economic factors, understand the dynamics of the political economy as well as stakeholders' needs. In addition, utility reforms must be aligned with national energy objectives and targets. Moreover, corporate management practices have to be implemented in order to improve operations efficiency and financial performance.

Finally, the energy access challenge must be included in utility reforms. Power utilities have a substantial role to play to reach universal access to clean energy in the region. Indeed, the current evolution of the power sector has to consider not only the provision of a reliable and sustainable service, but also ensure an affordable access to electricity to every African citizen. At the same time, financial viability is crucial to improve creditworthiness of public power utilities. Therefore, specific business models need to be developed, able to satisfy energy needs of the entire population and the sustainability of state-owned companies.

More details regarding power utilities and available solutions to tackle the clean energy access challenge across sub-Saharan Africa are provided in the "*Business model adaptation*" chapter.

4.5 Tariff Setting

Tariff setting is part of a comprehensive national energy strategy and aims at supporting the development of mini-grids and centralised power systems. Those two concerned sectors have different costs structures that need to be considered.

A tariff-setting process is politically sensitive since it needs to deal with social acceptability and affordability, while providing adequate financial returns to investors and enabling the formation of the necessary reserves. Therefore, tariff setting has a strong influence on the mobilisation of private capital and requires a constant monitoring of the market as well as consultation of all relevant stakeholders. Moreover, tariffs should be stable, reliable and predictable in order to provide sufficient clarity to market participants.

4.5.1 Mini-Grids

Together with connection fees and possible subsidies, electricity tariffs represent the revenue streams for a mini-grid project, being thereby strongly dependent on electricity demand and customer affordability.

4.5 Tariff Setting

It is not necessary to set one single tariffs for all mini-grids within a country or a region. They can differ according to several factors, like the installed capacity, the energy resource(s) used, the targeted population, the ownership structure and the existence of financial support. However, tariffs need to match the context in which the mini-grid is deployed and provide the necessary incentives to all market participants.

A proper methodology includes the involvement and the cooperation between public authorities, end-consumers and project managers, during the development and implementation of mini-grids. Indeed, those core stakeholders have different objectives that need to be aligned. Community-owned and operated mini-grids generally aim at reaching break-even, while private developers seek profitable business models, ensuring adequate financial returns. Simultaneously, both attempt to provide reliable power to end-consumers at an acceptable and affordable tariff. At the same time, regulators and policymakers seek to meet electrification objectives and implement tariff-setting processes perceived as fair by all other stakeholders.

4.5.1.1 Unregulated Tariffs

In the mini-grid sector, tariffs can be unregulated, thus reducing administrative duties for regulators. Usually, public authorities fix a maximum installed capacity under which selling prices are set by project developers. Accordingly, it may tempt the private sector to develop mini-grids that are exempted from tariff regulation, in order to avoid regulatory uncertainties and administrative burden.

Through unregulated tariffs, project developers serving not only households but also productive uses, may apply higher rates to commercial and/or better-off customers, supposing more solid financial situations. Those cross-subsidies allow to offer lower tariffs for low-income individuals, thus reducing the social acceptance and customer risks.

However, end-users are usually not aware of the costs associated with the development and management of a mini-grid system. Such situation offers the possibility for project developers to capitalise in asymmetry of information and introduces abusive tariffs. In addition, some mini-grid developers may find themselves in monopolistic conditions in certain territories where they experience insufficient competition and should therefore exert a monopolistic power.

In order to protect served communities, regulators may impose tariff caps, linked to technologies used, system sizes and/or targeted customers, as well as based on a clear calculation methodology. Moreover, some countries provide end-users with the opportunity to ask for a regulatory review if a significant part of the connected community considers tariffs as excessive.

4.5.1.2 Regulated Tariffs

When tariffs are regulated, various options exist for regulators. Automatically, the involvement of public entities in tariff setting limits flexibility. Yet, it should provide clarity for the private sector and protection for mini-grid customers.

- Uniform national tariffs

In this case, a single national tariff is applied for electricity, without distinction between on- and off-grid systems. Generally perceived as fair, this solution is politically preferable and decreases administrative burden. It may represent a good option for publicly owned installations.

However, uniform tariffs are in most cases too low to cover all costs[7] associated with mini-grids (CES, 2018). Indeed, centralised systems benefit from substantial economies of scale and are usually deployed in less remote areas. In addition, cost structures among mini-grids may widely vary depending on their location as well as the technologies and energy resources used.

Said situation implies the need to bridge those gaps in order to attract the private sector. A first option is the introduction of tariff subsidies and/or capital subsidies[8] to improve financial positions of mini-grids. By allowing the application of lower tariffs, those financial incentives also increase the addressable market. A second possibility is the application of a national tariff slightly higher to allow cross-subsidisation across the country, yet affordability might become an issue in certain territories.

- Cost-reflective tariffs

Public authorities can set tariffs that cover costs as well as allow mini-grid developers and investors to receive a reasonable financial return. This solution provides incentives to the private sector, since it intends to ensure the financial profitability of the project. Nevertheless, this mechanism could seem unfair as mini-grid customers would pay higher rates than those connected to the national grid.

In addition, regulators require specific information to propose appropriate cost-reflective tariffs in each context. Therefore, project developers benefit from information asymmetry that may be used strategically. In order to decrease this concern, public entities may involve mini-grid developers in the tariff setting process and/or fix tariff caps depending on the technologies used and incentives received. Moreover, tariffs can also be proposed by developers and approved or not by regulators.

- Public mini-grid auctions

Like power generation plants, auction schemes can be used for the deployment of mini-grid systems. Thanks to the introduction of competitive mechanisms, those processes may attract high-quality players bidding final tariffs that usually reflect their costs, thus decreasing information asymmetry. Nevertheless, public auctions require an adequate preparation and management in order to achieve the expected objectives. More details regarding public auctions and tendering processes are provided in the next subsection.

---

[7]Costs for mini-grids include development, generation, distribution, operation and maintenance, management and financial expenses.

[8]Capital subsidies are usually preferred as it decreases the risk of regulatory changes in the medium and long term (political risk).

4.5 Tariff Setting

4.5.2 National Grid

Like for the mini-grid sector, public regulators may set tariffs for electricity provided by the national grid, seeking to offer acceptable electricity prices for end-consumers while maintaining financial viability of centralised systems.

4.5.2.1 Feed-In-Tariffs (FIT)

This book considers full FIT,[9] namely a market-independent mechanism[10] that guarantees fixed prices set by the government for the power generated over a specific period of time. They can be set in local currency as well as partially or completely in hard currency, implying that part of the currency risk is assumed by the public sector.

FITs allow public authorities to send out a strong signal regarding long-term policy goals. Moreover, they stabilise the business environment by lessening uncertainty for power producers regarding future revenue streams. Some FITs can even consider technological advancements and decrease over time, thus reducing pressure on public finance. Indeed, support schemes such as FITs should be flexible enough to respond to failing production and technological costs. As technologies and markets mature, FITs may be gradually removed and replaced by feed in premiums or other support instruments that incentivise power producers to respond to market developments and innovations. As such, financial supports for clean and renewable energies should be limited to what is necessary, with the aim of strengthening their competitiveness in the market.

However, FITs require the collection of reliable information in order to properly set tariff rates. In addition, through FITs public authorities embrace a long-term process, including a potentially heavy financial burden. In the case the government is not able to fulfil its contractual obligations and retroactively asks for a FIT cut, the private sector' trust will be strongly eroded. Such risk materialised in Europe, where Germany, Spain and Czech Republic suddenly corrected their FIT levels or introduce additional taxes to compensate for overgenerous tariff designs, leading to loss of investor confidence in ongoing policies and regulations (UNEP FI, 2012).

4.5.2.2 Public Tenders/Reverse Auctions

Tenders or reverse auctions are procurement mechanisms soliciting bids from private actors for the realisation of specific projects. In the energy sector, this market-led approach is often applied to the development of power generation plants. Nevertheless, it may also be used to achieve certain outcomes linked to energy targets through off-grid systems.

---

[9]For simplicity purpose, the document uses the term FIT for full FIT.
[10]Not based on the spot market, thus reducing price volatility.

The selection criteria are not necessarily focused only on financial factors. Indeed, they may also include social, environmental and economic aspects. By doing so, public authorities seek to share the benefits of privatisation with local communities, protect cultural identities and the natural environment, as well as facilitate social acceptance. Moreover, private bidders sometimes have to fit specific requirements aimed at catalysing local economic development (i.e. local employment, manufacturing and financing).

Like FITs, public tenders are not based on the spot market. They aim at stabilising the business environment and providing a long-term policy signal. Therefore, they decrease volatility and improve transparency, thus facilitating financial forecasting and long-term planning for project developers, investors and the public sector. In addition, public tenders let private actors propose electricity tariffs, thus decreasing information asymmetry. Moreover, through specific requirements, they give national authorities the opportunity to diversify the technological mix and physical locations, in order to improve energy security and geographic dispersion.

Nevertheless, corruption within governments may disrupt the process and break its competitive nature. Furthermore, public tenders' success strongly depends on external factors linked the overall country situation[11] and the energy resources potential, which may affect participation and outcome. Accordingly, they should be accompanied by additional measures.

In addition, public tenders are complex and expensive processes. Their development and implementation necessitate specific expertise within the public sphere. Strict prequalification criteria (prefeasibility studies, environmental and social impact assessment, land and grid concessions, permits and licenses obtained, financial closure reached or letter of intent) can be required to ensure high-quality projects. Indeed, lack of sufficient prerequisites may lead to speculative bidding,[12] delays and even non-completion. However, burdensome requirements and administrative procedures as well as insufficient government guarantees may prevent the participation of high-quality, small and/or new players. Therefore, public authorities need to find the right equilibrium.

4.6 International Cooperation and Partnerships

International cooperation and communication among countries can support transboundary issues resolution and facilitate the conduct of rational diplomacy, thus increasing the probability to reach mutually beneficial agreements.

Early 2020, concerns over the construction and reservoir filling of a dam based in Ethiopia lead to a difficult geopolitical situation involving Egypt, Ethiopia and Sudan, attracting international attention amid rising fears of an armed conflict. Negotiations

---

[11] Investment climate, overall country risk, market size, transmission and distribution infrastructures, off-taker credit risk, etc.

[12] Player hoping that costs will decrease when the construction starts. If not, the project is abandoned.

4.6 International Cooperation and Partnerships

over the speed of the reservoir filling raised tensions. Concerns were expressed in regard to Ethiopian energy security and the downstream effects on Egyptian and Sudanese water access. The next step in this dispute is for the African Union to review progresses made and propose a way forward to encourage transboundary talks in order to avoid further diplomatic escalation (Meseret, 2020). This specific case shows the importance of international negotiations, even though the final resolution is still undefined at the time this book is being written.

International cooperation can also increase investors' confidence. In August 2020, the French group Total signed an agreement with the government of Mozambique to protect the installations of a gas exploitation project in the north of the country, a territory facing political turmoil at that time (AFP, 2020a). Such cooperation efforts may reduce certain investment risks linked to macroeconomic and political situations.

Similarly, cooperation and partnerships can help implement projects at a sub-national level, support technological and knowledge transfers and foster financial transactions between countries, for the benefit of the whole region. For instance, regional power pools present several benefits but need transboundary dialogue and collaboration to be implemented.

4.6.1 Regional Power Pools

Many end-users in Africa face electricity tariffs among the highest worldwide, due to high generation costs driven by stark imbalances in power supply and demand, poor utility performance and sometimes constraints on private and independent power producers (IPPs) (Attia, 2019). This situation makes cost recovery difficult, thus blocking investments in grid maintenance, upgrade and expansion.

Regional power pools can help improve the overall performance of centralised systems, by facilitating the balance between supply deficits faced by a majority of countries in sub-Saharan Africa and over-generation issues happening in few territories. Moreover, power pools offer massive potential saving opportunities in CAPEX and OPEX thanks to infrastructure linkage and economies of scale. They also improve the reliability of power systems and decrease the risk of power blackouts. Furthermore, regional power pools ease the integration of renewable energy resources in their network, allowing a full exploitation across borders and reducing concerns linked to intermittency.

Accordingly, regional power pools allow utilities to provide high-quality services at affordable tariffs for end-users, while at the same time reducing the power off-taker and curtailment risks (Deloitte, 2017). In addition, power utilities may be better positioned to modernise and expand the national grid.

Consequently, the formation of regional markets may help meet energy access targets in sub-Saharan Africa as well as decrease the reliance on fossil fuels for importing countries. Furthermore, regional market pools provide the opportunity to improve the overall business climate and decrease risk perception of potential private investors.

In order to strengthen and expand cross-border electricity markets, intergovernmental cooperation, coordination and planning are required to harmonise regulatory frameworks among countries and build the necessary transmission and distribution infrastructures.

Currently, there are five active regional power pools in the continent:

- The Southern African Power Pool (SAPP)
- The East African Power Pool (EAPP)
- The West African Power Pool (WAPP)
- The Central African Power Pool (CAPP)
- The Maghreb Electricity Committee (COMELEC)

4.7 Fiscal Incentives

Fiscal incentives are designed to induce behaviour changes by reducing or exempting tax burdens for certain sectors or market participants. Through their use, governments support the development of the targeted activities or the purchase of specific goods and services. Fiscal incentives do not involve a direct spending, but rather imply the use of public resources in terms of tax revenues forgone.

Favourable tax regimes can be directly granted to projects and organisations fostering the access to clean energy, thus improving net incomes and/or cash-flow positions. They can take the form of abatement or exemption of income taxes, VAT and/or custom duties, as well as accelerated depreciation of assets.

In addition, public authorities can encourage activities indirectly linked to energy access through fiscal incentives, such as mobile money transactions or research and development. Similarly, tax credit can be offered to capital providers investing in clean energy technologies as well as purchasers of specific products and consumers of targeted services.

For instance, Zimbabwe has introduced different fiscal incentives, used to support clean energy projects (IEA, 2016). Import duty exemptions are given for solar panels, while investments in renewable energy benefit from a ten-year income tax holiday.

4.8 Subsidies

A subsidy is a financial incentive providing a price signal, given to support the development of a sector and unlock its market potential. Even if they do not directly address a specific investment risk, subsidies improve competitiveness and may therefore attract private capital and project developers.

The selection of subsidy schemes strongly depends on market characteristics, public objectives, financial structures of targeted organisations as well as end-users' affordability. They can take several forms and intervene at different development stages.

4.8.1 Subsidies in the Clean Energy Sector

In the energy sector, subsidies may target a firm or a project (supply-side subsidy), thus strengthening their financial performance and competitiveness. They can also be directed towards individuals and households (demand-side subsidy), either directly or through financial intermediaries like microfinance institutions (MFIs) ensuring distribution to end-users. Both can be complementary.

Subsidies are an important tool in order to attract private capital and scale-up commercial operations, as they improve financial viability of the targeted sector. They might be needed when clean energy solutions are not cost-competitive relative to existing alternatives. Furthermore, affordable access to clean energy for the poorest segments of the population sometimes requires some forms of financial support. Therefore, subsidies may be used to decrease energy-related expenses for low-income customers.

Subsidies schemes can target energy asset prices, fuel payments (when applicable) as well as electricity tariffs. They may also focus on connection fees related to the national grid and mini-grid systems, ideally after an independent verification of working installation and proof of use of service through billing records.

However, subsidies represent a substantial financial burden for the public sector. The government needs the ability to support the associated costs. Accordingly, they are not an ideal tool for an economy which is already facing financial constraints and has difficulties in fulfilling associated obligations.

In addition, universal subsidies are more beneficial to citizens with higher incomes and financial means as they generally consume larger quantities of energy. Indeed, an estimated 45% of fossil fuel subsidies in Africa benefit the richest 20% of the population, while on the other hand only 7% of these subsidies goes to the poorest 20% (Wesseh et al., 2016). A lower final price may even lead to over-consumption by better-off households, thus using public resources without effectively achieving the intended objectives. Moreover, subsidies may create technology lock-in and cause fuel scarcity if they focus on a specific energy device without considering the whole range of solutions to tackle the clean energy access challenge.

Accordingly, subsidy schemes must be carefully designed and monitored in order to ensure that they achieve the expected results and are pass on to the targeted end-users. To increase the likelihood of success of subsidy schemes, governments have to focus on specific outcomes within a particular sector and not on preselected technologies. They can efficiently reach poor households without access to clean energy by heavily subsidising basic consumption (targeted subsidies), thus avoiding an inefficient use of public resources.

Phasing-out of clean energy subsidies should occur when the targeted sectors are competitive enough and can strive without financial incentives, as well as when every household has sufficient financial resources to cover energy-related costs. Nevertheless, this process can be politically difficult. Therefore, the right timing as well as proper communication is crucial.

4.8.2 Subsidy Reform

Several countries across Africa provide financial incentives, such as fossil fuels subsidies, that negatively affect the deployment of clean energy solutions and create market distortion. In 2017, fossil fuel subsidies, direct and indirect, reached $400 billion globally (Bridle et al., 2018). They allow carbon-intensive technologies to stay in place and hinder the deployment of cleaner ones. This considerable amount of public money could be in part shifted away from fossil fuels in order to support access to clean energy, thus aligning subsidy schemes with energy targets and policies. In addition, a properly designed subsidy reform could help to achieve other important social and environmental targets, such as GHG emissions reduction, increase in the share of renewables and prevention of health issues linked to air pollution. Finally, it decreases the reliance on fossil fuels and the exposure to volatile energy markets.

Considering the negative externalities generated by fossil fuels, the rationale for subsidy reforms may be evident, yet implementation can be complex. First, fossil energies are strongly linked with economic growth, especially in exporting countries, causing opposition from certain groups with vested interests and potentially strong political influence. Second, the removal of fossil fuel subsidies would imply a sizable impact on households and industries counting of them, particularly in the poorest segments of the populations that use a large share of their revenues in energy needs. Finally, behavioural patterns may also influence the expected outcomes of public policies.

In view of the important role of energy in the economy, governments need a holistic approach to overcome those implementation barriers. Subsidy reforms have to be aligned with public energy strategies and complemented by additional measures to protect and compensate low-income households for any negative impact of a rise in fossil fuel prices. A proper evaluation of the direct and indirect consequences of a fossil fuel subsidy removal is necessary to obtain a comprehensive understanding of the economic and social implications, especially for poor communities (move from universal to targeted subsidies). In any case, the phasing-out of subsidies is generally a complex and difficult process for many governments.

Many sub-Saharan African countries are sometimes forced to remove financial supports in order to allocate public money in other critical sectors of the economy or because of dwindling revenues. In 2008, the Ethiopian government removed an annual $800 million subsidy on all fuels (CI-ACA, 2019), using the money to ease the spiralling costs of food items, caused by a combination of drought and high global food prices (Reuters, 2008). Similarly, the coronavirus pandemic and the resulting economic slump pushed the Nigerian government to end fuel subsidies, affecting many households and economic sectors (AFP, 2020b). In the same period of time, electricity tariffs almost doubled, generating anger among the population.

Both examples show the complexity behind subsidy reforms in developing and emerging economies. Indeed, limited public budgets restrain flexibility. Moreover, compensation schemes are crucially needed to avoid adverse consequences on the poorest segments of the population. Consequently, multilateral agencies and development banks have an important role to play in the implementation of subsidy reforms.

4.9 Priority Sector Lending

This finance policy is a sector-based mechanism aimed at giving a shape to the economy and ensuring that sufficient funding supply flows into specific segments considered as important for a territory.

It consists of predefined lending levels in certain domains of activities that specific financial institutions have to reach. It can be boosted with preferential lending conditions (lower interest rates, longer grace periods and/or tenors). Priority sector lending implies that targeted financial institutions support particular objectives set by the government and contribute to the sustainable development of the country. In addition, it aims to promote social equity and facilitate investments in less developed sectors and/or regions.

Nevertheless, opponents to this finance policy claim that it causes market distortion and becomes an economic burden for subjected financial institutions, by limiting investments in other sectors and diverting funds from potentially profitable industries (Udit, 2016). Moreover, some financial institutions may lack expertise in the priority sectors, seeing therefore their operations and possible expansion affected.

However, complementary solutions exist to decrease those negative perceptions. First, the bankability of projects and companies active in the priority sectors can be improved through additional supportive mechanisms. Second, regulation may be adapted to the specificities of financial entities, considering their experiences and geographic presence.

Back in 2015, the Reserve Bank of India introduced renewable energy resources into its priority sector lending (PSL) policy, with the objective to incentivize investments in this segment of its economy. The program is mandatory for national banks and foreign banks with operation in India, and it includes preferential interest rates for the targeted sectors. Moreover, a trading scheme allowing to exchange PSL certificates in order to reach predefined targets was created by the government. In case of non-compliance, banks have to provide capital to a special-purpose investment vehicle, the Rural Infrastructure Development Fund.

4.10 Obstacles and Opportunities for a Fast and Comprehensive Implementation—The Political Economy of Policy Implementation

Public policies are government interventions that should represent the values and vision of a territory and respond to specific concerns. They state a plan of actions to achieve future objectives, therefore implying changes that may cause confusion, resistance and frustration.

Their formulation and implementation are two key steps of the policy life cycle that face different challenges. The development of a good policy does not necessarily ensure the achievement of the expected outcomes. Indeed, the application within a certain context can be influenced by various external factors and stakeholders, as well as different interpretations. In addition, it is strongly dependant to political commitment and public governance.

In order to avoid implementation gaps, potential barriers need to be identified, analysed and mitigated. The following factors are obstacles that could influence the effective implementation of a public policy, implying distancing, leading to resistance and even sabotage (Omoniyi, 2018):

- Weak institutional capacities
- Improper planning and management, lack of proper direction
- Inability to involve all relevant stakeholders, public and private, resulting in policies perceived as unfavourable and externally imposed without consultation
- Lack of consideration of specific factors linked to the local context
- Financial constraints and unavailability of necessary resources (material, human)
- Bureaucratic bottlenecks
- Lack of political will, corruption and political patronage
- Vested interests and political opposition

To avoid an implementation gap, public authorities first need to have legitimation. To do so, they should take all the necessary means to decrease corruption, create confidence and improve transparency. The government has to prove its commitment and sensitiveness to the underlying challenges and its will to respond to the population's needs. Moreover, an effective energy policy implementation requires coherence and synergies with national objectives and strategic planification in order to reduce confusion and guide priorities.

Moreover, the goal-setting process has to be realistic and adapted to the local context, the targeted challenges and the available resources. It is not necessary to elaborate energy policies for an entire country. However, they should target specific requirements and objectives, while considering prevailing peculiarities, circumstances and aspirations.

In addition, public entities have to ensure a proper understanding and interpretation of the overall process through adequate communication at all stages of the policy life cycle. Targeted issues and proposed responses need to be clearly explained, including solid arguments to justify specific choices.

Equally important is the necessity to involve all relevant stakeholders, from problem identification and policy formulation to implementation, monitoring and evaluation. This requires organisation and coordination, but allows the public sector to spark a debate, exchange information and increase engagement and cooperation. It aims at creating a consultative and participatory approach and closing the gap between policy conception and implementation.

Furthermore, the public sector needs to consider the interest of internal and external parties as well as their ability to influence the implementation of an energy policy, in order to avoid tension between opposing stakeholders. Dialogue should be encouraged to take into account all situations and consequences for various stakeholders.

4.10 Obstacles and Opportunities for a Fast and Comprehensive …

Finally, a constant monitoring and assessment of the impact and progresses made is necessary, allowing the introduction of the required modifications and increasing the likelihood of success. Pilot and temporary measures may be implemented in order to get regular feedbacks and improve commitment of different stakeholders.

Here again, multilateral agencies can support national and local governments in the implementation of energy policies, providing technical assistance and advisory services to improve capabilities and increase policy efficiency.

References

AfDB (2013b). *African development bank: Initiative for risk mitigation. Needs assessment for risk mitigation in Africa: Demands and solutions*. African Development Bank, March 2013.
AFP (2020a). *Total Signe un Accord avec le Mozambique pour Protéger les Installations de son Project Gazier*, Agence Française de Presse, August 24, 2020.
AFP (2020b). *Price hikes anger Nigerians as fuel subsidy ends*. Retrieved October 1, 2020, from https://ewn.co.za/2020/09/14/price-hikes-anger-nigerians-as-fuel-subsidy-ends.
Attia, B. (2019). *Big solar bankability and utility performance can benefit from power pools*. Energy for Growth Hub, September, 2019.
Attia, B., Shirley, R. (2018). *Distributed models for grid extension could save African utilities billions of dollars*. Green Tech Media, June, 2018.
Bridle, R., Halonen, M., Klimscheffski, M., Merril, L., Tommila, P., Zinecker, A. (2018). *Swapping fossil fuel subsidies for sustainable energy*. Nordic Council of Ministers, 2018.
CES (2018). *Tariff-setting approaches for rural electrification*. Clean Energy Solutions, Webinar released on April 25, 2018, online at https://cleanenergysolutions.org/training/tariff-setting-approaches-rural-electrification.
CI-ACA (2019). *Carbon pricing approaches in Eastern and Southern Africa. Annexure A: Country chapters*. Collaborative Instruments for Ambitious Climate Action. April, 2019.
Concern Worldwide, Mercy Corps (2020). *At what cost? How chronic gaps in adaptation finance expose the world's poorest people to climate chaos*. Concern Worldwide, Mercy Corps, July, 2020.
Deloitte (2017). *Sub-Saharan Africa power trends: Power disruption in Africa*, Deloitte, 2017.
IEA (2016). *Tax incentives for renewable energy*. International Energy Agency, April, 2016. Retrieved September 29, 2020, from https://www.iea.org/policies/6006-tax-incentives-for-renewable-energy.
IEA (2019). *Africa energy outlook 2019*. International Energy Agency, Paris. www.iea.org/reports/africa-energy-outlook-2019.
IISD (2019). *Policy approaches for a kerosene to solar subsidy swap*. Global Subsidies Initiatives, International Institute for Sustainable Development.
IPP Projects (2020). *Independent power producer procurement programme*. Retrieved September 10, 2020, from https://ipp-renewables.co.za.
IRENA (2016). *Policies and regulations for private sector renewable energy mini-grids*. IRENA, Abu Dhabi, 2016.
Lighting Africa (2020a). *Quality Assurance*.Lighting Africa. Retrieved October 15, 2020, from https://www.lightingafrica.org/what-we-do/quality-assurance/.
Lighting Africa (2020b). *Consumer education*. Lighting Africa. Retrieved August 28, 2020, from https://www.lightingafrica.org/what-we-do/consumer-education/.
Meseret, E. (2020). *Ethiopia denies report government has started filling dam*, AP News, July 15, 2020.

Omoniyi V. A. (2018). *The challenges of policy implementation in Africa and sustainable development goals*. Lagos State University, February, 2018.

Pérez-Arriaga, I. (2017). *New regulatory and business model approaches to achieving universal electricity access*. Institute for Research in Technology (IIT), Comillas Pontifical University Madrid, Spain, Center for Energy & Environmental Policy Research, Massachusetts Institute of Technology (MIT), Cambridge, USA.

Res4Africa (2020). *Scaling up Africa's renewable power: The need for de-risking investments and the case for RenewAfrica*. Res4Africa Foundation, July 2020.

Reuters (2008). *Ethiopia ends fuel subsidy, increases pump prices*. Thomson Reuters Foundation, October 4, 2008.

SEforAll (2020). *Access to electricity (% of population)*. Database from the SE4ALL Global Tracking Framework, World Bank Group, International Energy Agency, Energy Sector Management Assistance Program. Retrieved September 27, 2020, from https://data.worldbank.org/indicator/EG.ELC.ACCS.ZS?end=2018&locations=IN&start=1990&view=chart.

Transparency International (2020). *CPI 2019: Sub-Saharan Africa*. Transparency International, January 23, 2020.

Udit, R. (2016). *Priority sector lending in India*. Published on Legal Services India. Retrieved October 23, 2020, from http://www.legalservicesindia.com/article/2417/Priority-Sector-Lending-In-India.html.

UNEP FI (2012). *Financing renewable energy in developing countries: Drivers and barriers for private finance in sub-Saharan Africa*. UNEP Finance Initiative, Innovative Financing for Sustainability, February, 2012.

USAID (2018). *What are the best ways for governments to create an enabling investment climate for mini-grids*. USAID, February 12, 2018. Vallée, M. (2018). *PPP laws in Africa: Confusing or clarifying?*. Published on Getting Infrastructure Finance Right, February 22, 2018.

WB (2019). *Rethinking power sector reform in the developing world*. World Bank Group, 2019.

Wesseh P. K., Boqiang L., Atsagli P. (2016). *Environmental and welfare assessment of fossil-fuels subsidies removal: A computable general equilibrium analysis for Ghana*, December 1, 2016.

Open Access This chapter is licensed under the terms of the Creative Commons Attribution 4.0 International License (http://creativecommons.org/licenses/by/4.0/), which permits use, sharing, adaptation, distribution and reproduction in any medium or format, as long as you give appropriate credit to the original author(s) and the source, provide a link to the Creative Commons license and indicate if changes were made.

The images or other third party material in this chapter are included in the chapter's Creative Commons license, unless indicated otherwise in a credit line to the material. If material is not included in the chapter's Creative Commons license and your intended use is not permitted by statutory regulation or exceeds the permitted use, you will need to obtain permission directly from the copyright holder.

Chapter 5
Direct and Indirect Investments in the Energy Sector

> *This chapter focuses on financial investments, coming either from public or private asset managers and institutions. It has two main targeted readers (without any exclusion): (i) public and private capital providers, with the objective of presenting traditional and alternative financial instruments and schemes capable to align risk-return profiles of several investment opportunities in the clean energy sector, (ii) project developers, in order to increase awareness of the financial mechanisms available in the market.*
>
> *The first part of this chapter starts by highlighting the role of public finance in the allocation of private capital towards clean energy companies and projects. Thereafter, it presents traditional and alternative direct financial instruments, with the aim of giving a comprehensive overview of the solutions that can foster the financing of clean energy access. In addition, it exposes the role of special-purpose investment vehicles.*
>
> *The second part of this chapter focuses on alternative financial structures able to enhance financial flows towards clean energy access in sub-Saharan Africa, including blended finance, crowdfunding platforms and structured finance. Finally, the last sub-section is dedicated to the financing of large and complex energy projects, as well as the mechanisms available to decrease the risk perception and foster their funding.*

In addition to energy policies and targeted initiatives, the public sector also uses its financial resources to directly or indirectly fund clean energy activities. Apart from subsidy schemes, public institutions may use additional financial instruments and mechanisms as well as collaborate with private actors through public–private partnerships (PPPs).

As previously reported, public money will not be sufficient to bridge the financial gap associated with the access to clean energy in sub-Saharan Africa. Thus, private capital providers should be encouraged to invest in related initiatives. Moreover, private investors have a broad set of financial schemes at their disposal to meet the requirements of the supply and demand of capital.

5.1 The Role of Public Finance

Public financial institutions have a crucial role to play in the financing of clean energy access in sub-Saharan Africa, especially by paying the way for the private sector and creating an enabling investment climate.

Public financial resources are used to develop and implement public policies and regulations as well as specific programs supporting the growth of the clean energy sector. In addition, the public sphere directly invests in public and private initiatives supporting energy access, mainly through grants and (concessional) lending. On top of that, recent years have seen the deployment of innovative financial structures and mechanisms, such as guarantees, liquidity facilities and derivative instruments, aimed at addressing specific investors' concerns and leveraging private capital (IRENA, 2016). Even though some projects may still require direct public funding, an increasing use of mobilisation tools is important considering the limited availability of public money. Indeed, they are necessary to bridge the financing gap in the access to clean energy in sub-Saharan Africa.

Public funding sources include government spending, multilateral agencies, public export agencies and climate finance institutions. All can invest in publicly and privately owned organisations. Those public finance entities should provide capital to underinvested sectors that generate a positive economic, social and environmental impact, using various financial instruments. They usually offer funds on concessional terms, thus reducing the overall cost of capital for investees. In addition, the presence of public money may also decrease the risk perception associated with a project or a company and therefore catalyse private investors.

5.2 Traditional and Alternative Financial Instruments

This subsection presents traditional financing schemes (grant, debt and equity financing) used by capital providers to fund energy projects and companies. Those financing instruments are generally used by public institutions, commercial and investment banks as well as institutional investors.

In addition, alternative instruments can be mobilised to finance clean energy initiatives in sub-Saharan Africa, as they present specific features that may be well-suited for specific financial structures and projections. Indeed, they can adapt to particular constraints and cash-flow forecasts, thus reducing pressure on financial statements in the short run. Moreover, this flexibility may give time and space to project developers to understand their markets, develop projects responding to customer needs and

5.2 Traditional and Alternative Financial Instruments

validate their business model for subsequent rounds of financing. Alternative financial instruments may bear early-stage risks and prepare for scaling, thus catalysing mainstream capital at later development stages. This is particularly important as behavioural changes may take long and a significant part of potential customers are poor in sub-Saharan Africa. Finally, those alternative financing structures provide additional options for investors to exit their investments, essential in illiquid sectors and underdeveloped capital markets.

Nowadays, alternative financial instruments are underutilised in many sectors, mainly because both investors and investees are not familiar with those innovative financial structures or not aware of their existence. Furthermore, certain jurisdictions may not be adapted to their application. However, they have the potential to achieve a win–win situation, especially for off-grid and clean cooking companies. Indeed, they have the potential to match the supply and demand of capital and provide more flexibility by aligning financial obligations and capabilities over time. Accordingly, they offer additional options to fund companies, in particular those without a sufficient track record for traditional debt investors such as commercial banks.

It is important to mention that the development and use of new financial products and schemes must strike the right balance between necessary innovation and familiarity to capital providers. In addition, common standards as well as supporting policies and regulations are required in order to reach a significant scale.

5.2.1 Grants

Grants can fund initiatives at different development stages. Since they do not involve interest rate, they represent an entry of capital free of charge, thus de-risking the aided project. Furthermore, grants may encourage mission alignment and help achieving impact objectives.

Grant funding may support preliminary activities of a project. At later stages, it provides the opportunity to set lower selling prices and/or affordable tariffs and connection fees for end-users. Moreover, grants may cover financing needs of technical assistance programs as well as awareness campaigns.

Grants can be **recoverable**, meaning that all or part of the principal must be repaid to the granter at a specific moment in time. Another form of grant funding which is increasingly prevalent in international climate finance is **result-based financing**. This ex-post funding scheme bases the distribution of funds upon the achievement of predefined results such as serving hard-to-reach segments or entering new market(s). Therefore, it provides strong incentives for recipients to reach those objectives, while letting them autonomy and flexibility on the means. At the same time, grantees must have access to upfront capital to be able to respond to those incentives, which may be challenging in certain cases.

In addition, public finance institutions as well as private capital providers may use **convertible grants**, giving the possibility to shift from grant funding to interest-bearing loan financing once a particular milestone is reached (i.e. feasibility study completion, pilot project achievement, financial closure, number of customers served). Therefore, it offers the opportunity to support projects during phases with insufficient capacities to cover the entirety of financial expenses, without removing the potential to benefit from interest payments should the desired outcome materialise. Moreover, public convertible grants may facilitate access to private capital by reducing financial constraints before conversion and accompanying projects towards the realisation of specific objectives. Convertible grants are part of the set of financial instruments used by the Electrification Financing Initiative (ElectriFI[1]), an impact investment facility funded by the European Union with the mission to support the access to clean energy in developing countries.

5.2.2 Debt-Like Instruments

Debt financing is commonly used by capital providers and may include either traditional or concessional terms. The latter offers advantageous financial conditions, including below-market interest rates, long-term tenors and/or longer grace periods.

As an example, ResponsAbility, an impact investor with headquarters in Switzerland, proposes flexible debt financing solutions for energy access companies active in Africa and Asia Pacific (ResponsAbility, 2020). They include flexible ticket sizes, maturities ranging from 6 to 36 months, funding in various currencies, as well as disbursement and repayment structures tailored to cash-flow projections.

A market-based lenders' approach usually requires the provision of collaterals, an adequate debt to equity ratio and an acceptable debt service coverage ratio (DSCR), preventing the use of debt-like instruments for many early-stage and growing companies. In contrast to traditional fixed repayment schemes, certain lenders may include additional conditions and concessionary terms in order to adapt to financial projections. Indeed, debts can be subordinated, offer longer grace periods and/or bullet payments, as well as reduce their collateral requirements. Those debt-like instruments are well-suited for companies at development stage, when scaling requires additional funding but cash-flows do not necessarily cover financial obligations at the moment of investment. Moreover, they avoid dilution for project developers, may optimise fiscal positions and are usually less expensive than equity-like instruments.

Subordinated debt and **shareholder loans** may be provided to clean energy projects or companies, with the objective of enhancing credit ratings and catalysing private capital. Also known as junior securities, subordinated debts are unsecured loans that are repaid after senior debt securities, meaning they rank below with respect to claims on assets or earnings. A shareholder loan is an interest-bearing debt provided by the owner(s) of a company in order to cover temporarily cash shortage and remove the necessity to seek external financing in the short run. By having a lower cash-flow priority in the capital stack, subordinated debts and shareholder loans can

---

[1] For more information: https://www.electrifi.eu.

thus catalyse private capital and reduce the cost of financing as they decrease part of the liquidity risk for senior debt investors.

Like for grant funding, lenders may use **convertible loans** to finance projects in the clean energy sector. This mezzanine[2] instrument offers the option to convert the outstanding balance into an equity investment during a period of time and at predefined conditions, usually when an agreed milestone is reached (the trigger). A **SAFE** is in many aspects similar to a convertible note, with the difference that the loan bears no interest. The potential upside returns of those two debt-like instruments may be attractive for private investors.

Private capital providers may use convertible loans to fund companies at seed or early stages as well as for bridge financing,[3] usually converting at the next investment round. Convertible loans generally do not require an immediate payment of interest, but rather the latter get accrued and converted to equity, thus reducing pressure on cash-flows in the short term. Moreover, the execution of convertible notes is usually faster than equity financing, as an agreement on valuation is not needed at the time of the investment.

Similarly, convertible loans can be used by public institutions to finance early-stage activities, thereby assuming development risks. For instance, in case a project is successfully developed and thus catalyses private capital for construction, operations or scaling, the public investment is repaid as a traditional debt and private investors benefit from a more stable situation. Otherwise, project developers are diluted but avoid going bankrupt as the debt is converted to equity.

Finally, **revenue-based financing** is a debt mezzanine instrument, increasingly used by investors, where a percentage (fixed or variable) of the investees' revenues[4] is used as source of return for lenders. This structure, thus, follows the seasonality of a company and is designed to stop paying investors when total payments have reached a prenegotiated return, expressed as a multiple of the principal. Company's payments may be made monthly, quarterly or yearly, depending on the lending agreement. This financial instrument is particularly well-suited for companies with existing operations and revenues streams, looking for financing for scaling but that do not fulfil all requirements of traditional lenders such as commercial banks. Moreover, financial expenses associated with this scheme lessen pressure on cash-flows since they are usually based on revenues realised by the company.

---

[2] Mezzanine financing is a layer of financing that fills the gap between senior debt and equity in a company. It can be structured either as preferred stock or as unsecured debt, and it may provide investors with an option to convert to equity interest.

[3] Bridge financing is an interim financing option used by companies and other entities to solidify short-term positions until long-term financing can be arranged. It can take the form of debt or equity.

[4] In the case of a demand dividend (in many aspects similar to revenue-based financing), the percentage is on operating cash-flows rather than on the revenues.

5.2.3 Equity-Like Investments

Public finance institutions may directly hold shares of companies, being a minority or majority investor. Moreover, equity-like instruments allow public authorities to participate in the management of investees, giving the opportunity to align enterprise strategies with national public objectives.

Similarly, equity financing can also be used by private investors, involving the purchase of common or preferred stocks. The equity-financing process can be done directly, thus applying to private companies, or through a secondary market, referring to companies listed on an exchange.

Equity investors may include special features in order to provide more flexibility to their portfolio companies and adapt their expected returns to the risks taken, ranging from warranties to buy back options.

Redeemable shares and **performance aligned stocks** are types of equity securities where the company buys back the outstanding shares of an investor over time or at a specific moment in time. Payments are divided by a ratio of dividend payments and share redemptions. They can be triggered by pre-agreed terms such as a percentage of revenues, redemption rights or repurchase schedules, and negotiated at the time of investment, thus offering a structured exit[5] for capital providers. According to the financing contract, shares can be repurchased on monthly, quarterly or yearly basis as well as with a bullet payment at maturity, thereby adapting to the company's financial forecasts.

5.3 Special-Purpose Investment Vehicles

Financial institutions can develop special-purpose investment vehicles focusing on specific development objectives such as clean energy access. The pool of money can either come from public, private and blended sources.

Those funds may be used to invest directly in projects and companies as well as to provide guarantees targeting specific investment risks or third-party collateralization, thus improving bankability. More information regarding the use of special-purpose vehicles to mitigate certain investment risks is provided in the following sections.

Nowadays, the clean energy sector presents a set of interesting businesses and investment opportunities with a potential for attractive financial returns. Therefore, financing vehicles dedicated to the access to clean energy are more and more emerging. For instance, Energy Access Ventures (EAV[6]) is a hands-on investor in the next generation of smart infrastructure companies in sub-Saharan Africa. EAV I, a $75 million fund, focuses on distributed energy enterprises.

---

[5]Other methods exist to exit an equity investment: corporate acquisition, equity sale on the secondary market, initial public offering (IPO). However, they may sometimes be particularly difficult to apply in current sub-Saharan African contexts.

[6]For more information: https://eavafrica.com.

5.4 Alternative Financial Structures

This following subsection focuses on alternative financial mechanisms and structures, adapted to the specificities of certain investment opportunities in the clean energy sector. Indeed, in many situations, project developers and entrepreneurs require innovative schemes to fulfil their financing requirements. This necessity may come from different factors, such as early development stages and the types of business or the risk-return profiles.

5.4.1 Blended Finance

Blended finance is a structuring approach that uses public or philanthropic capital with the aim of increasing private investments in development and sustainable objectives (Fig. 5.1) (Convergence, n.d.). It allows different capital providers to invest together, while targeting their own goals, whether financial returns, positive social and environmental impact or a combination of both.

This structure can be applied to various types of financial transactions, including special-purpose funds, direct investments and other facilities. Blended finance is primarily employed when the expected financial returns are considered as too low compared to the perceived risks for private investors. Public or philanthropic capital is

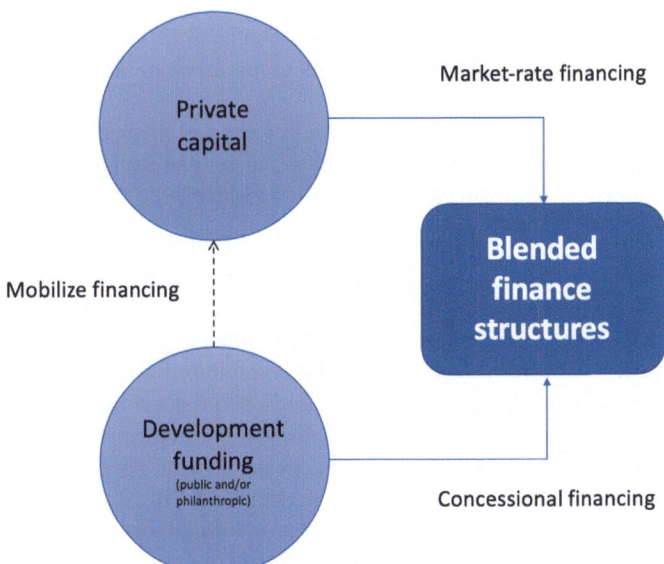

Fig. 5.1 Blended finance. *Source* Authors' elaboration, based on https://www.convergence.finance/blended-finance

then used to reduce the risk perception through concessional financing[7] or guarantees, thus crowding in investments on commercial terms and helping direct private investments towards social and environmental goals. Furthermore, the mix of concessional and commercially oriented capital increases the competitiveness of clean energy solutions as well as enables acceptable and affordable tariffs for end-users.

Considering the limited amount of public and philanthropic funds, they must be deployed strategically to unlock the potential of markets and sectors perceived as risky by commercially oriented capital providers. Multilateral agencies and development banks are particularly well-positioned to scale up the deployment of blended finance, using their resources and expertise as well as their relationships with the international investment community.

Blended finance provides the opportunity to share skills, experience and network as well as cumulate resources and capabilities. Similarly, this approach enables a better management of risks associated with a financial transaction. Moreover, it allows the deployment of tailored financing structures through mechanisms and instruments used by public and private actors.

Even though blended finance is an interesting mechanism to leverage private capital and expertise, its use remains limited across the African continent and is mainly concentrated in a few countries (Izuwah and Rana, 2018). As a matter of fact, some existing barriers hamper its development and implementation, including among other:

- Inappropriate legal and regulatory frameworks
- Corruption
- Political and economic instability
- Lack of suitable skills and experience among both public and private players
- Lack of cooperation, poor definition of roles and responsibilities
- Time-consuming and complex processes
- Lack of investment-ready projects suitable for blended finance
- Lack of public financial and fiscal incentives, such as sovereign guarantees, able to catalyse private actors in blended finance structures.

Source: Bindzi Zogo (2017) Dentons (2018), Olusola Babatunde et al. (2015), Vallée (2018)

In order to overcome those barriers, public financial institutions may start with small projects to gain experience in Africa, before embarking on larger ones based on the lessons learned. Moreover, public authorities can improve risk-return profiles of targeted projects by mitigating some of the associated risks, thus improving attractiveness for the private sector. As an example, the government of Pakistan issued a wind risk guarantee to compensate investors when wind speed is unfavourable compared to a predefined benchmark (Izuwah and Rana, 2018).

In addition, some of those barriers can be overcome with the support of multilateral agencies providing advisory services and technical assistance in the structuring, execution and management of blended finance schemes.

---

[7]Through cost, structure, terms, rank or a combination.

Some encouraging examples of blended finance structures and public–private partnerships have started to emerge across the sub-Saharan African region. For instance, the Rwandan government collaborated with several private companies to deploy off-grid solar systems in remote locations, providing access to affordable electricity to approximately 600,000 rural households (Cornell University, 2018). Moreover, the United Nations Development Programme (UNDP) partnered with the Swedish impact investment platform TRINE, with the objective of contributing to the achievement of SGD 7, initially focusing on Kenya, Rwanda Nigeria, Tanzania and Zambia (UNDP, 2018).

5.4.2 Crowdfunding Platforms

Crowdfunding platforms have surged in popularity in recent years and are used as funding options in various sectors. They have started to emerge after the 2008 financial crisis, in response to the difficulties faced by many enterprises attempting to raise private capital.

Those virtual platforms provide small-scale and retail capital providers with the opportunity to invest little amount of money into private companies, initiatives and ideas. Therefore, crowdfunding platforms hold the potential to democratise climate investments, by increasing awareness and encouraging public participation in the realm of social and environmental change.

In addition, they offer an alternative potential funding option for private organisations as well as a diversification of financing, outside the traditional sources of capital. Without representing a disruption or competition to larger investors, crowdfunding platforms can potentially increase the amount of finance available for small to medium clean energy projects. They are particularly well-adapted to overcome the initial financing gap in investments that do not required large ticket sizes and due diligence processes (Globalfields, 2020).

Many types of crowdfunding exist, but generally speaking they fall into two broad categories: non-investment and investment crowdfunding. Non-investment crowdfunding refers to funding driven by donations and rewards, excluding financial returns expectations. This category includes systems using recoverable grants such as the Kiva[8] platform which provides loans that need to be paid back without interest charges. By contrast, investment crowdfunding usually involves larger sums and includes both debt and equity financing. They are regulated by public authorities, generally unlike non-investment platforms. For project developers, it is important to select the right platform when using crowdfunding, focusing of the adequate type(s) of financial instruments and targeted sector(s).

This financing solutions can be applied to clean energy access, by providing funds to early-stage and established projects and companies. Indeed, several platforms

---

[8] https://www.kiva.org/businesscenter/crowdfunding-with-kiva.

Table 5.1 Examples of companies that raised capital through crowdfunding platforms

Company	Amount raised (USD)	Platform	Campaign type	Country of activity
WakaWaka	1,266,166	Oneplanetcrowd	Equity	Various
Buffalo grid	719,550	Crowdcube	Equity	Uganda, India
Mobile Solarkraftwerke Africa	384,615	Bettervest	Debt	Mali
SunTransfert	263,958	Bettervest	Debt	Kenya
Vitalite	111,000	Trine	Debt	Zambia
SimGas	111,000	Lendahand	Debt	Tanzania

Source Authors' elaboration, based on E4I (2017)

specialised in renewable resources and energy access have started to appear (i.e. M-Changa,[9] Energise Africa,[10] Trine,[11] Bettervest,[12] Triodos Crowdfunding,[13] etc.). Even though the sums invested can reached millions of US dollars, crowdfunding platforms are well-adapted to small-scale energy projects, such as mini-grids, stand-alone systems and clean cooking companies.

Between 2015 and June 2019, $77 million have been raised for energy access through crowdfunding, with capital coming primarily from Europe, Japan and the USA (Cogan, 2019; E4I, n.d.). Crowdfunding platforms are supported by a new generation of investors, mainly Millennials, concerned with using their financial resources in a different way, aligning their investments with their personal values.

Even though this number is impressive, it is still far from the total financing gap associated with energy access. Nowadays, crowdfunding platforms are still under-utilised to finance projects aimed at fostering the access to clean energy, mainly because this practice is still little known, and thus many project developers do not think about this alternative source of funding to raise private capital (Cogan, 2019).

However, several energy companies active in sub-Saharan Africa have successfully raised capital through crowdfunding platforms (see Table 5.1). In addition, other energy companies targeting other markets have raised significant amount of money thanks to crowdfunding. One of them is GoSun, which has raised over $2.6 million for the development of a diverse portfolio of energy projects, ranging from clean cooking devices and solar-powered coolers, to a water purification system (Casey, 2020). Another example is Allpowers, a firm that rose close to $1.5 million (14,800% of its funding target) for the commercial production and distribution of a massive 1.287 Wh solar-powered charger (ibid.). Those two success stories suggest that clean

---

[9] https://www.changa.co.ke.
[10] https://www.energiseafrica.com.
[11] https://trine.com.
[12] https://www.bettervest.com/en/.
[13] https://www.triodoscrowdfunding.co.uk.

energy projects have the potential to raise considerable amount of money through crowdfunding.

Crowdfunding presents several advantages, such as the opportunity to have access to a large pool of potential investors, the ability to validate a project as well as the possibility to leverage off/online platforms to gain traction. In addition, project developers usually face less bureaucratic hurdles and may have quicker access to funding compared with the use of traditional financing sources.

Nevertheless, several barriers need to be overcome. The main one is to convince capital providers using unilateral communication. This can be very challenging, especially when presenting unknown technologies and new business models, therefore pushing project developers to be clear, innovative and efficient. Furthermore, investors have to be aware that they fund organisations without the opportunity to realise a solid due diligence process. Finally, regulatory frameworks to protect stakeholders and increase citizen engagement are underdeveloped, even though this trend is rapidly changing.

5.4.3 Structured Finance

In order to bridge the gap associated with the financing of clean energy access in sub-Saharan Africa, investment opportunities in the related sectors have to be available and attractive for "mainstream" investors as well. This means they should have the adequate ticket sizes and risk-return profiles, as well as acceptable transaction costs for both parts of the transaction.

Structured finance mechanisms offer the opportunity to decrease costs related to due diligence processes, improve clarity through standardisation and/or isolate investment risks and financial returns from project originators. Moreover, they may tackle the ticket size challenge linked to small-scale projects and address the issue of illiquidity in certain capital markets.

Therefore, structured finance encompasses financial schemes aimed at responding to the complexity and sophistication of financing needs of certain projects or companies, which cannot be satisfied by conventional financing. In addition, it is used to manage certain investment risks related to complex situations, such as small ticket sizes or future receivables.

Structured finance includes aggregation, securitisation and Yieldco structures. In the subsequent subsections, these different schemes are explained.

5.4.3.1 Aggregation

In order to provide universal access to clean energy in sub-Saharan Africa, different initiatives exist that broadly vary in size and financial needs, ranging from small companies selling solar products in rural areas to large power generation plants connected to the national grid. However, transaction costs and due diligence processes tend to be somehow similar, negatively affecting small-scale projects' attractiveness. Moreover, some capital providers may lack internal capacity and/or willingness to assess individual energy projects and structure deals for direct investments in relatively small initiatives.

By pooling several small-scale clean energy projects presenting similar features, aggregation offers various benefits, including (UNDP and ETH Zurich, 2018)

- Increased total financing requirements
- Reduced transaction costs relative to each project
- Access to a broader pool of financing sources and new asset classes
- Diversification benefits across a portfolio of energy projects.

Even though aggregation requires government support (mainly for standardisation) as well as consensus among industry stakeholders, it represents an interesting opportunity to attract the capital of large private investors such as pension funds and insurance companies towards small-scale energy projects.

The Climate Aggregation Platform (CAP[14]) is an initiative implemented by the United Nations Development Programme (UNDP), in partnership with the Global Environment Facility (GEF) and the Climate Bonds Initiative. It has the objective to promote a large-scale use of financial aggregation and reduce the cost of capital for small-scale and low-carbon energy projects in developing countries. The CAP is structured around three core activities: (i) engagement and coordination among industry stakeholders, (ii) development of standardised tools and (iii) technical assistance (IRENA, 2016).

5.4.3.2 Securitisation

Securitisation is a process in which a company pools some of its assets and sells their underlying cash-flows in the form of an asset-backed security (Fig. 5.2). This scheme requires a group of homogeneous assets generating regular and predictable payment streams.

In this financial scheme, the originator creates a special-purpose vehicle (SPV), established as a subsidiary, that can issue asset-backed notes. These notes are secured by the unpaid portions of sales contracts. By transferring specific assets and isolating them into a new legal entity, it separates the associated risks with the ones directly linked to the originator (operational risks related to business expansion for instance).

The assessment of the SPV strongly depends on the nature of the sales contracts, the associated track record (default and delinquency rates), the payment collection system as well as the quality of the customer services and underlying assets.

In the clean energy sector, securitisation is well-adapted to clean cooking companies and distributed energy service companies (DESCOs) using PAYGO systems, leasing products or offering multiple payment schemes. In those specific cases, enterprises have to support the total expenses of energy devices but need to wait several

---

[14] For more information: https://climateaggregation.org.

5.4 Alternative Financial Structures

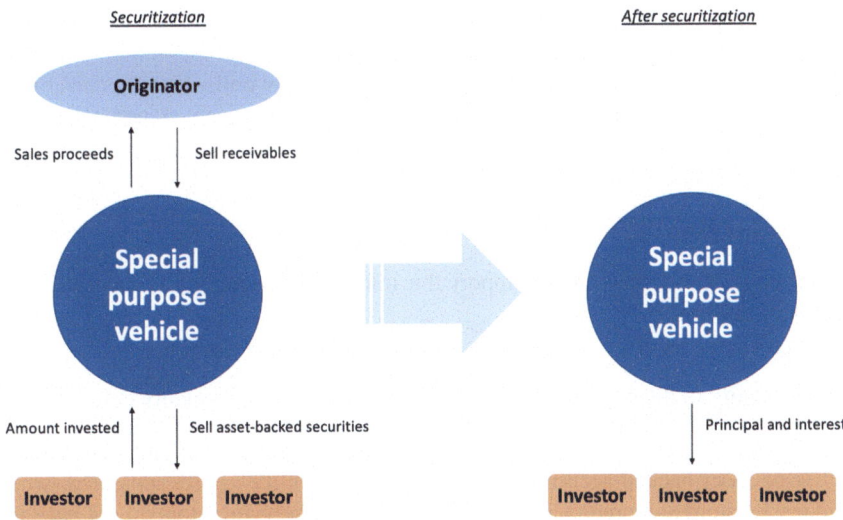

Fig. 5.2 Outline of a securitisation process. *Source* Authors' elaboration

months or years to fully recover the costs of goods sold. In addition, this period of time increases the exposure of those companies to currency risk when assets are acquired in hard currencies.

Therefore, when a portfolio of customers reaches a significant size, substantial capital is required to cover those asset receivables. While equity-like instruments would not be well-suited, securitisation could be an important cornerstone for the financing of working capital of mature and growing clean cooking companies and DESCOs in sub-Saharan Africa. It provides access to new asset classes and types of investors, mainly large-scale and commercially oriented lenders.

In order to foster the use of securitisation in the clean energy sector, governments need to implement legal frameworks supporting the creation of SPVs. In addition, multilateral agencies and development banks could invest in the riskiest part of the SPV in case several investment tranches are proposed with different risk-reward profiles, thus attracting risk-averse private investors.

However, the use of securitisation in sub-Saharan Africa presents different challenges:

- Large customer portfolio

A large customer portfolio is needed in order to create an asset-backed security with a significant size and solid track record, able to create economies of scale, cover transaction costs and attract investors. Nevertheless, many companies across the continent have not reached the required size yet.

- High transaction costs

The transaction costs are mainly linked to the SPV creation and may decrease in case securitisation becomes more frequent across sub-Saharan Africa.

- Limited asset isolation

In the clean energy sector, the originator usually directly collects the receivables. Therefore, a complete separation of the activities is challenging. A vertical disintegration of the clean cooking and off-grid sectors could increase the possibility to isolate assets included in the SPVs.

- Underdeveloped capital markets

Capital markets are needed to support the trading of asset-backed securities on secondary markets.[15]

Nevertheless, securitisation confers important advantages such as

- Opportunity to diversify the financing sources through high-quality debt

Companies may attract new types of investors such as institutional ones. Moreover, they issue asset-backed securities from a subsidiary entity legally separated, with solid track record and predictable cash-flows. Accordingly, investors do not have to bear certain risks linked to the originator as well as development and scaling-related risks. Consequently, the use of this financial scheme may potentially decrease the overall cost of capital in the clean energy sector in the long run.

- Access to financing including hedging instruments

Large-scale investments with underlying cash-flows are more likely to be swapped in hard currencies compared to small ticket sizes.

- Access to financing in local currency

Securitisation may be aligned with investment constraints faced by large local investors such as pension funds and insurance companies.

Solar securitisation for Rwanda is a first-of-its kind initiative that pools loans associated with multiple solar stand-alone systems into a tradable asset-backed security, freeing up capital for market expansion and providing project developers access to more liquid financing (CFL, 2019). The project, still under development in early 2021, is being led by the Development Bank of Rwanda, which has over 15 years of experience in energy finance, and targets three of the largest solar home system companies active in the country. The initial issuance is planned at $9 million and should enable the deployment of around 175,000 solar home systems. The instrument will be split into two tranches, with the first one being sold to commercial and retail investors as senior debt. The second tranche, serving as subordinated, will be financed by development finance institutions, providing first loss credit enhancement and downside protection for senior tranche investors.

However, if energy is sold as a service, then clients never purchase or lease assets. It is, for instance, the case of mini-grid companies. Therefore, no fixed financing contracts linked to predictable cash-flows generated by underlying assets can be sold

---

[15] See Chap. 6 for more information on capital market development.

5.4 Alternative Financial Structures

to a SPV. In that case, other financial schemes exist in order to separate specific revenue streams. For instance, Yieldco structures offer this possibility.

5.4.3.3 Yieldco Structures

A Yieldco is a new company created to own operating assets generating predictable cash-flows. The parent company usually maintains an active role, commonly through operation and maintenance (O&M) contracts or supply agreements, meaning it could thus be replaced in case of bad performance or financial concerns.

Those structures have started to emerge in the US energy sector (i.e. NRG, SunEdison Power) and are therefore built around some unique features based on the country's regulation. Their use in other continents may, thus, require an adaptation of legal frameworks.

A company may allocate all contractual rights related to a group of customers (i.e. service contracts, ownership of used assets, etc.) to a Yieldco. The latter benefits from a higher credit quality since it only bears risks related to operations with existing clients. Construction and expansion risks are carried out by the parent company.

Accordingly, Yieldcos may potentially draw capital at lower cost to finance operating energy assets. They may be funded through debt, equity[16] or a combination of both, depending on the nature of the underlying cash-flows.

Consequently, a Yieldco structure allows the separation of specific assets from the balance sheet of the parent company and eases the financial analysis for potential investors. In addition, it expands the investor base, providing access to a wider range of capital providers, with different risk appetites.

5.4.4 *Financial Structures for Large and Complex Energy Projects*

This section presents specific financial structures and mechanisms aimed fostering the allocation of capital in large-scale and complex projects, such as infrastructures and power generation plants. Depending on circumstances, they could be applied to smaller energy initiatives as well.

5.4.4.1 Off-Balance Sheet Financing

Also known as project finance, this financing structure offers an interesting opportunity for capital allocation in the clean energy sector. Off-balance sheet financing is commonly used for complex and multiparty projects, requiring substantial funding and characterised by long payback periods.

---

[16]For equity investors, there are also certain tax benefits using this financial scheme.

In contrast to corporate finance where investments are made into companies and thereby consider their entire assets and liabilities, off-balance sheet financing provides capital to a specific project. A special-purpose vehicle (SPV) without previous business record is created, with the sole objective of carrying out the targeted activities.

Project finance limits the exposure of shareholders' resources by separating the specific project from their own balance sheets, thus limiting their financial liabilities. They are only liable up to the extent of their equity investments. Accordingly, lenders' recourse is limited to the SPV's assets in case of default, shifting part of the associated risks from the shareholders to the lenders. Investment criteria are, therefore, different and only focus on the activities of the SPV, its associated risks and potential financial returns.

Off-balance sheet financing is generally a complex and time-consuming process, involving high transaction costs and engaging several stakeholders. The underlying project will have expected revenues and costs, generating cash-flows that will be dedicated to the payments of principals and interests linked to its indebtedness and provide financial returns to shareholders.

Every equity investor is committed to the underlying project and has thus incentives to perform well. Potential project sponsors may include the following actors:

- Public administration

Public authorities may use public tendering processes to select adequate private actor(s) to develop, build and manage a specific project. Furthermore, they can fund part of the related project.

- Private project developers

They are actors bringing not only capital but also skills and experience into the project. They are usually selected through a bidding process managed by public authorities.

- Financial institutions

Equity investors providing capital to the project.

A typical project finance structure, including the contractual agreements, is represented in Fig. 5.3.

In order to attract private capital providers in this financial structure, project-related risks shall be properly identified and allocated during both the precompletion and operational phases. Furthermore, the solidity of the entire network and the inter-relations between parties have to be ensured, as it strongly affects the rating of the project and thus influences the cost of its financing.

Off-balance financing is particularly well-suited for power generation plants, a sector in which revenue streams are likely to be fixed by a power purchase agreement (PPA), including when using renewable energy resources. This implies that no revenue is collected during the construction phase for greenfield projects, increasing

5.4 Alternative Financial Structures

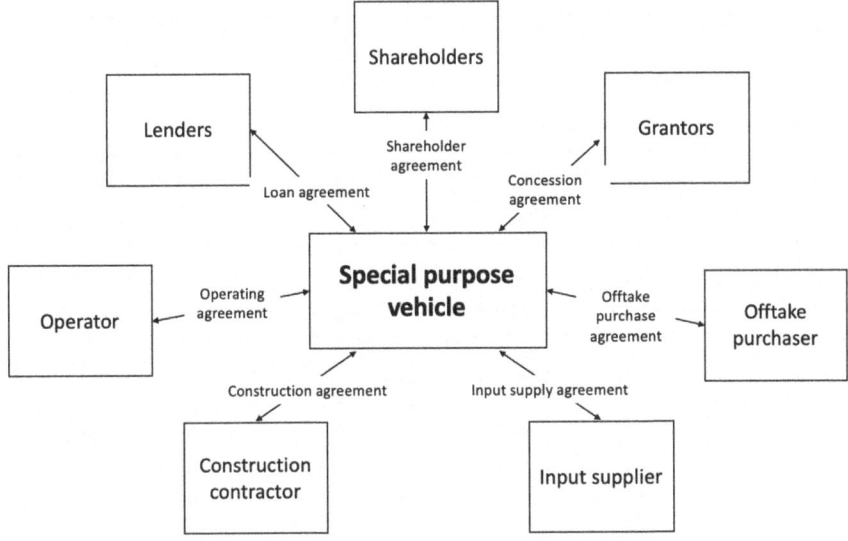

Fig. 5.3 Project finance. *Source* WB (2016)

the risks for lenders and equity investors, exclusively depending on cash-flows coming from the SPV. Therefore, a specific financial structure needs to be built, able to attract sponsors and debt investors for the financing of the SPV.

So as to keep the retained risk to a minimum level, investment risks can be allocated in two different ways:

- Through the completion of contractual agreements between internal parties

For instance, EPC[17] and O&M contracts state the required conditions for the construction and operations of the project.

- Through insurance contracts and guarantee instruments with external partners

Other investment concerns such as environmental risk or social acceptance risk may not be allocated through contractual agreements between internal parties. Therefore, the project can work with external public and private companies providing guarantees and insurance products targeting specific risks associated with the underlying project.

5.4.4.2 Loan Syndication

Loan syndication allows the distribution of risks among a group of lenders, therefore limiting each capital provider's risk exposure as well as money invested. This financial structure applies particularly to projects requiring large-scale investments

---

[17] Engineering, procurement and construction contracts.

and perceived as risky. In addition to combining financial resources, syndication contributes to making each participant's skill set and competencies available to a specific project. However, being a time-consuming process, it can be more broadly exposed to changes in economic conditions and political situations.

The participation of multilateral agencies or development banks in loan syndication can be reassuring for other lenders and even decrease the overall cost of borrowing. Indeed, those institutions bring their experience and knowledge of the local context. Therefore, it may facilitate the involvement of local and foreign commercial banks. Moreover, multilateral agencies or development banks may, for instance, lead early rounds of financing using concessional terms, paving the way for private investors through knowledge gained and interest raised.

In addition, development institutions can use **B-loan structures** in syndicated loans, retaining a portion of the entire loan (A-loan) and selling the remaining part (B-loan) to participant lenders. Through this scheme, clean energy projects can obtain large-scale financing with lower transaction costs and simplified administrative processes by signing a single loan agreement with a public financial institution. Meanwhile, private capital providers engage in a sub-participation with development agencies, instead of directly lending to projects, allowing the public institutions to negotiate on behalf of all lenders. Thence, the latter benefit from higher credit rating, strong ability to manage certain investment risks and close relationships with national governments.

References

Bindzi Zogo, E. C., Wei, L. P. (2017). *Investment motivation in renewable energy: A PPP approach*. School of Economics, Wuhan University of Technology, China.

Casey, J. P. (2020). *Clean energy Crowdfunding: Successes and failures*. Power Technology, Published on July 27, 2020.

CFL (2019). *Solar securitization for Rwanda*. Climate Finance Lab. Retrieved September 25, 2020 from https://www.climatefinancelab.org/project/solar-securitization/.

Cogan, D. (2019). *Too risky for the crowd? Assessing the potential of Crowdfunding for energy access*. Next Billion, Guest Articles, October 30, 2019.

Cornell University, INSEAD, and WIPO (2018). *The global innovation index 2018: Energizing the world with innovation*. Ithaca, Fontainebleau, and Geneva.

Dentons (2018). *The emergence of public-private partnerships (PPPs) in the middle East and Africa*, May, 2018.

E4I (2017). *Crowd power: Can the crowd close the financing gap?* Energy4Impact, July, 2017.

Globalfields (2020). *Crowdfunding for development and climate finance*. Globalfields Insight, November, 2020.

IRENA (2016). *Unlocking renewable energy investment: The role of risk mitigation and structured finance*. IRENA, Abu Dhabi, 2016.

Izuwah, C., Rana, F. (2018). *Infrastructure & Africa's development—The PPP imperative*. Published on Getting Infrastructure Finance Right, January 23, 2018.

Olusola Babatunde, S., Perera, S., Udeaja, C., Zhou, L. (2015). *Barriers to public private partnerships projects in developing countries*. Northumbria University, UK, November, 2015. https://doi.org/10.1108/ECAM-12-2014-0159.

References

Vallée, M. (2018). *PPP laws in Africa: Confusing or clarifying?* Published on Getting Infrastructure Finance Right, February 22, 2018.

ResponsAbility (2020). *Debt financing, energy access companies in Africa and Asia Pacific.* Retrieved October 10, 2020, from https://www.responsability.com/en/energy-access-companies-africa-and-asia-pacific.

UNDP (2018). *UNDP and TRINE partner to scale-up private investment in high-impact energy projects.* Posted on April 26, 2018. Retrieved October 7, 2020, from https://www.undp.org/content/undp/en/home/news-centre/announcements/2018/partnership-to-scale-up-private-investment-in-high-impact-energy.html.

UNDP & ETH Zurich (2018). *Derisking renewable energy investment: Off-grid electrification.* New York, Zurich, Switzerland: United Nations Development Programme, ETH Zurich, and Energy Politics Group.

WB (2016). *Project finance—Key concepts.* World Bank Group, September 6, 2016. Retrieved September 10, 2020, from https://ppp.worldbank.org/public-private-partnership/financing/project-finance-concepts.

Open Access This chapter is licensed under the terms of the Creative Commons Attribution 4.0 International License (http://creativecommons.org/licenses/by/4.0/), which permits use, sharing, adaptation, distribution and reproduction in any medium or format, as long as you give appropriate credit to the original author(s) and the source, provide a link to the Creative Commons license and indicate if changes were made.

The images or other third party material in this chapter are included in the chapter's Creative Commons license, unless indicated otherwise in a credit line to the material. If material is not included in the chapter's Creative Commons license and your intended use is not permitted by statutory regulation or exceeds the permitted use, you will need to obtain permission directly from the copyright holder.

Chapter 6
Capital Markets for the Financing of Clean Energy Access in Sub-Saharan Africa

> *After having presented various financial instruments and mechanisms available for financing clean energy access projects and companies, this chapter focuses on a key element enabling an efficient use of some of the schemes exposed in the previous section. Indeed, well-functioning capital markets not only increase the trust of potential capital providers, but also enhance financial flows among countries and actors.*
>
> *This chapter explores different solutions strongly depending on capital markets, in particular the bond market, encompassing green bonds as well as alternative and emerging forms of bonds.*
>
> *Furthermore, an entire sub-section is dedicated to carbon pricing and carbon finance, with a focus on sub-Saharan Africa. It includes an analysis of the current situation in the subcontinent, as well as the shortcomings associated with the implementation of carbon pricing and the use carbon finance.*
>
> *Finally, this chapter aims at presenting the current status of capital markets and banking systems in sub-Saharan African countries, as well as potential solutions to strengthen and reinforce the trust of potential capital providers, domestic and international.*

Financial regulations such as Basel III[1] or Solvency II[2] impose restrictions on certain types of capital providers, limiting investments in illiquid markets and risky

---

[1] Basel III (or the Third Basel Accord or Basel Standards) is a global, voluntary regulatory framework on bank capital adequacy, stress testing and market liquidity risk. This third instalment of the Basel Accords was developed in response to the deficiencies in financial regulation revealed by the financial crisis of 2007–08. It is intended to strengthen bank capital requirements by increasing bank liquidity and decreasing bank leverage.

[2] Solvency II is a Directive in European Union law that codifies and harmonises the EU insurance regulation. Primarily this concerns the amount of capital that European insurance companies must hold to reduce the risk of insolvency.

securities. In this particular context, capital markets have a crucial role to play in the financing of clean energy access in sub-Saharan Africa, by improving liquidity, providing long-term financing and allowing the use of specific financial instruments.

6.1 Green Bonds

Green bonds are traditional bonds labelled as "green". Accordingly, those debt securities offer the opportunity to raise large-scale, long-term and non-banking financing for environmental-friendly and climate-related initiatives. Green bonds may be used to finance new projects or for refinancing purposes, focusing on mitigation and adaptation to climate change (IRENA, 2020a).

Currently, renewable energy is the dominant recipient of those fixed-income securities' proceeds, followed by energy efficiency and clean transport (Fig. 6.1). Thus, green bonds offer interesting opportunities for investors, especially large ones with experience in bond markets and willingness to invest in the clean energy sector.

Green bonds can be issued by public and private entities, as well as financial and non-financial institutions (i.e. sub-national agencies, national and local governments, development banks, commercial banks, private entities). Moreover, they can take different forms: project bonds, asset-backed securities,[3] revenue-back bonds, corpo-

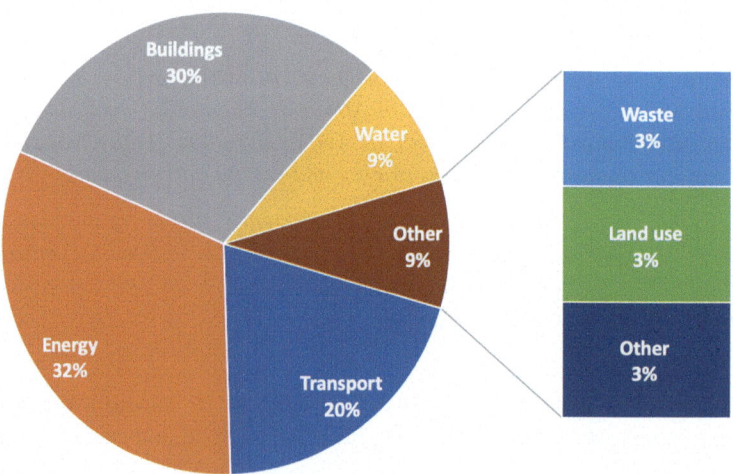

Fig. 6.1 Green bonds: use of proceeds (2019). *Source* Authors' elaboration, based on CBI (2020b)

rate bonds, subordinated bonds, Sukuk,[4] bonds with warrants, etc. Even though the US dollar and the euro are still overrepresented (accounting for more than 80% of issuance), green bonds were issued in 30 diverse currencies in 2018 (IRENA, 2020a).

This form of bond attracts different types of capital providers, ranging from institutional investors looking for sustainable investment opportunities and insurance companies willing to reduce their exposure to the climate risk, to commercially oriented investors. By providing access to "green" projects, it offers the possibility to diversify their assets under management (AUM). In addition, green bond investments usually positively impact the reputation of investors and issuers.

Even though the impact of the "green" label on the cost of capital is still not clear yet, it may increase confidence of investors as well as save costs and time during due diligence processes. Indeed, the "green" label is directly related to the specific assets or project(s) financed by the bond, not to the issuers, thus reducing the analysis requirements regarding environmental factors.

Three different ways exist to issue a bond labelled as "green":

- Self-labelling

This option is based on reputation and was mainly used for the first green bond issuances. Nowadays, investors may require stronger arguments to really trust the "green" label.

- Second-party opinion (SPO)

A methodology of assessment is created by external reviewers with experience in the environmental sector. Usually, the evaluation is aligned with the Green Bond Principles (GBP) and aimed at assessing the overall objectives and processes, without basing the analysis on a particular governance structure.

- Third-party opinion

In this case, the evaluation is based on external standards and released by an approved verifier, improving the independence and transparency of the assessment and allowing a clear taxonomy across the market. The use of a third-party opinion has a cost, but reduces complexity and may increase investors' confidence.

The Climate Bonds Initiative is an approved verifier providing unique and global standards for a broad range of sectors that can possibly be funded through green bonds. Regarding the energy sector, wind, solar, geothermal and marine energies can be certified, while hydro, bioenergy and electrical grids criteria are currently under development or due to commence.

---

[3] Pooling and securitization of small-scale projects/assets, increasing attractiveness for large capital providers and decreasing transaction costs.

[4] A Sukuk is an Islamic financial instrument, comparable to a bond in Western economies, that complies with the Sharia. As interest-paying bond structures are not permissible under the Islamic religious law, the issuer of a Sukuk basically sells a certificate and then uses the proceeds to finance a specific project that investors have direct partial ownership. This issuer makes a contractual promise to buy back the bond at par value at a future date.

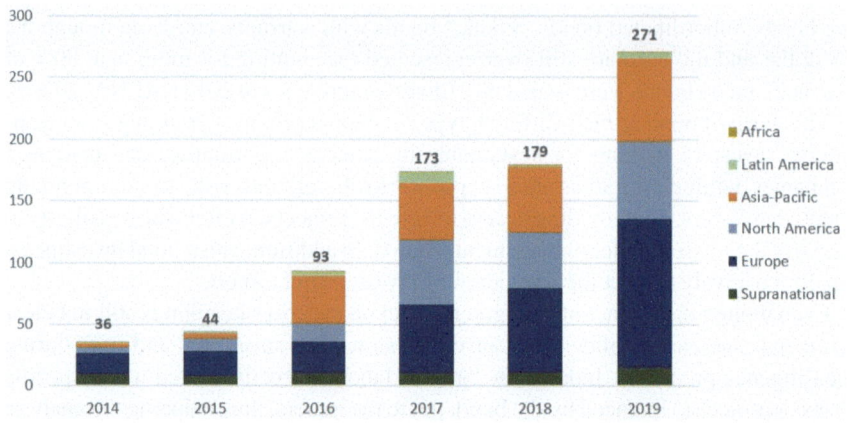

Fig. 6.2 Annual green bonds issuance per region, 2014–2019, USD billion. *Source* IRENA (2020b), based on data from the Environmental Finance Bond Database (subscription required)

The green bond market has been growing at impressive rates in emerging as well as industrialised countries over the last 10 years. In many cases, green bonds were even over-subscribed (The Economist, 2020). Even though the green bond market remains small compared to traditional bonds,[5] it reached over $50 billion worldwide in 2019 (CBI, 2020a).

However, the use of green bonds is still very limited in Africa, mainly because of underdeveloped capital markets (Fig. 6.2). Like the overall bond market, green bonds are catalysed by stock exchanges. Therefore, their deployment strongly depends on the development of the financial sector.[6] Moreover, additional market barriers include: lack of awareness of the benefits of green bonds, lack of clarity regarding guidelines and standards, shortage of projects, higher transaction costs compared to traditional bonds (IRENA, 2020a).

Public authorities can foster the use of green bonds for the financing of clean energy initiatives by establishing supporting policies, providing financial incentives as well as developing specific standards and guidelines. Furthermore, policymakers and regulators may review investment restrictions of institutional investors in order to increase financial flows to environmentally friendly projects.

Similarly, multilateral agencies and development banks have a strong role to play to unlock the potential of green bonds. They are particularly important for markets that are new to green bonds such as Africa, where the African Development Bank has issued more than 80% of the outstanding green bonds at December 2018 (Tiyou, 2019). Thanks to their high credit rating, they can issue such bonds with a lower cost of capital. Moreover, they may provide technical assistance and capacity building to public and private issuers.

---

[5] The global bond market is currently valued at around $100 trillion (IRENA, 2020a).

[6] For more details, refer to Sect. 6.3 dedicated to the development of capital markets in sub-Saharan Africa.

At a European level, the European Investment Bank (EIB) created the Project Bond Credit Enhancement Facility (PBCE), aimed at providing a subordinated tranche of debt and granting project guarantee facilities through a revolving letter of credit (EIB, 2012). Thus, it enhances the credit rating of bonds issued and help leverage more private investment in Europe. Something similar could be developed in the African continent, to encourage the use of green bonds in the continent.

In addition, sub-Saharan Africa could expand the experience of the Amundi Planet Emerging Green One Fund, a special-purpose investment vehicle developed in partnership with the International Finance Corporation (IFC) and created to finance SDG-linked debt in emerging markets. It uses a first-loss junior tranche to achieve credit uplift for countries' sovereign debts, thus possibly leveraging senior tranche private investors interested in gaining exposure to SDG investments (Hugman et al., 2020).

At the end of April 2019, for the first time in South Africa a private bank issued green bonds to finance four renewable energy projects, one wind farm and three solar farms (A21, 2019). Indeed, Nedbank planned to raise $177 million through green bonds. However, the operation generated close to $380 million in offers, an oversubscription explained by the bank's managers as an increasing investors' appetite for environmentally friendly projects (ibid.). The bonds were listed on the green segment of the Johannesburg Stock Exchange (JSE), highlighting the importance of solid capital markets to catalyse private investments in the clean energy sector.

6.1.1 Other Financing Opportunities in the Bond Markets

In addition to green bonds, other labelled debt securities exist that may be exploited to finance the access to clean energy in sub-Saharan Africa: social bonds, transition bonds, sustainability-linked bonds, SDGs bonds, etc.

Moreover, innovation is gaining the African bond markets, seeking untapped sources of financing and new ways of raising private capital. For instance, the government of Nigeria issued its first diaspora bond in 2017, raising $300 million (130% subscribed) for investments in local Nigerian infrastructures from Nigerians overseas. This success can be partly explained by an offering linked to development concerns (Benson, 2019) as well as an anti-corruption campaign launched by public authorities (Kazeem, 2017). Furthermore, Kenya became the first country to sell government bonds via mobile phones to its citizens in 2017 (BBC, 2017).

Both examples show the various opportunities to provide funding to development challenges, as well as the need to explore innovative tools attracting new sources of capital, such as diaspora remittances. Similarly, instruments like green Sukuk could fit into the energy strategies of many sub-Saharan African countries and help tackle energy poverty issues and climate change.

6.2 A Price on Carbon: Carbon Pricing and Carbon Finance as Sources of Capital

Many jurisdictions across the world have started to internalise the negative social and environmental externalities of conventional technologies and activities by putting a price on carbon through taxes or/and establishing emission trading systems (ETS), affecting costs of production and/or final prices.[7] A carbon tax fixes the price of carbon in an economy and is generally easier to implement (price-based instrument). Moreover, it generates additional revenues for public authorities. In contrast, ETS, also referred to as cap and trade systems, determine the maximum volume of GHG emissions in a specific territory by imposing a cap on different sectors (quantity-based instrument). If an entity emits more than the assigned amount, additional allowances can be acquired in an open market.

Those market-based schemes aim at correcting market failures using the "polluter pays" principle and achieving emission targets at a country or territory level. They can exploit possible behavioural responses and influence decision-making (potentially in a more efficient manner than command and control (CAC) mechanisms and subsidies), through their flexible and least-cost approach as well as the stimulation of innovation.

Even though they are gaining momentum globally, significant disparities across jurisdictions in prices and coverage dilute their efficacy and impose the implementation of border carbon adjustments that may affect trade relationships yet leverage other countries to participate in climate agreements.

Considering poverty eradication priorities and low energy intensity in many sub-Saharan African economies, it is difficult to justify a local implementation of such mechanisms. In addition, even though GHG emissions are currently low compared to other regions of the globe, they are expected to raise in the decades to come (CI-ACA, 2019). Therefore, the value of carbon pricing may lie less in the potential to curb actual emissions but more on prospects offered for expected emission growth.

Moreover, considering the prevailing socioeconomic circumstances in the majority of sub-Saharan African countries, the implications caused by the introduction of a carbon tax and/or an ETS would be difficult to bear. Both would need to be implemented gradually to give the economy the necessary time to adapt. Furthermore, complementary mechanisms[8] should be introduced in order to anticipate potentially negative consequences linked to carbon finance for market participants (carbon leakage, competitivity concerns, other impacts on trade and the labour market, decreased government revenues and availability of abatement opportunities), foster decarbonisation at a global level and address additional obstacles not targeted by such mechanisms (mainly non-price and financial barriers[9]). On top of that, the choice and design of such tools is highly important and needs (i) to be tailored to

---

[7] Please refer to Annex 5 for additional features associated with carbon taxes and ETS.

[8] Free allowances, tax exemption, support low-carbon investments with complementary policies.

[9] Additional initiatives can be implemented to address those barriers and create enabling environments, for instance: standard establishment, public green investment vehicles, R&D.

country-specific factors and macroeconomic conditions (such as GHG-intensity and trade exposure of the targeted sectors), (ii) to complement the overall (climate) policy mix as well as (iii) to consider barriers to implementation.[10]

In addition, a fully fledged ETS requires sufficient as well as dynamic supply and demand of carbon credits, currently not available in many countries across the region due to their relatively small economies. This may explain why there are currently no African emission trading systems. A carbon tax has been implemented in South Africa on all fossil fuels. A similar scheme is currently under consideration in Senegal and Côte d'Ivoire (WB, 2020).

Regional systems could represent an interesting possibility to access carbon finance in Africa as it allows significant trading volume compared to what is possible solely domestically. However, their implementation is challenging given the distinct legal frameworks across the continent. Nevertheless, institutions like the East African Development Community (EAC) could support those initiatives.

All of this implies the exploration of different approaches enabling the use of carbon finance for clean energy access projects located in sub-Saharan Africa. An interesting opportunity consists of using existing systems based on international markets. Indeed, developing countries usually have a comparative advantage in supplying the global market with carbon credits as emission reduction may potentially be achieved at a relatively lower cost. Thus, it offers the possibility to reduce the cost of compliance for entities located in industrialised countries. At the same time, it represents additional revenue streams for project developers in developing and emerging economies and associated investors, thus improving bankability and potentially leveraging private investments.

International carbon markets offer an attractive solution to channel new investments into the African energy sector and can help countries meet specific targets associated with clean energy access, share of renewables in the energy mix and emission reduction. Moreover, carbon markets are an interesting alternative to traditional international funding, especially public sources of capital coming from tax payers, currently under pressure due to austerity efforts in several countries. Indeed, international carbon markets are decentralised and do not require direct government budgeting, but rather private finance. However, the proper design, implementation and management of a carbon tax and/or an ETS are crucial to ensure well-functioning carbon markets and achieving the expected economic, environmental and social outcomes.

The relevance of carbon markets has been reaffirmed under the Article 6 of the Paris Agreement in 2015. Those market-based mechanisms are used for compliance with quantified emission targets placed in industrialised and emerging countries as well as on voluntary basis. Diverse set of systems were created for the trading of GHGs "pollution rights", corresponding to allowances, permits or credits. Two are

---

[10]Barriers to implementation and functioning include (non-exhaustive list): lack of political consensus on the role of carbon pricing, management of negative consequences caused by carbon pricing, market functioning (for ETS mainly), stakeholder engagement, change in legislation, administrative concerns, means and capacity to design and implement such mechanisms, market concentration and illiquidity (for ETS mainly).

particularly relevant for the financing of clean energy access in sub-Saharan Africa: Clean Development Mechanism (CDM) and voluntary carbon markets (VCMs).

6.2.1 Clean Development Mechanism (CDM)

The CDM[11] is a project-based and offset system focused on GHG emission reduction, that entered into effect under the Kyoto Protocol in 1997. It provides an opening for substantial international resource transfers as it allows entities in industrialised countries (Annex 1 countries) to purchase carbon credits from projects located in developing economies (non-Annex 1 countries). It has the objective to contribute to the reduction of global GHG emissions, while fostering the flow of financial resources for specific climate change mitigation projects based in developing countries. Regarding the scope of this book, fuel shift as well as renewable energy resources has traditionally been good sources of emission reduction credits through CDM projects (Fig. 6.3).

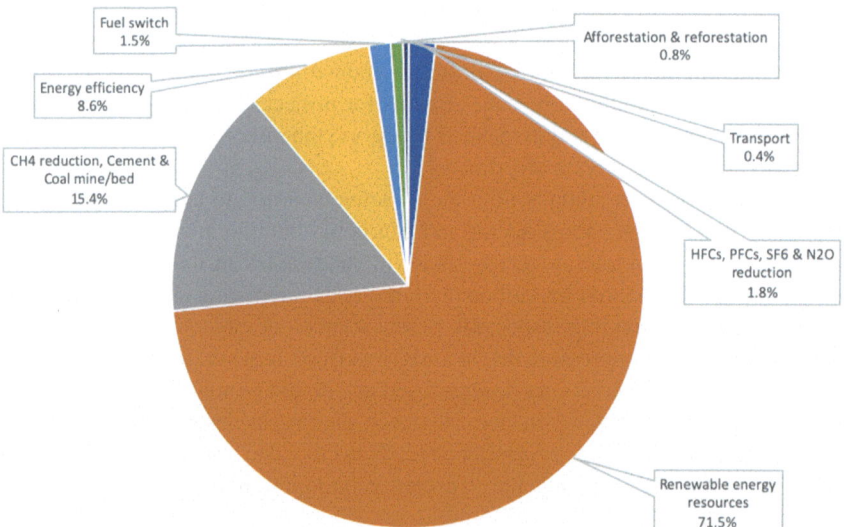

Fig. 6.3 CDM per project type. *Source* UNEP DTU Partnership (2020)

---

[11] For additional information: https://unfccc.int/process-and-meetings/the-kyoto-protocol/mechanisms-under-the-kyoto-protocol/the-clean-development-mechanism.

6.2 A Price on Carbon: Carbon Pricing … 111

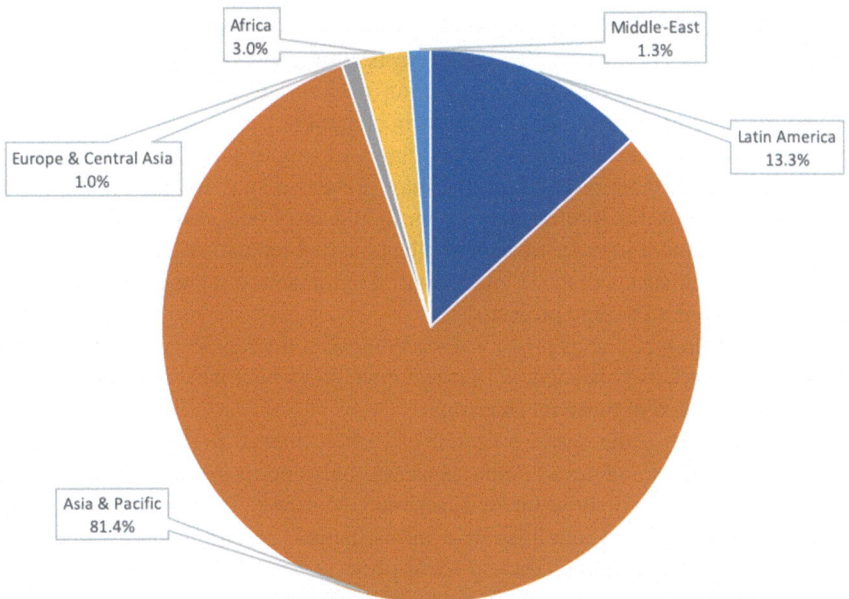

Fig. 6.4 CDM per region. *Source* UNEP DTU Partnership (2020)

6.2.2 Voluntary Carbon Markets (VCMs)

Voluntary carbon markets are similar to CDM with the difference that they are not regulated by the UNFCCC. Yet, different standards are applied. Renewable energy resources and fuel switching can be considered by VCMs (AfDB, n.d.). They are generally used by private individuals, companies and investors that seek to offset their carbon footprints and enhance their reputation.

Nowadays, Africa is participating in international carbon markets mainly using CDM. Even though those market-based instruments could help reach national clean energy access targets, the continent is still under-represented at an international level (Fig. 6.4).

6.2.3 Carbon Market Shortcomings

Accessing international carbon market mechanisms is highly demanding. Many actors have expended significant efforts and costs in accreditation, registration and monitoring. Processes are laborious and time-intensive, which increases transaction costs (AfDB, n.d.). Moreover, projects have to comply with specific and stringent requirements as well as carry out rigorous and burdensome reporting.

In addition, a favourable investment climate as well as adequate legal and institutional frameworks is necessary. Indeed, projects require upfront financial resources for construction and development, as carbon markets are result-based financing schemes, improving bankability of projects in operation.

Furthermore, uncertainties linked to the future of supply and demand for carbon credits as well as their price volatility may prevent a massive participation of investors. On top of that, project developers should carry out solid social and environmental assessment in order to decrease the potential reputational risk for participants, linked for instance to the displacement of indigenous communities due to the implementation of an energy project.

Finally, a solid pipeline of projects complying with the requirements of international carbon markets is needed, yet project developers may lack awareness about opportunities related to those mechanisms.

In order to realise the entire potential of carbon finance in African countries, multilateral agencies and development banks should support the public and private sector in the utilisation of those financial schemes. Moreover, countries can establish national institutional and administrative infrastructures for the identification and implementation of potential CDM and VCM projects.

The Deutsche Gesellschaft für Internationale Zusammenarbeit (GIZ) launched in 2018 a project in East Africa, aimed at strengthening capacities among public and private decision-makers regarding the use of international carbon markets (GIZ, n.d.). It focuses on sharing successful approaches and experiences of CDM projects, as well as piloting activities to utilise carbon finance mechanisms to achieve NDCs[12] implementation. Policymakers and regulators receive technical assistance to create an enabling environment and promote opportunities that carbon markets entail. Local private enterprises are provided with all necessary information related to entry requirements and procedures.

Initiatives at regional level already exist, with the mission to strengthen the capacity of member countries and foster regional approach towards international carbon market mechanisms and climate finance: the Eastern Africa Alliance for Carbon Markets and Climate Finance, the West Africa Alliance on Carbon Markets and Climate Finance.

6.3 The Financial Sector and Capital Markets in Africa

Every country has its own development needs. However, all regions at a global level need access to capital and long-term financing to support socioeconomic prosperity. It is generally accepted that the financial sector has an instrumental role to play in capital allocation and the financing of projects and companies (Levine, 1997). Therefore,

---

[12]Nationally Determined Contribution (NDCs) are intended reductions in greenhouse gas emissions expressed by countries under the United Nations Framework Convention on Climate Change (UNFCCC).

capital markets and the banking sector need to be complementary in order to bridge the financial gap related to universal clean energy access across sub-Saharan Africa.

6.3.1 The Development of Capital Markets

Capital markets are crossing points where suppliers of capital (retail and institutional investors) and entities that need it for productive uses (businesses, public entities) can meet and exchange securities. They involve various stakeholders[13] and have the objective to enhance transactional efficiency. Accordingly, the development of well-functioning domestic capital markets may provide significant benefits for the financing of clean energy access.

The benefits include:

- Increased capital inflows and enhanced liquidity

First, capital markets increase the funding supply as well as provide higher visibility and exposure for traded securities to active and passive investors,[14] thus improving liquidity and decreasing dependency on foreign markets. Moreover, they offer additional exit options for (early stage) investors.

- Access to secondary and derivative markets

Second, they enable access to secondary (Table 6.1) and derivative markets, thus complementing traditional bank services, increasing the availability of financing mechanisms and potentially underpinning the (green) bond markets. This can be useful when conventional funding dries up, which is an important concern across the continent as African firms rely extensively on banks for external financing (Otchere et al., 2017). Moreover, it allows the use of new risk management mechanisms like hedging instruments as well as facilitates the sterilisation of large capital inflows and long-term investing. The increased trading volume and funding supply may even possibly result in a reduced cost of capital in the long-run (van der Putte et al., 2020).

- Improve transparency

Third, capital markets may improve corporate governance and transparency by imposing public disclosure requirements, leading to better-informed investment decisions and reducing information asymmetry.

Capital markets are crucial for equity financing. As an example, the Morgan Stanley Capital International (MSCI) Emerging Markets Index helps capital providers evaluate equity market performance in emerging markets. Moreover, it

---

[13] Governments, policymakers, regulators, investors, corporations, etc.

[14] Active investing requires a hands-on approach, in which a portfolio manager oversees a team of analysts who look at qualitative and quantitative factors in order to actively manage a portfolio. Passive investing often results in investors buying index funds or other mutual funds.

Table 6.1 Proceeds raised (USD billion) via IPOs[a] and FOs[b] and number of deals in global and African equity capital markets, 2010–2019

	2010	2011	2012	2013	2014	2015	2016	2017	2018	2019
IPO proceeds raised—global	299.1	178.8	142.5	195.6	274.3	206.9	142.5	209	223.6	199.2
IPO proceeds raised—Africa	2.5	1.1	0.4	0.9	1.7	2	1.5	3	2.2	1.2
% of proceeds raised in Africa (%)	**0.86**	**0.62**	**0.28**	**0.46**	**0.63**	**0.98**	**1.11**	**1.48**	**1.00**	**0.63**
FO proceeds raised—global	642	479.9	509.3	588.2	613.5	685.8	551.1	620.8	462.6	457.8
FO proceeds raised—Africa	7.8	4.4	5.4	5.1	9.4	11.1	7.4	10.7	6.2	3.5
% of proceeds raised in Africa (%)	**1.22**	**0.93**	**1.07**	**0.87**	**1.54**	**1.61**	**1.35**	**1.73**	**1.33**	**0.76**
Number of deals (IPO)—global	1258	1041	728	865	1167	1185	1013	1523	1198	1040
Number of deals (IPO)—Africa	23	17	13	23	27	32	24	30	17	9
% of IPO in Africa (%)	**1.83**	**1.63**	**1.79**	**2.66**	**2.31**	**2.70**	**2.37**	**1.97**	**1.42**	**0.87**
Number of deals (FO)—global	3562	2902	2508	3046	3178	3323	3186	3571	2839	2733
Number of deals (FO)—Africa	71	65	52	50	75	93	73	95	79	59
% of FO in Africa (%)	**1.99**	**2.24**	**2.07**	**1.64**	**2.36**	**2.80**	**2.29**	**2.66**	**2.78**	**2.12**

Source Authors' elaboration, based on PwC (2020)
[a]Initial public offerings, referring to the process of offering shares of private corporations to the public in a new stock issuance
[c]Further offers

6.3 The Financial Sector and Capital Markets in Africa

is commonly used by investors to channel investments. However, no African countries are currently represented in this index, with the exception of Egypt and South Africa (MSCI, 2019). They should therefore explore the necessary requirements[15] to upgrade their status from frontier to emerging markets in order to make the most of the previously mentioned benefits.

As reported above, capital markets are also vital for the development of fixed-income markets, especially a green bond market in the case of the clean energy sector. With the aim of encouraging their growth and uptake, African stock exchanges and regulators need to develop and implement green bond guidelines as well as specific listing rules and standards.

Additionally, capital markets targeting SMEs should also be implemented. Indeed, small- and medium-sized enterprises are essential for an economy, as they tend to be more dynamic than larger firms in driving innovation and developing sustainable business models. To do so, they need access to growth capital, beyond what is possible through venture capital funding.

Currently, many African countries have weak financial systems, which limit the pool of domestic finance, deter international investors and deteriorate countries' credit ratings. Even though development stages vary across the continent, capital market infrastructures and stock exchanges are generally underdeveloped. In addition, the region faces critical challenges related to the low-income levels and asset accumulation, as well as a limited number of large enough institutions able to provide the required funds to ensure the solidity and efficiency of capital markets (McKinsey, 2017).

Indeed, building vibrant secondary and derivative capital markets requires a nationwide or even regional approach, designed for a sustainable rather than fast development. Firstly, a set of preconditions are needed to create the foundations for long-term capital market establishment and drive investors' confidence, encompassing sound and stable macroeconomic policies as well as strong institutional and legal settings.

Secondly, a critical mass of investors is required to obtain market depth and liquidity. Institutional investors are ideal candidates for the position of cornerstone institutions. However, in case national levels do not reach the necessary size, regional solutions should be promoted in order to avoid illiquid markets. Even though it requests coordination and harmonised legal frameworks allowing investors and issuers to freely operate across member states, regional capital markets represent an interesting solution to improve international cooperation and financial efficiency.

Finally, market architecture needs structural reforms to provide clarity and vision, strengthen stakeholders' protection, introduce supervisory and legal frameworks as well as new financial schemes. On top of that, market regulators have a central role to play in the development and functioning of local capital markets and thereby need to be empowered to ensure adequate surveillance and regulatory enforcement. Furthermore, modern technologies should be put at their disposal to facilitate fair trading, information flow exchange and transparent disclosure.

---

[15] For more information see Annex 6.

Knowing that the development of capital markets is a complex process, multilateral agencies and development banks can work alongside regulators and policymakers as well as build capacity among market participants, by providing practical recommendations and sharing experience.

6.3.2 African Banking Systems

The banking system is growing across Africa. Moreover, innovation is transforming how people conduct financial transactions and save money in the continent, even though patterns vary by gender and income levels.

Yet, retail services are still underdeveloped and the unbanked population is significant, resulting in a widespread use of cash and informal saving schemes, limited access to long-term and affordable financing, high transaction costs, complex processes and poor geographic coverage.

Nevertheless, the sector presents several opportunities and innovations such as

- The use digital technologies and mobile phones to overcome the underuse of banking facilities
- The provision of tailored-made saving, borrowing and investing services
- Optimization in order to decrease operational complexity and costs
- Support of consumer finance and securitization

As previously reported, a large part of external financing of African SMEs comes from commercial banks, highlighting the importance of this industry across the continent. Nevertheless, many entrepreneurs tend to rely on their savings to start a business rather than borrow for it.

Accordingly, it is important to reinforce the capacity of the banking sector in order to foster local financing and capital allocation in clean energy access solutions. Moreover, saving mobilisation may provide additional sources of capital to start and grow clean energy access projects.

Even though the gross savings in percentage of GDP have had a declining trend in the last decades in sub-Saharan Africa, some countries present significant saving rates[16] that could in part be used to bridge the financing gap in clean energy access (WB, 2019). In 2019, sub-Saharan Africa had gross domestic savings as a percentage of GDP of 22%, which represents around $380 billions, part of which could be invested in sustainable development in the case enticing investment opportunities with tailored risk-return profiles are available to retail investors (ibid.).

---

[16] Here, it should be added that due to significant income inequalities around the subcontinent, a small share of the population holds an important part of the domestic savings.

References

A21 (2019). *South Africa: Nedbank issues green bonds for renewable energy*. Afrik21. Published on May 8, 2019. Retrieved August 25, 2020, from https://www.afrik21.africa/en/south-africa-nedbank-issues-green-bonds-for-renewable-energy/.

AfDB (n.d.). *Carbon markets and Africa: A quick fact sheet for journalists*. Retrieved October 7, 2020, from https://www.afdb.org/fileadmin/uploads/afdb/Documents/Generic-Documents/Carbon%20Market%20Quick%20Facts%20%20ACF%202012.pdf.

Benson, J. (2019). *How bonds aimed at the diaspora can raise crucial funds for Africa*. African Arguments. Published on July 10, 2019. Retrieved September 1, 2020, from https://africanarguments.org/2019/07/10/how-bonds-aimed-at-the-diaspora-can-raise-crucial-funds-for-africa/.

BBC (2017). *Kenya starts selling bonds via mobile phones*. BBC. Published on March 23, 2017. Retrieved August 21, 2020, from https://www.bbc.com/news/business-39364885.

CBI (2020a). *2019 green bond market summary*. Climate Bonds Initiative, February, 2020.

CBI (2020b). *Green bonds: Global state of the market 2019*. Prepared by Climate Bonds Initiative, 2020.

CI-ACA (2019). *Synthesis report: Carbon pricing approaches in Eastern and Southern Africa*. Collaborative Instruments for Ambitious Climate Action. April, 2019.

EIB (2012). *An outline guide to project bonds credit enhancement and the project bond initiative*. European Investment Bank, December 12, 2012.

GIZ (n.d.). *Building up the global carbon market in East Africa: Project description*. Deutsche Gesellschaft für Internationale Zusammenarbeit. Retrieved October 3, 2020, from https://www.giz.de/en/worldwide/42196.html.

Hugman, M., Pinzón A., Robins, N. (2020). *How could sustainable finance help avoid an emerging market sovereign debt crunch*. Grantham Research Institute on Climate Change and the Environment, May 26, 2020.

IRENA (2020a). *Renewable energy finance: Green bonds*. Renewable Energy Finance Brief 03, January, 2020.

IRENA (2020b). *Financing the global energy transformation: Green bonds*. Article published March 03, 2020.

Kazeem, Y. (2017). *Nigeria's first ever diaspora bond has raised $300 million*. Quartz Africa. Published on June 26, 2017. Retrieved August 27, 2020, from https://qz.com/africa/1014533/nigeria-has-raised-300-million-from-its-first-ever-diaspora-bond/.

Levine, R. (1997). Financial development and economic growth: Views and agenda. *Journal of Economic Literature, 35*, 688–726.

McKinsey (2017). *Deepening capital markets in emerging economies*. McKinsey & Company, April, 2017.

MSCI (2019). *MSCI market classification framework*. June, 2019, available at https://www.msci.com/documents/1296102/1330218/MSCI_Global_Market_Framework_2019.pdf/57f021bc-a41b-f6a6-c482-8d4881b759bf.

Otchere, I., Senbet, L., Simbanegavi, W. (2017). Financial sector development in Africa–an overview. *Review of Development Finance, 7*, 1–5.

PwC (2020). *African capital markets watch 2019*. PricewaterhouseCoopers, March 2020.

The Economist (2020). *The climate issue: The flourishing world of climate finance*. The Economist, August 24, 2020.

Tiyou, T. (2019). *Can Africa green bonds be the future of funding? Climate bonds initiative expert tells us all*. Renewables in Africa. Published on August 7, 2019. Retrieved November 17, 2020, from https://www.renewablesinafrica.com/can-africa-green-bonds-be-the-future-of-funding-climate-bonds-initiative-expert-tells-us-all/.

UNEP DTU Partnership (2020). Centre on Energy, Climate and Sustainable Development, Content of CDM/JI Pipeline. Retrieved November 5, 2020, from https://cdmpipeline.org/index.htm.

Van der Putte A., Campbell-Holt, Littlejohn G. (2020). *Financing the energy transition*. In M. Hafner & S. Tagliapietra (Eds.), *The geopolitics of the global energy transition*, Springer; Waissbein, O.,

Glemarec, Y., Bayraktar, H., Schmidt, T.S. (2013). *Derisking renewable energy investment. A framework to support policymakers in selecting public instruments to promote renewable energy investment in developing countries.* New York, NY: United Nations Development Programme.

WB (2019). GDP (current US $), World Bank National Accounts Data. Retrieved November 5, 2020, from https://data.worldbank.org/indicator/NY.GDP.MKTP.CD?name_desc=false.

WB (2020). *Carbon pricing dashboard.* World Bank Group. Retrieved October 15, 2020, from https://carbonpricingdashboard.worldbank.org/map_data.

Open Access This chapter is licensed under the terms of the Creative Commons Attribution 4.0 International License (http://creativecommons.org/licenses/by/4.0/), which permits use, sharing, adaptation, distribution and reproduction in any medium or format, as long as you give appropriate credit to the original author(s) and the source, provide a link to the Creative Commons license and indicate if changes were made.

The images or other third party material in this chapter are included in the chapter's Creative Commons license, unless indicated otherwise in a credit line to the material. If material is not included in the chapter's Creative Commons license and your intended use is not permitted by statutory regulation or exceeds the permitted use, you will need to obtain permission directly from the copyright holder.

Chapter 7
Risk Mitigation Instruments Targeting Specific Investment Risks

> *This chapter focuses on instruments aimed at mitigating specific investment risks, including political, credit, currency and liquidity risks. It explores solutions emanating from both the public and private sectors.*
>
> *It primarily targets project developers, with the objective of providing a global overview of the available schemes that currently exist. In addition, it targets policy-makers as well as public and development agencies, exploring some solutions capable to increase the use and improve the accessibility of those schemes in the clean energy sector.*
>
> *The chapter starts by targeting guarantee instruments and insurance, as well as their availability in the clean energy sector. In particular, it focuses on solutions to improve the accessibility of such mechanisms for small- and medium-scale projects and companies.*
>
> *Moreover, emphasis is put on the currency and liquidity risks, considering the complexities of sub-Saharan African contexts and the energy sector. Indeed, those two investment risks are critical for many project developers and capital providers. Therefore, this chapter presents different actions in order to manage and mitigate those risks, using either internal or external solutions.*

7.1 Guarantee Instruments and Insurance

By providing financial protection against events that negatively impact a project or a company, guarantee instruments and insurance give the opportunity to make investment opportunities more attractive for private capital providers while using limited financial resources. Guarantees and insurance can be issued by public and private entities. In the former case, potential financial losses are transferred to the public sector.

Guarantee instruments and insurance may cover a broad range of investment risks relevant for the clean energy sector. Nevertheless, moral hazard[1] is a well-known potential consequence associated with those risk mitigation instruments, that may compromise their initial objectives and lead to substantial additional costs for issuing institutions. In order to reduce moral hazard issues, two options are available for guarantee and insurance issuers:

- Conduct a rigorous due diligence process before issuing guarantees and insurance, thus rewarding high-quality projects
- Provide a partial coverage of potential financial losses to decrease financial exposure

Even though guarantee instruments and insurance are widely used in project finance and the fossil fuel industry, their use is still moderate in the clean energy sector (IRENA, 2016). A study realised by IRENA highlights the following factors as the main barriers to the use of guarantees and insurance in clean energy investments (ibid):

- Little financial resources dedicated to those instruments in public financial institutions
- Elevated transaction costs
- Lack of product awareness among project developers
- Time-consuming and complex processes
- High due diligence requirements

In addition, guarantees and insurance are sometimes not available in specific geographic areas and/or for small investment sizes. Therefore, the clean energy sector has today a limited experience in using those potentially powerful instruments to mobilise private capital.

The public sphere has an important role to play in the deployment of guarantee instruments and insurance reflecting specific requirements of clean energy initiatives. More resources should be devoted to those mobilisation tools. In addition, solutions adapted to smaller investment tickets are needed. Public entities may for instance create guarantee funds to meet the needs of the off-grid and clean cooking sectors.

7.1.1 Guarantees Issued by Governments

Before investing in developing countries, private investors often require guarantees issued by public authorities to reinforce the financial viability of targeted projects. Indeed, governments have a competitive advantage in backing certain investment

---

[1] Moral hazard arises when a party to a transaction has the incentive to take unusual risks because he/she is unlikely to suffer potential consequences.

7.1 Guarantee Instruments and Insurance

barriers such as currency and political risks, as well as credit risk associated with state-owned companies.

However, governments' financial constraints and sometimes low creditworthiness may prevent the state's ability to provide guarantee instruments, forcing capital providers and project developers to look for other issuers like development agencies, export credit organisations or the private sector.

7.1.2 Political Risk Guarantees and Insurance

Coverage focuses on risks related to governments actions or inactions and may include political turmoil, currency convertibility, asset expropriation, breach of contracts involving a public entity and change of policies and regulations without negotiations. Moreover, political risk insurance provides the opportunity to enhance creditworthiness of state-owned companies such as public power utilities, by covering grid interconnection risk and financial default.

Multilateral and development agencies are well-positioned to issue political risk insurance thanks to their strong creditworthiness and close relationships with member states. Currently, the largest issuer of political risk insurance in terms of volume is the Multilateral Investment Guarantee Agency (MIGA), a member of the World Bank Group. Other providers include export credit agencies and private insurers.

7.1.3 Credit Risk Guarantees

Those guarantee instruments mitigate the credit risk as they cover losses in the event of a default on debt obligations, without differentiation of the cause(s) of non-payment. Those mechanisms may help borrowers gain access to commercial capital and potentially decrease the cost of debt.

The available instruments include:

- Partial credit guarantees, covering part of the debt service
- Full credit guarantees, covering the entire amount of the debt service
- Export credit guarantees, insurance covering losses for exporters or lenders financing projects tied to the export of goods and services

7.2 Currency Risk Mitigation

Efforts to mitigate the foreign exchange risk faced by private investors and project developers can be categorised into two distinct areas: (i) approaches that directly deal with the foreign exchange rate and (ii) methods to facilitate local currency financing and support the development of the bank market.

The public sector, including national governments and multilateral agencies, as well as private players, has the following options at their disposal:

- Hard currency PPAs

By offering power purchase agreements (PPAs) in hard currency, governments bear potential financial losses linked to a devaluation of the local currency. Therefore, the currency risk is passed on to the public sector.

This option may potentially incur high costs for public finance and is not applicable for small-scale electricity projects and the clean cooking sector, as they usually do not use PPA mechanisms.

- Currency risk guarantee funds

There are special-purpose funds created by public entities and aimed at covering the difference in exchange values over a period of time. Governments can use public money or charge fees to participants to access guarantee funds.

They offer less expensive options compared to traditional hedging instruments (see next point) and allow access to currency risk mitigation tools for small-scale projects. However, this option does not enable the public sector to hedge its exposure and may therefore be expensive in the event of strong local currency devaluation.

- Currency hedging instruments

Commonly provided by the private sector, hedging instruments such as foreign exchange swaps and forward contracts allow to lock the differential between two currencies in advance, thus artificially eliminating value fluctuations.

Currency hedging is generally expensive and thereby increases the overall financing costs. Moreover, those mechanisms are usually available for large-scale investments and for certain currencies.

- Local currency financing

Local currency financing may be provided by the public sector, through state-owned financial institutions, multilateral agencies and development banks. Moreover, investors located in African countries are increasingly becoming an important source of capital (World Bank Group, 2014). They include domestic financial institutions, such as banks, as well as institutional investors (i.e. pension funds,[2] insurance companies, sovereign wealth funds[3]). The latter usually finance large-scale projects and/or invest indirectly through funds, thus requiring developed capital markets.

Stimulating domestic investment entails several advantages. It avoids foreign exchange exposure, contributes to local economic prosperity and helps develop local

---

[2] African pension assets are often concentrated in large public pension or social security funds. In certain countries like Kenya and South Africa private corporate pension plans exist. However, private and voluntary pension savings currently form a tiny part of the market (WB, 2014). Due to their specific mandates, pension funds usually face investment restrictions.

[3] In Africa, sovereign wealth funds exist mainly in natural-resource-rich countries.

financial sectors. In addition, domestic sources of capital may potentially add significant value by bringing their experience and knowhow of the local contexts and engaging their network to build strong pipelines.

Even though the interest among local capital providers in clean energy initiatives is on the rise, several barriers still exit to increase their commitment. Most of the time, they do not have a proper mandate for clean energy access financing. Additionally, they may lack experience in investing in this sector, making the assessment of risks and deal structuring complex. Finally, some local financial institutions may have a limited access to capital, preventing them to enter young sectors (such as the clean energy sector) and waiting until they reach maturity.

To overcome those barriers, different solutions exist, first by strengthening capacity building among local investors as well as informing them about available de-risking strategies and innovative financial mechanisms. Moreover, public authorities can establish fiscal incentives and finance policies such as priority sector lending. Governments or public development finance institutions may also increase their use of mobilisation tools like nonperforming buyouts[4] and guarantee instruments.

In addition, multilateral agencies and development banks (sometime also national governments, depending on their creditworthiness and financial constraints) can provide access to capital to local financial institutions through **on-lending structures**. Those facilities may have a significant impact on the financing of clean energy activities in sub-Saharan Africa. By using their high credit rating and access to international financial markets, public financial institutions provide capital at lower cost to local banks and make it available for particular development sectors. Therefore, the banks' costs are reduced and liquidity is increased. This lower cost of capital can thus be on-lent to local projects and companies at lower rates than what was previously possible, without currency mismatch.

Those revolving lines of credit are better adapted for short-term financing (i.e. working capital, seasonality) and are usually targeting small- to medium- scale investments. In order to increase the efficiency of these mechanisms, on-lending facilities may include training and consultancy services to ensure a proper understanding of the investment environment. An example of on-lending facilities in Africa is the World Bank's Tanzania Energy Development Assistance Program, which intends to provide medium- and long-term loans to projects engaged in energy access, applying more favourable financial conditions (WB, 2016).

Regarding larger investment sizes, **co-lending**,[5] through direct investing or specialised funds, may reduce the risk perception of lenders, by distributing risks and limiting financial exposures. Local lenders may be more willing to participate in clean energy financing using this structure.

---

[4]Through nonperforming buyouts, a public financial institution commits itself to buy nonperforming loans detained by a commercial bank.

[5]For more details, see Sect. 5.4.4.2 dedicated to loan syndication.

7.3 Liquidity Risk Mitigation

Several clean energy projects may face liquidity constraints and cash-flow shortfall periods, increasing the risk of payment default. Different options are available to enhance creditworthiness and decrease the risk perception of potential capital providers.

7.3.1 Public External Liquidity Facilities

Public external liquidity facilities usually concentrate on power generation plants. Indeed, their revenues strongly depend on future payments generally stipulated under a purchase power agreement (PPA), therefore decreasing uncertainties regarding sale price during a predefined period of time. However, power off-takers, often public power utilities, frequently face financial difficulties, causing cash-flow issues and making the provision of cash collateral difficult (IRENA, 2016).

Accordingly, the liquidity risk hinders access to affordable financing for project developers, as investors may price a liquidity premium, thus increasing the financing costs for power generation plants and affecting projects' competitiveness.

Usually provided by multilateral agencies and development banks, external liquidity facilities are created to improve a project's liquidity profile by covering potential off-taker defaults. They aim at loosening the tensions on public utilities' financial statements, providing a credit line or letter of credit to IPPs, thereby resolving short-term liquidity concerns without requiring additional cash from power off-takers. This should thus decrease the liquidity risk for capital providers, and therefore facilitate financial closure and access to affordable capital.

Such facilities could also be created for small-scale projects, following the model of currency risk guarantee funds but applied to liquidity constraints in the off-grid and clean cooking sectors. Public financial institutions can create a central liquidity facility available for clean energy companies active in a predefined territory. This special-purpose fund could be backed by public entities and act as lender of last resort in case of difficulties faced to pay capital providers on due time. A membership fee might be covered to companies to benefit from this facility. The challenge here is to determine the amount of this fee.

7.3.2 Liquidity Guarantees

High perceived risks combined with a lack of experience in investing in the clean energy sector may create maturity mismatch between capital providers and project developers. For instance, the construction of a power generation plant requires long-term financing. However, some investors may propose financial terms not necessarily aligned with the timing of such projects. In addition, certain jurisdictions restrict the maximum duration of lending activities.

Liquidity guarantees allow to extend tenors when necessary, reducing the refinancing risk linked to power generation plants and improving cash-flow management. Generally used by multilateral agencies and development banks, this mechanism permits the repayment of a debt instrument when due through a new loan, automatically increasing the entire duration and matching the financial requirements of power generation plants.

Similarly, put options allow commercial lenders to sell their bonds at maturity in exchange for a premium to multilateral and development institutions. The latter repay the principal and ensure that financial obligations are honoured at maturity.

7.3.3 Internal Liquidity Facilities

Project developers and operators can undertake various actions aimed at mitigating the liquidity risk linked to their specific project or company. This will help ensure timely payments to capital providers, bridge short-term cash-flow issues and cover unexpected expenses.

A first easy-to-implement solution is to establish a separate reserve account, by accumulating cash above what is require by the business itself, including financial expenses. It can of course be done once operations have started and revenues are earned. It will thus improve the liquidity position of the company or project.

Over-collateralisation, meaning that more collaterals than required are posted, is another option to secure financing and potentially lower the cost of capital. It can be difficult or unfeasible in certain situations such as project finance where a special-purpose vehicle (SPV) is created. The assets of the originator, not involved in the new legal entity, can indeed not be used as collaterals.

Any form of contingent equity[6] may also reduce the liquidity risk. In this case, when a predefined occurrence happens, debt-like instruments and shares with fixed dividends are converted into common equity, thus reducing fixed financial obligations associated with certain forms of financing.

References

IRENA. (2016). *Unlocking renewable energy investment: The role of risk mitigation and structured finance*. IRENA, Abu Dhabi

WB. (2014). *Institutional investment in infrastructure in emerging markets and developing economies*. World Bank Group

---

[6]For more details, see Sect. 5.2 dedicated to financial instruments.

WB. (2016). *Increasing electricity access in Tanzania to reduce poverty.* World Bank Group, 6 Dec 2016. Retrieved 21 Sept 2020, from https://www.worldbank.org/en/results/2016/12/06/increasing-electricity-access-in-tanzania-to-reduce-poverty

Open Access This chapter is licensed under the terms of the Creative Commons Attribution 4.0 International License (http://creativecommons.org/licenses/by/4.0/), which permits use, sharing, adaptation, distribution and reproduction in any medium or format, as long as you give appropriate credit to the original author(s) and the source, provide a link to the Creative Commons license and indicate if changes were made.

The images or other third party material in this chapter are included in the chapter's Creative Commons license, unless indicated otherwise in a credit line to the material. If material is not included in the chapter's Creative Commons license and your intended use is not permitted by statutory regulation or exceeds the permitted use, you will need to obtain permission directly from the copyright holder.

Chapter 8
Business Model Adaptation

> *This chapter primarily targets project developers and managers. Apart from the public policies and initiatives, as well as the private financial schemes previously presented, private actions emanating from the persons behind clean energy access projects have also a crucial role to play in the allocation of capital. Capital providers, profit-oriented or not, usually value the way a business is conducted, including how potential risks are managed as well as the capacities of the team to deal with complex situations.*
>
> *This section presents different actions available to private actors, targeting specific risks linked to the various investment opportunities previously explored. More specifically, it focuses on strategies for risk transfer, avoidance and compensation, principally targeting customer, political, counterparty, business and social acceptance risks (cf. Chap. 3 for a complete definition of investment risks considered in this book). Moreover, additional solutions are explored to support internal risk management processes and business management in the energy sector.*
>
> *Since this book does not concentrate on a specific country or market, this section does not pretend to be exhaustive. In addition, innovative approaches to manage risks in the energy industry are constantly emerging around the world, with different levels of performance that should be properly analysed. Nevertheless, this chapter has the objective to offer some avenues to be explored in order to manage the risks associated with different energy companies or projects, with a particular focus on sub-Saharan African contexts.*

Project developers may adapt their business models to improve the risk perception of potential capital providers. In order to upgrade their risk-reward profiles, several alternatives are available, depending on the context, sector and type of business.

The first step consists of ensuring a comprehensive understanding of the risks, real and perceived, associated with a specific business model through an adequate

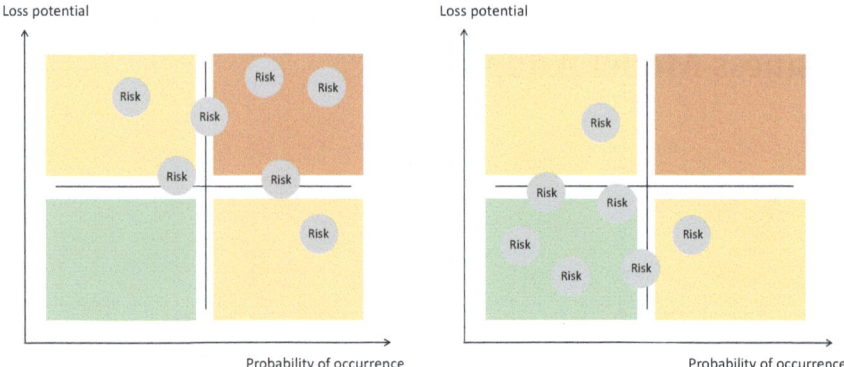

Fig. 8.1 Loss potential and probability of occurrence before (left) and after (right) risk treatment. *Source* Authors' elaboration, based on Alliance for Rural Electrification et al. (2015)

mapping. Those investment barriers should be properly assessed using associated loss potential and probability of occurrence.

Once a comprehensive analysis of risks has been realised, effective risk management approaches need to be developed and implemented in order to avoid, mitigate or transfer them, when technically and financially feasible.

A successful risk management process should result in a notable reduction in the loss potential and the probability of risk occurrence, as presented in Fig. 8.1.

Several industries have tailored-made risk management procedures that are clear and easy-to-handle for all stakeholders. They provide key information to investors and decrease knowledge and language gap with project developers. Moreover, they allow an understanding of existing risk mitigation actions within the specific sector.

Those mechanisms are generally available when an industry reaches maturity. For instance, microfinance institutions have developed several risk management techniques. In addition, they disclose specific information and ratios to properly communicate with capital providers and other stakeholders active in the industry. Even though global standards and risk management solutions do not exist for every business model within the clean energy sector, certain initiatives have started to emerge over the years.

8.1 Strategies for Risk Transfer

Some of the business models considered in the present book have the opportunity to transfer part of the risks associated with their activities to external entities, either public or private ones, by using insurance and guarantee instruments.

As previously mentioned, those mechanisms can target various investment risks, ranging from political to currency and counterparty risks. However, the related costs can be high and therefore not affordable for certain business models. Moreover, those instruments are usually created for large-scale investments and project finance and may not be available and/or accessible for smaller energy projects, such as clean cooking companies or the off-grid sector.

In addition, project developers may use products and assets including warranties, decreasing the counterparty and social acceptance risk. This practice can be applied when a company is selling energy devices as well as energy as a service.

Risk transfer schemes are powerful tools to catalyse private investments, as they improve risk-reward profiles of investment opportunities and clearly establish the consequences may an unexpected event occur. Nevertheless, their use is still low in the clean energy sector, with the exception of off-balance sheet financing and large-scale investments in power generation plants. Accordingly, public and private actors should develop new risk transfer mechanisms, adapted to various financing structures and ticket sizes, as well as foster their utilisation by raising awareness around those instruments and increase their affordability.

8.2 Strategies for Risk Avoidance and Compensation

Those strategies aim at significantly decreasing the probability of occurrence of an event that may negatively affect a company or a project. In addition, this subsection includes some actions outside risk transfer instruments that may compensate, partly or entirely, potential financial losses should this event occur.

8.2.1 Customer Risk in the Off-Grid and Clean Cooking Sectors

In order to mitigate the risk of customer non-payment, project developers active in the off-grid and clean cooking sectors have several schemes at their disposal to improve the collection rate.

- Flexible payment methods

In the off-grid and clean cooking sectors, different payment schemes can be envisaged in order to be aligned with financial capacities and constraints of targeted customers:

- Fixed or flexible payment plans spread over several months or years
- Lease systems, either lease-to-own or perpetual lease
- Pays-as-you-go (PAYGO), a scheme whereby customers unlock an energy system with irregular payments according to their consumption

Mobile money penetration has paved the way for flexible and digital payment schemes. It has become one of the most significant technology advancements in the enhancement of clean energy access in many developing and emerging countries.

- Clear consequences of non-payment

Project developers can define in advance specific consequences for customers in case of payment default. Depending on the business model and payment schemes, penalties can be imposed due to payment delay. Moreover, the energy supply can be cut-off through the use of smart metres. Finally, the company may retake possession of the energy device and reuse it for further transactions.

- Increase the capacity and willingness to pay

By providing high-quality services and maintaining good relationships with customer and the communities, companies may increase the willingness to pay of customers. Moreover, they can ease bill settlements and bureaucratic procedures in order to reduce burdensome processes for their clients.

In addition, project developers can promote and support productive uses, thus linking electrification with entrepreneurship initiatives and commercial activities in order to increase incomes within the served community.

Smiling Through Light[1] is a social enterprise that focuses on clean electricity access in Sierra Leone. By setting up distribution networks and supporting women-led businesses, the company focuses on the last mile distribution to help communities access safe and clean light technologies, while simultaneously improving income levels. Thus, the organisation is able to foster economic growth, strengthen environmental awareness and address air pollution through its dual approach targeting the creation of thriving business opportunities as well as the provision of clean energy access. In addition, profits are reinvested to acquire new solar products as well as provide training and ongoing support to local women.

- Portfolio diversification and management

By serving customers in different geographic areas and with distinct socioeconomic profiles, project developers minimise the default risk through portfolio diversification. In addition, management systems for large portfolios are available to monitor customers, providing clear data and reporting as well as assessing credit default risk.

Regarding the lack of information related to energy consumption and socioeconomic status of targeted clients, two distinct options, non-mutually exclusive, are open to project developers to mitigate this customer-related risk:

- Prefeasibility and market study

Project developers can release by themselves a feasibility and market study in order to get information about socioeconomic conditions and energy demand in their addressable market. Even though financial and human resources are needed to do so, it may help develop a business model tailored to the local context.

- Start with small-scale projects

Especially in the mini-grid sector, lack of adequate information regarding energy consumption may push project developers to deploy installations with over-capacity,

---

[1] For more information: https://www.smilingthroughlight.com.

implying expensive maintenance costs not covered by revenues. Starting with lower installed capacity and a flexible power generating system let mini-grid projects the opportunity to adjust installations based on energy demand, without incurring significant additional expenses and within a reasonable time frame.

OnePower Africa[2] is a fast-growing energy start-up that is currently planning to install 25 mini-grids across Lesotho. Rather than looking at each system in isolation, the company has bundled construction and operation into an efficient portfolio approach. The mini-grids aim to serve remote communities, varying in sizes and locations but similar in consumption patterns. On top of this, OnePower recognises the challenges inherent in deploying power systems for previously unconnected customers, with little-to-no historical data about energy consumption and uses. In response, the company developed an innovative tool aimed at determining the optimal installation configuration, based on available data, such as population, sun radiation, as well as on energy demand projected from similar communities.

- Satellite imagery

New methodologies to estimate energy access and consumption through satellite imagery are being developed and tested, allowing a better understanding of energy status, especially in remote areas (Falchetta et al. 2019a, b).

8.2.2 Power Utilities and Low-Income Households

As previously reported, grid extension and last-mile distribution are complex and require substantial investments. In addition, many African power utilities run on quasi-fiscal deficits due to several factors such as (Attia and Shirley, 2018):

- Non-cost-reflective tariffs
- Line losses and system underperformance
- Power theft
- Payment delinquency
- Mis-management and corruption

Consequently, it may be difficult to extend their services in hard-to-reach zones and to low-income households.

Additionally, even when grid extensions are completed, they often result in unprofitable projects, mainly due to high marginal costs and low-consumption levels. On top of that, illegal connections may be frequent in previously unconnected areas, thus worsening financial performances (WB, 2015).

As an example, Kenya Power and Lighting Company (KPLC), the national utility, launched the Last Mile Connectivity Project back in 2015 (Attia and Shirley, 2018). This $150 million project aimed at extending power distribution network as well as introducing a subsidised connection fee in low-income areas. Even if the customer

---

[2]For more information: https://1pwrafrica.com.

base increased significantly, the project faced cost overruns owing to low concentrated power demand. Moreover, many newly connected households did not own sufficient financial resources to cover connection expenses, even at a subsidised rate.

Accordingly, many poor households across sub-Saharan Africa are not connected to the national power network, even though some live in areas where the grid has already expanded (Attia and Shirley, 2017). This is mainly due to non-affordable connection costs and electricity tariffs, lack of access to formal billing channels and/or little consideration towards certain low-income and marginalised consumers from power utilities.

However, reaching new communities would not only electrify unconnected individuals, but also increase the utilities' customer bases. Therefore, it may potentially improve the attractiveness for capital providers, if the appropriate schemes are proposed, namely offering affordable and reliable services while securing positive financial margins.

Certain solutions exist to provide electricity services adapted to low-income communities and extend them in unconnected zones:

- Understanding of customer electricity needs

Power utilities could start by releasing customer surveys to understand electricity uses and consumption within their addressable market. As a result, they are better able to develop tailored-made services adapted to financial capacities and energy needs, when technically and financially possible. Furthermore, investing in prepayment metres may decrease financial risks associated with the elasticity of demand as well as illegal connections.

- Tailor-made services

When technically and financially feasible, power utilities can improve the affordability of connection costs and electricity tariffs in two different ways. First by offering payment plans adapted to financial constraints, including payments spread over several months or years. Second by cross-subsidising certain neighbourhoods where low-income households are living.

In addition, power utilities can support poor customers with their electricity bills, by hiring local persons to serve as bill collection agents for instance. On top of that, this customer engagement strategy may improve uptake and retention of clients.

- Public–private partnership

Through utility concessions or distribution franchising, publicly owned utilities can involve private actors in the distribution and transmission sector. However, considering the low financial returns generally associated with this part of the power value chain, additional public measures would be needed, such as subsidies and guarantees.

- Decentralised business model

Where energy consumption is low, power utilities can support the deployment of decentralised solutions, being less expensive and faster to install than an extension of the national grid. Furthermore, off-grid systems may adapt their installed capacities to power demand, set specific tariff schemes and be connected to the main grid when it reaches the area.

This can be done through rural electrification cooperation, privately owned companies or direct involvement of public power utilities. Indeed, moving away from the binary thinking of on- and off-grid solutions may allow the access to electricity for many unconnected communities across sub-Saharan Africa within a reasonable time frame.

The Moroccan case is an interesting example of well-performing utility-led rural electrification. As a matter of fact, the national utility successfully used a combination of grid extension and decentralised solutions to increase the electrification rate from 20% in 1995 to 100% in 2020 (SEforAll, 2020), adapting energy services to customers' financial constraints and consumption. Three main principles are considered to have contributed to a rapid improvement of levels of electrification: (i) a clear vision and political commitment, (ii) a solid institutional framework allowing the involvement of both national and international players and (iii) a financial model that includes all core stakeholders (Nygaard and Dafrallah, 2016).

In order to ensure high-quality services in rural areas, the national power utility decided to outsource the off-grid component to the private sector, through an international bidding process for ten-year concession contracts (ibid). This public–private partnership strengthened the entire approach and facilitated the mobilisation of international funding (ibid).

At the same time, some specific factors helped achieve those outcomes: (i) a relatively high GDP compared to many sub-Saharan African countries and (ii) a high level of urban electrification, allowing cross-subsidisation (ibid).

8.2.3 Political Risk

Project developers can lessen the risks linked to political decisions and possible legislative changes by continuously engaging with and consulting local public authorities during development, implementation and operations, as well as constantly seeking dialogue.

Of course, this is easier said than done, and the outcomes are not assured. Yet, those efforts can significantly influence political commitment and foster decisions that would best achieve energy access objectives.

8.2.4 Strategic Partnerships

By establishing and maintaining strategic partnerships, project developers active in the clean energy sector can decrease business risks linked with their supply chain and internal operations as well as ease the access to affordable financing.

Business models offering energy devices may partner with microfinance institutions (MFIs). Indeed, access to modern energy services might be facilitated if potential customers have access to tailored financial services to cover the costs related to their energy consumption. Moreover, MFIs can help energy companies reach new markets, benefiting from a wider outreach and distribution channels. From an MFI perspective, energy products allow portfolio diversification and present an opportunity to expand their client base, since the addressable market is significant (Qayyum, 2017).

Similarly, energy-related projects can look for strategic agreements in order to strengthen their business model and decrease the associated perceived risks. As an example, corporate purchase power agreements (corporate PPAs) may reduce financial uncertainties for project developers, thus removing a significant roadblock to financing. They are long-term contracts under which a business agrees to purchase electricity directly from a power producer. Therefore, with a financially strong counterparty, corporate PPA is an interesting component to improve the bankability of an energy facility. Moreover, it increases certainty for the power off-taker, by fixing the electricity price in the long run and relying on a consistent energy supply.

Moreover, strategic partnerships have the potential to decrease other business-related risks, associated with fuel supply or decommissioning to name a few. Indeed, project developers should create a network of high-quality partners, following the project finance approach described in the corresponding section, in order to strengthen their business models. In the same vein, agreements can be reached with anchor consumers with strong creditworthiness, thus reinforcing the soundness of their commercial network.

Furthermore, similar agreements may be concluded with strategic investors with significant experience and know-how in the clean energy sector in sub-Saharan Africa. Besides, close relationships with key capital providers may also facilitate the access to affordable and bridge financing, thus increasing the supply of capital and reducing the refinancing risk.

8.2.5 Operational Risk

Several actions can be undertaken to improve operational efficiency, including:

- Standardisation of procedures
- Integration of internal rules and processes
- Staff training
- Establishment of good governance practices (including for financial management[3])
- Adoption of technical standards

---

[3]Good financial management can facilitate the access to affordable capital and decrease the refinancing risk.

In addition, once the sector is mature enough and project developers get a comprehensive understanding of their whole value chain, vertical disintegration may bring specialisation (i.e. manufacturing, distribution, operation, financing) and improve efficiency of the entire industry.

8.2.6 Social Acceptance Risk

Several initiatives can be undertaken by project developers to decrease the social acceptance risk, including:

- Community involvement from development to operations
- Partnership with local organisations
- Proper stakeholder management
- Community-owned systems

Community-owned businesses offer the possibility to develop a sense of ownership as well as an equitable distribution within a community. Moreover, they may potentially decrease electricity tariffs, as they are driven by financial sustainability rather than profit maximising models. However, there is a need to build capacity among community members to ensure proper operation and maintenance of the system.

8.3 External Consulting

Additionally to those internal actions, project developers may be supported by external actors in order to improve their risk-reward profiles as well as to strengthen their business models and value propositions.

Incubators, accelerators and consultants[4] support project developers at different development stages to launch and grow their businesses, using advisory services and technical assistance. They provide companies with tailored mentorship, sound expertise and facilitated networking. Moreover, they can assist entrepreneurs in financial structuring and fundraising processes. Those initiatives may be created by the state or private players.

As an example, INDIE (Smart Investment Strategy)[5] is a consulting company specialised in financial strategies and financial modelling for small growing businesses (SGBs). It has the objective of fostering the access to affordable capital and support the growth of promising and innovative business models active in the energy, agriculture, water, recycling and fintech sectors to name a few. The team provides

---

[4]For more information: https://ventureburn.com/2020/01/accelerators-incubators-african-startups-2/.
[5]For more information: https://indie.holacebras.com/En.

tailored consulting services with the aim of optimising financing strategies at any development stage and mitigating some investment risks. It also collaborates with capital providers (public and private) and incubators, in order to enhance the use and effectiveness of innovative financial instruments and schemes, capable of aligning risk-return profiles.

References

Alliance for Rural Electrification, Hochschule New-Ulm University of Applied Science, Institute ID-EEE, Deutsche Gesellschaft für Internationale Zusammenarbeit. (2015). *Risk management for mini-grids: A new approach to guide mini-grid deployment*, January 2015.

Attia, B., Shirley, R. (2017). *Living under the Grid: 110 Million of Africa's unconnected customers represent a massive opportunity*. Green Tech Media, December 8, 2017.

Attia, B., Shirley, R. (2018). *Distributed models for grid extension could save African utilities billions of dollars*. Green Tech Media, June 2018.

Falchetta, G., Pachauri, S., Parkinson, S., Byers, E. (2019a). *A High-Resolution Gridded Dataset to Assess Electrification in Sub-Saharan Africa*, Nature, July 2019.

Falchetta, G., Noussan, M. (2019b). Interannual variation in night-time light radiance predicts changes in national electricity consumption conditional on income-level and region. *Energies*, December, 2019.

Nygaard, I., Dafrallah, T. (2016). Utility led rural electrification in morocco: combining grid extension, mini-grids, and solar home systems. *Wiley Interdisciplinary Reviews: Energy and Environment*, 5(2), 155–168, https://doi.org/10.1002/wene.165.

Qayyum, S. (2017), *Microfinance and energy access*. Published on November 5, 2017, Retrieved September 19, 2020, from https://saadiaqayyum.wordpress.com/2017/11/05/microfinance-and-energy-access/.

SEforAll. (2020). *Access to electricity (% of population)*, database from the SE4ALL Global Tracking Framework, World Bank Group, International Energy Agency, Energy Sector Management Assistance Program, Retrieved September 27, 2020, from https://data.worldbank.org/indicator/EG.ELC.ACCS.ZS?end=2018&locations=IN&start=1990&view=chart.

WB. (2015). *Bringing electricity to Kenya's slums: hard lessons lead to great gains*. World Bank Group, August 20, 2015, Retrieved September 25, 2020, from https://www.worldbank.org/en/news/feature/2015/08/17/bringing-electricity-to-kenyas-slums-hard-lessons-lead-to-great-gains.

Open Access This chapter is licensed under the terms of the Creative Commons Attribution 4.0 International License (http://creativecommons.org/licenses/by/4.0/), which permits use, sharing, adaptation, distribution and reproduction in any medium or format, as long as you give appropriate credit to the original author(s) and the source, provide a link to the Creative Commons license and indicate if changes were made.

The images or other third party material in this chapter are included in the chapter's Creative Commons license, unless indicated otherwise in a credit line to the material. If material is not included in the chapter's Creative Commons license and your intended use is not permitted by statutory regulation or exceeds the permitted use, you will need to obtain permission directly from the copyright holder.

Chapter 9
The Role of Multilateral Agencies and Development Banks

This chapter concentrates on multilateral and development agencies, either located in Africa or pursing activities in the continent. The main objective is to understand what are their role in the financing of clean energy access in sub-Saharan Africa.

The chapter primarily targets professionals collaborating with development agencies as well as public administrations of the countries involved in their management.

It starts by presenting the inclusion of environmental considerations within those agencies, in addition to the historical objective to address social concerns as well as market failures. Moreover, this chapter aims at going beyond direct investments made by those institutions. Even though direct investments are crucial to bridge the financing gap associated with clean energy access, complementary solutions are needed to attract private capital at scale in this sector. Thanks to their international network and reputation, multilateral and development agencies have the potential to play an important role in this crucial development matter. Therefore, additional solutions are explored, such as advisory services and technical assistance (targeting public agencies, project developers and capital providers), stakeholder engagement, as well as mobilization tools to attract private financial actors.

Finally, this chapter ends with a proposal of business model evolution for multilateral and development agencies, including (i) the integration of complementary activities to attract private capital, (ii) the support of the creation of an enabling business and investment environment, and (iii) the mitigation of potential associated barriers to implementation.

Multilateral agencies and development banks are national, bi- and multilateral development institutions whose original mission is to spur economic development and alleviate poverty, by providing advisory services, technical assistance and funding to the public and private sectors.

In the past decades, many multilateral agencies and development banks have started to link social and economic objectives with sustainability and environmental concerns. Indeed, several institutions announced their willingness to stop or limit their financing in coal, oil and gas projects, align their activities with the Paris Agreement and back initiatives with beneficial impact on the climate and the environment (Boston University et al., 2020).

The involvement of multilateral agencies and development banks in clean energy initiatives may increase confidence among investors thanks to their reputation and credibility as well as regional presence and extensive experience. Moreover, their assistance to member countries allows senior claims on public authorities and a high level of influence. Accordingly, they have a critical role to play in the financing of the access to clean energy in sub-Saharan Africa and are uniquely positioned to pave the way for the private sector.

In order to tackle the energy access challenge across the region, multilateral agencies and development banks have different means of action at their disposal as follows:

- Capacity building and technical assistance
- Direct investments
- Mobilisation tools
- Stakeholder engagement and management.

9.1 Capacity Building, Technical Assistance and Advisory Services

9.1.1 Public Sector

Those services can target various public actors, including policymakers, regulators, rural energy agencies and public financial institutions. They aim at assisting public authorities in creating an enabling business climate for clean energy initiatives, by lowering market and financial barriers that prevent private investments.

Multilateral agencies and development banks can support governments in establishing political stability as well as clear policies and regulations, harmonised with national energy roadmaps. They may also provide assistance in the design and implementation of cost-effective and socially beneficial public measures and help phase out counterproductive instruments such as fossil fuel subsidies. Through the expertise of multilateral agencies and development banks, public authorities can elaborate stable and clear legal and regulatory frameworks, with a long-term vision and ambitious targets, tailored to country-specific challenges and opportunities.

Moreover, multilateral agencies and development banks can assist governments in overcoming the governance gap as well as in improving management capabilities and technical skills in state-owned companies such as public power utilities. Furthermore, they may participate in the design of bidding mechanisms as well as the development of pipeline facilities and project evaluation tools, in order to foster funding processes and financial closure.

9.1.2 Project Developers

Multilateral agencies and development banks can support project developers in activities such as feasibility studies, procurement processes, financial structuring and due diligence preparation, as well as economic, social and environmental impact assessment. Moreover, they may assist promising projects in the participation of tendering and bidding processes. This increases the availability of high-quality and investment-ready projects and helps establishing dynamic and competitive industries.

9.1.3 Financial Institutions and Capital Providers

Multilateral agencies and development banks can also provide technical assistance to private and public investors in order to increase their willingness and capacities to invest in the clean energy sector. They can raise awareness regarding financial mechanisms, deal structuring and risk assessment tools aimed at fostering investments in specific projects and companies. Finally, they can support local currency financing, by facilitating access to affordable capital for public and private domestic financial institutions and providing cross-currency swap[1] to country members.

9.2 Direct Investments

Compared to other financial institutions, multilateral agencies and development banks have a different attitude regarding investments as they are expected to be profitable but without the necessity to adopt a profit-maximising approach. Moreover, they face less financial and regulatory restrictions than other commercially oriented investors, allowing more flexibility as well as longer investment horizons. Nevertheless, their investing activities are constrained by the importance of maintaining a high credit rating, primordial to ensure credibility and gain access to affordable capital on international financial markets.

---

[1] Money provided without exchange risk for a predefined period of time to members.

Direct investments realised by multilateral agencies and development banks should have the objective to improve the competitiveness and attractiveness of clean energy initiatives that are beyond private investors' risk appetites. In addition, the allocation of capital shall be strategic and targeted towards underinvested sectors and specific development stages, such as emerging technologies, greenfield projects or power transmission and distribution activities.

Because their financial resources are limited, investment activities of multilateral agencies and development banks should not enter in competition with the private sector nor overcompensate for the risks taken. They might even disengage when investment opportunities are mature enough, in order to free up their resources and avoid crowding out private capital. Accordingly, it is important to determinate whether an investment opportunity requires public, private or blended financing, ensuring the most effective use of the available capital.

By providing financing to clean energy initiatives, multilateral agencies and development banks reinforce the confidence of investors and contribute to the building of a solid track record of successful projects with improved risk-reward profiles. As such, they offer the opportunity to catalyse private capital in key sectors providing positive externalities and help meet investors' requirements.

In addition, multilateral agencies and development banks can create attractive investment opportunities for investors that are reluctant to take on construction and development risks or be the first movers into new and unmatured markets, by investing at early development stages. This may support the mobilisation of capital coming from institutional investors, being typically large-scale and risk-adverse capital providers.

Multilateral agencies and development banks use a broad range of financial instruments and structures, such as concessional financing,[2] equity investing, traditional loans and green bonds, as well as special-purpose investment vehicles, credit lines and liquidity facilities. In addition, they often make use of blended finance and risk-sharing mechanisms like syndicated loans, in which they may act as lead investor to reinforce confidence and increase private involvement.

9.3 Mobilisation Tools

In addition to investing activities, multilateral agencies and development banks are increasingly using other mechanisms to improve the attractiveness of investment opportunities and mobilise private capital.

Mainly through to their close relations with governments of member's countries, multilateral agencies and development banks have a competitive advantage in covering certain risks and are therefore uniquely positioned to provide guarantee instruments. In particular but without limitation, they can cover political, credit and

---

[2] Including grants, subsidies, soft loans, first loss-capital, junior/subordinated debt.

counterparty risks when public authorities do not own the necessary resources and/or credibility to do so, thus improving investors' confidence.

Regarding the currency risk, the private sector may be reluctant to provide mechanisms to hedge less-traded currencies. Multilateral agencies and development banks can fill this gap by fostering local financing[3] and establishing foreign exchange liquidity facilities to address the high-cost issue related to hedging instruments.

As an example, the Currency Exchange Fund (TCX[4]) was created in 2007 to offer solutions to manage currency risk in developing and frontier markets. It consists of financial mechanisms (swaps and forward contracts) enabling TCX's investors to provide loan financing in over 70 currencies, shifting the foreign exchange risk to the fund. Capital providers are, thus, protected from currency volatility. This initiative was funded mainly by multilateral agencies and development banks and aims at providing access to currency protection to a wider range of market participants (GOGLA, n.d.).

Moreover, multilateral agencies and development banks can support the development of local capital markets in order to facilitate the use of secondary financial markets, derivative products and green bonds. Additionally, they can work closely with the banking sector to expand the range of available financial products and risk mitigation tools emanating from private actors, as well as build an inclusive financial sector fostering access to affordable capital for consumers and enterprises.

Finally, their local presence and in-house expertise provide multilateral agencies and development banks with a comprehensive understanding of the investment environment. Thus, it offers the possibility to develop new and tailored risk mitigation tools targeting unaddressed investment barriers. This task requires consultation and engagement of all relevant stakeholders involved in the clean energy access challenge.

9.4 Stakeholder Engagement and Management

In order to take adequate actions and respond to the needs of different private and public actors, it is important to increase cooperation and dialogue among stakeholders. Thanks to their intensive network and understanding of the sub-Saharan African energy access challenge, multilateral agencies and development banks can ensure coordination and strengthen relationships between parties. In addition, they may increase the commitment of core stakeholders to national energy strategies and stimulate their participation in addressing development concerns.

Moreover, multilateral agencies and development banks can share relevant information and best practices with market players, increasing awareness on risk mitigation tools and supporting better-informed investment decisions.

Finally, multilateral agencies and development banks are well-positioned to promote project bundling, cross-border collaboration and the integration of regional

---

[3]Using for instance non-performance buyout and third-party collateralisation.
[4]For more information: https://www.tcxfund.com/about-the-fund/.

power markets, thus allowing economies of scale as well as facilitating access to international finance and risk mitigation mechanisms.

9.5 Business Model Evolution

The role multilateral agencies and development banks is evolving, shifting from a focus on grant-based development assistance to an approach driven by private sector development and involvement. In addition, those institutions have to ensure that collaboration is strengthened and their activities are not distorting markets and/or competing with other key stakeholders.

Traditionally, multilateral agencies and development banks have focused on addressing market failures and providing capital to projects, enterprises and financial intermediaries. In order to achieve SDG 7, more actions to mobilise private investments as well as an increasing presence in riskier markets are required, without compromising financial viability. Accordingly, an extension of multilateral agencies and development banks' focus is needed to address investment barriers and foster the allocation of funds towards the greatest economic, social and environmental challenges of our time, such as energy poverty. A new approach needs to be adopted, allowing the adaptation to new and risker contexts as well as complementing activities of other market participants.

Multilateral agencies and development banks need to use their resources to create an attractive investment environment for private capital. This requires a transition towards a wider use of risk mitigation and mobilisation tools, effective collaboration with public and private players, as well as stronger support to capacity building and the development of financial markets.

To effectively do so, multilateral agencies and development banks need to

- Understand what hampers capital allocation in the clean energy sector
- Align action with countries' targets, needs and programs
- Raise awareness around mobilisation tools, internally and externally.

Moreover, a different allocation of multilateral agencies and development banks' resources necessitates a reorientation of their internal culture, by increasing awareness and building capacity around mobilisation and risk mitigation tools. It does not mean those institutions should stop direct financing, but rather continue investing activities in sectors in which private capital is not available, while expanding actions aimed at creating an attractive business environment.

However, such changes do not come overnight and may face the following implementation barriers:

- Cultural biases against risk mitigation actions as well as engagement with the private sector.
- Donors' interests are dominating operations and might not be aligned with a reorientation of activities.
- Risk mitigation tools generate generally less revenues than direct investments.

9.5 Business Model Evolution

Table 9.1 Differences and complementarities between development and commercial finance

Development finance	Commercial finance
Development mandate	Commercial mandate
Longer-term lending	Shorter-term lending
Profit seeking	Profit maximising
Economic rates of return	Financial rates of return
Public–private partnerships	Public–private partnerships
Capacity building	–
Project preparation	–

Source Authors' elaboration, based on Boston University et al. (2020)

Part of those issues is related to internal incentives. Indeed, investment teams within multilateral agencies and development banks are sometimes rewarded based on the amount of money invested, rather than on the impact generated. In addition, some pressure exists to maintain high credit rating.

In order to overcome those challenges, multilateral agencies and development banks need innovative financial structures such as special-purpose vehicles (SPVs) where risk is contained and separated from originators. Moreover, they need to improve the measurement and transparency of their direct and indirect impacts and ensure that the development results are not double counted. Finally, new benchmarks, metrics and key performance indicators (KPIs) are needed to engage the entire internal workforce.

Table 9.1 presents the main differences and complementarities between development and commercial finance.

References

Boston University, University of Pretoria, The Southern Africa Development Community Development Finance Resource Center, The Development Bank of Southern Africa. (2020). *Expanding renewable energy for access and development: The role of development finance institutions in Southern Africa*, 2020. Global Development Policy Center, Boston University

GOGLA. (n.d.). *The currency exchange fund (TCX)*. Retrieved September 27, 2020, from https://www.gogla.org/about-us/members/the-currency-exchange-fund-tcx

Open Access This chapter is licensed under the terms of the Creative Commons Attribution 4.0 International License (http://creativecommons.org/licenses/by/4.0/), which permits use, sharing, adaptation, distribution and reproduction in any medium or format, as long as you give appropriate credit to the original author(s) and the source, provide a link to the Creative Commons license and indicate if changes were made.

The images or other third party material in this chapter are included in the chapter's Creative Commons license, unless indicated otherwise in a credit line to the material. If material is not included in the chapter's Creative Commons license and your intended use is not permitted by statutory regulation or exceeds the permitted use, you will need to obtain permission directly from the copyright holder.

Chapter 10
Conclusions and Policy Recommendations

The first chapter of this book presented the energy access challenge in sub-Saharan Africa and the negative consequences that energy poverty has on populations and the environment across the region. In order to tackle this pressing development concern, technical solutions exist, adapted to urban and rural zones of the continent. However, substantial financial investments are needed to allow their deployment.

The second chapter presented different investment opportunities for capital providers within the power and clean cooking sectors, including the drivers behind those energy solutions and the associated investment risks. These risks were classified into four distinct categories: (i) economic and financial factors, (ii) overall country situation, (iii) business environment and (iv) environmental and social considerations. In addition, core stakeholders, which can directly or indirectly influence investors' risk perception, were identified and described.

This comprehensive mapping of investment risks and key stakeholders led the analysis to the second part of this book, namely the definition of risk mitigation strategies and innovative financing schemes, available to the public and private spheres. Those mechanisms and initiatives have the following objectives: (i) foster capital allocation in projects and organisations aimed at addressing the clean energy access challenge in sub-Saharan Africa, (ii) mobilise private investments and (iii) decrease the cost of financing in the power and clean cooking sectors across the region.

This book did not focus on specific countries. Accordingly, its final objective was not the selection of an adequate set of tools able to redirect capital allocation in clean energy solutions in a particular country. However, it provided a general overview of public and private strategies able to improve the attractiveness and competitiveness of the selected clean energy initiatives. This toolbox of public and private actions considered in this book was classified into four distinct spheres of interest: (i) public policies and initiatives, (ii) public financial and fiscal mechanisms, (iii) private financial structures and mechanisms and (iv) private initiatives.

In addition, this book included important concerns that may inhibit the deployment of public and private risk mitigation strategies. First, it described approaches to overcome political economy considerations in the implementation of targeted public policies and initiatives. Second, it underlined the necessity to develop capital markets in sub-Saharan Africa, crucial for the use of several financial mechanisms presented here.

Finally, the last chapter emphasised the role of multilateral agencies and development banks in the clean energy access challenge in sub-Saharan Africa. In particular, it focused on an efficient use of their limited resources in order to leverage private capital in the clean energy sector, thus increasing the utilisation of mobilisation tools, technical assistance and stakeholder engagement, alongside direct investing activities.

The various investment barriers mentioned above are interrelated and simultaneous. Indeed, their combined effect strongly influences the financing of clean energy access solutions in sub-Saharan Africa. Therefore, when developing energy strategies, the public sphere, including policymakers and international public institutions, has to consider the overall situation in order to design and implement integrated mechanisms, rather than isolated schemes. Hence, public actions need to be interconnected and complementary to each other.

Accordingly, the public sector, both domestic and international, shall focus simultaneously on three distinct areas of work when addressing the clean energy access challenge in sub-Saharan Africa:

1. The creation of an enabling investment and business environment
2. The improvement of risk-reward profiles
3. The mobilisation of private capital.

10.1 Creating an Enabling Investment and Business Environment

As previously highlighted, the region is perceived as highly risky by the private sector. This does not only apply to the energy sector, but to the entire economy. Thus, an adequate business and investment climate needs to be created and maintained in order to attract high-quality project developers and mobilise private capital at scale.

- Formulation and communication of a national energy masterplan

Acting as overall guidelines, national energy strategies are the first step for any government addressing energy-related challenges, allowing to define the vision for the country's future. They should include nationwide energy objectives, complemented by specific time frames as well as the role clean resources are expected to play in the energy pathway.

From the perspective of private players, setting-up clear, transparent and coherent targets is central. Moreover, it creates the basis to subsequently design targeted measures and mechanisms in order to achieve energy objectives. Furthermore, it allows to monitor energy objectives as well as to assess the effectiveness and efficiency of public actions.

10.1 Creating an Enabling Investment and Business Environment

By showing political commitment and determination, governments send a strong message to the private sector and to the civil society, related to the direction public authorities are taking for the national energy journey. A declaration establishing specific energy targets also gives the opportunity to define a social contract and articulate how those goals can contribute to the sustainable socio-economic development of the country.

In addition, the energy access challenge must be integrated in national energy strategies, including centralised and decentralised power systems as well as clean cooking solutions. The latter is too often considered as a second-level priority, even though universal access to clean and efficient cook stoves would bring an enormous positive social and environmental impact in the region. Furthermore, rural electrification plans have to be clearly formulated, mentioning the technologies as well as energy resources used in different areas. They should represent a central part of national energy masterplans.

Several public actions must be taken to achieve universal energy access in sub-Saharan Africa, including but not limited to: mainstreaming decentralised power systems and clean cooking solutions in national energy strategies; elaborate and implement specific regulations and policies as well as fiscal and financial support mechanisms dedicated to all technical solutions and geographical areas.

- Mitigation of country risk

National governments must mitigate investment barriers linked to the overall country situation for capital providers and project developers. Specific reforms need to be implemented at the country level, including anti-corruption measures as well as sound management and governance practices. Public authorities must also strengthen law enforcement within their respective territories and increase disclosure and transparency.

Additionally, by streamlining administrative requirements, decreasing bureaucratic burdens and creating pipeline facilities, the public sector can largely reduce the barriers to entry in the energy sector and facilitate access to the market. Moreover, one-stop-shops, representing public authorities and dedicated to the supervision of the energy industry, will increase the overall efficiency of the industry and foster the implementation of clean energy initiatives. They should be accessible in urban as well as rural zones, in order to assist in the execution of administrative tasks as well as ease the functioning to public mechanisms.

Moreover, power utility reforms must be aligned with national energy strategies, be committed to the clean energy access challenge and include targeted actions to strengthen the financial position of state-owned utilities. In addition, concerns related to the access to the national electric grid have to be considered, in order to send a clear message to potential market participants.

Considering the complexity and extensiveness of the country risk in many developing and emerging economies, mitigation without external support is usually complicated. Therefore, the international community should be actively involved, proposing risk mitigation instruments such as political risk guarantees, as well as developing targeted initiatives aimed at decreasing the risk perception of private stakeholders.

- Encouragement of international cooperation

Public authorities can also contribute to the development of an enabling investment and business environment through international and mutually beneficial collaboration, within and outside the sub-Saharan African region.

International cooperation enhances the transfer of technologies and knowledge between countries. Moreover, it has the potential to improve the perception of the overall country situation as well as to reinforce investors' confidence.

In addition, through collaboration with nearby states, properly functioning regional power market pools should be created to increase the efficiency of the sector and allow the provision of electricity at lower tariffs, thus making power affordable and accessible to a wider part of the population.

10.2 Improvement of Risk-Reward Profiles of Investment Opportunities

In addition to an enabling investment and business climate, the attractiveness of clean energy initiatives needs to be improved to leverage private capital at scale in sub-Saharan Africa. Two non-mutually exclusive options are available: (i) increasing expected financial returns and (ii) reducing risk perception.

- Measures adapted to local contexts and energy objectives

To that end, the public sphere has a broad set of tools at its disposal. Each scheme presents advantages and disadvantages. Furthermore, the selection process of the most efficient and cost-effective mechanisms has to consider social and cultural circumstances as well as local opportunities and challenges associated with the domestic energy market. In addition, they should be aligned with national energy objectives.

- Encourage the use of risk mitigation tools

Moreover, public actors are uniquely positioned to incentivise the utilisation of specific risk mitigation tools adapted to the clean energy sector. Indeed, the use of risk mitigation tools for clean energy is still low compared to other industries, with some exception such as off-balance sheet financing for large-scale power generation plants.

In addition, governments as well as multilateral agencies and development banks have to support the creation of new and innovative structures, tailored to small- and medium-scale energy investments. In particular, few strategies and mechanisms

10.2 Improvement of Risk-Reward Profiles of Investment Opportunities

aimed at mitigating the currency and liquidity risks in the clean cooking and decentralised power sectors exist. However, their impact would be huge. Thus, the public sector should fill this gap.

- Avoid market distortion

Moreover, several policies currently in place in many emerging and industrialised economies are distorting markets as well as negatively affecting the competitiveness of clean energy solutions. Indeed, public subsidies in sub-Saharan Africa should be progressively shifted away from polluting fossil fuels and redirected towards cleaner alternatives.

Furthermore, targeted subsidy schemes should be developed, in order to support the poorest segments of the population and avoid over-consumption of energy by better-off households. Besides, any subsidy reform has to be completed by additional measures aimed at compensating poor individuals for whom energy expenses generally represent a significant part of their incomes.

10.3 Deployment of Mechanisms Aimed at Catalysing Private Capital

Even though public financial resources are crucial to bridge the energy access gap in sub-Saharan Africa, private investments are strongly needed, first because of limited public finance availability and second to avoid unsustainable debt to GDP ratios. Therefore, the public sector needs to use part of its resources to attract private capital providers, commercially oriented and not, local and international.

- Mobilisation of international financial resources

Financial resources can be made available by industrialised countries through various channels:

First, multilateral and development agencies as well as public climate funds have a central role to play in the financing of clean energy access in sub-Saharan Africa. Apart from directly investing in clean energy activities using money coming from tax payers and donors, those public institutions may increase their utilisation of mobilisation tools (guarantee instruments, currency hedging, development of local capital markets, fostering local financing, ...) in order to leverage private capital. As explained in Chap. 9, some internal and cultural changes (increased awareness, internal capacity building and incentives, improved impact assessment and KPIs, ...) may be required to incentivise an effective use of the limited resources.

Second, international carbon markets present an interesting opportunity to mobilise private capital from emitters based in industrialised economies. Public authorities have the potential to foster the use of carbon finance within their territories, by supporting promising projects able to fulfil all the requirements of international carbon market mechanisms.

- Development of domestic capital markets

In addition, the public sector has to help develop capital markets in the sub-Saharan African region, in order to increase the flow of capital in the clean energy sector, provide more visibility, as well as improve the liquidity of the market. Moreover, capital markets are crucial for the use of certain financial mechanisms such as green bonds and offer more exit options for investors using equity-like instruments.

- Legal frameworks supporting innovative financial schemes

By encouraging the use of alternative and innovative financial instruments and/or mechanisms, the public sector can support tailored financing structures adapted to the needs of several clean energy initiatives as well as risk profiles of different capital providers. Yet, innovative financing schemes can be deployed at scale and used by market participants provided that adequate legal frameworks are built and implemented in sub-Saharan African countries.

- Support domestic financing

Domestic financing has to be developed and increased as it cancels the currency risk and allows the strengthening of the local financial sector. A significant amount of capital is available in sub-Saharan Africa. However, adequate frameworks need to be designed, and attractive investment opportunities should be available to local private capital providers.

In addition, the public sector has to support domestic financial institutions, by reinforcing capacity in investing in specific industries considered important for the development of the country, such as the energy sector. Moreover, multilateral agencies and development banks should use their high credit rating to access low-cost capital and put it at disposal of local financial institutions under certain conditions, through the use of on-lending structures.[1]

Open Access This chapter is licensed under the terms of the Creative Commons Attribution 4.0 International License (http://creativecommons.org/licenses/by/4.0/), which permits use, sharing, adaptation, distribution and reproduction in any medium or format, as long as you give appropriate credit to the original author(s) and the source, provide a link to the Creative Commons license and indicate if changes were made.

The images or other third party material in this chapter are included in the chapter's Creative Commons license, unless indicated otherwise in a credit line to the material. If material is not included in the chapter's Creative Commons license and your intended use is not permitted by statutory regulation or exceeds the permitted use, you will need to obtain permission directly from the copyright holder.

---

[1] Multilateral agencies and development institutions provide capital at lower cost to local banks and make it available for particular sectors, thus increasing the liquidity. This lower cost of capital can thus be on-lend to local projects and companies at lower rates than what was previously possible, without currency mismatch. For more details on on-lending structures, please refer to Chap. 7.

Chapter 11
Further Areas of Work

This book presented investment risks associated with the sub-Saharan African clean energy industry and an overview of risk mitigation strategies and innovative financing schemes available to public and private players, while focusing on the power and clean cooking sectors and specific energy resources.

Starting from this basis, we identified the following areas for future work:

- Quantification of investment risks

This book described specific investment risks linked to the power and clean cooking sectors. Even though they are all relevant in the sub-Saharan African context, some may be seen as critical by investors, while other may be considered as secondary. In addition, the risk perception may vary from one place to another.

Accordingly, a quantification of investment risks, from the perception of different capital providers and based on specific contexts, may help the public and private sectors effectively allocate their resources where most needed, in order to improve the risk-reward profiles of clean energy initiatives.

- Selection of risk mitigation actions and their impact on the cost of capital

It is important to take into consideration socio-economic and cultural factors to select and implement an effective and efficient set of tools aimed at mobilising affordable capital in the clean energy sector.

Accordingly, in-depth analysis for specific case studies should be realised at a country level, with the objective to define a tailor-made strategy for each country across sub-Saharan Africa. This may involve the consultation of all relevant stakeholders as well as including an analysis of where does the public money come from (taxpayers, national budget, international donations, etc.).

In addition, each analysis should include the impact of risk mitigation actions on the cost of capital. Here again, a specific research should be realised for each country, as the risk perception is context-dependent and may significantly vary from country to country.

- Sectors and energy resources

In order to foster the financing of a fair energy transition in sub-Saharan African countries, more sectors should be analysed, such as transportation, energy efficiency, heating and cooling.

Moreover, other interesting energy resources may be considered (i.e. nuclear power, advanced biofuels) that also have the potential to tackle the clean energy access challenge across the region and facilitate the transition towards a low-carbon economy.

- Subsidies

This book presented an outline of the opportunities and challenges associated with public subsides. However, further work on analysing the impact of (fossil fuel) subsidies as well as possible approaches to effectively implement subsidy reforms in developing and emerging economies may significantly improve the attractiveness of clean energy investments.

Open Access This chapter is licensed under the terms of the Creative Commons Attribution 4.0 International License (http://creativecommons.org/licenses/by/4.0/), which permits use, sharing, adaptation, distribution and reproduction in any medium or format, as long as you give appropriate credit to the original author(s) and the source, provide a link to the Creative Commons license and indicate if changes were made.

The images or other third party material in this chapter are included in the chapter's Creative Commons license, unless indicated otherwise in a credit line to the material. If material is not included in the chapter's Creative Commons license and your intended use is not permitted by statutory regulation or exceeds the permitted use, you will need to obtain permission directly from the copyright holder.

Chapter 12
Annex

12.1 Annex 1: Definition of the Tiers of the Multitier Framework (MTF) Initiative

Multitier matrix for access to household electricity

	Tier 0	Tier 1	Tier 2	Tier 3	Tier 4	Tier 5
Power capacity	–	Min 3 W	Min 50 W	Min 200 W	Min 800 W	Min 2 kW
AND daily capacity	–	Min 12 Wh	Min 200 Wh	Min 1 kWh	Min 3.4 kWh	Min 8.2 kWh
Services	–	Task lighting and phone charging	General lighting and phone charging and television and fan (if needed)	Tier 2 and any medium-power appliances	Tier 2 and any high-power appliances	Tier 2 and very high-power appliances
Duration (hours per day)	–	Min 4 h	Min 4 h	Min 8 h	Min 16 h	Min 23 h
Duration (hours per evening)	–	Min 1 h	Min 2 h	Min 3 h	Min 4 h	Min 4 h
Reliability	–	–	–	–	Max 14 disruptions per week	Max 3 disruptions per week of total duration < 2 h

Source Authors' elaboration, based on ESMAP (2015)

Multitier matrix for access to clean cooking solutions

	Tier 0	Tier 1	Tier 2	Tier 3	Tier 4	Tier 5
ISO's performance targets (default ventilation) PM2.5 (mg/MJ d)	>1030	Max 1030	Max 481	Max 218	Max 62	Max 5
ISO's performance targets (default ventilation) CO (g/MJ d)	>18.3	Max 18.3	Max 11.5	Max 7.2	Max 4.4	Max 3
Cookstove efficiency	Max 10%	>10%	>20%	>30%	>40%	>50%
Convenience—fuel acquisition and preparation time (h/week)	–	–	<7	<3	<1.5	<0.5
Convenience—stove preparation time (min/meal)	Min 15	Min 15	<15	<10	<5	<2

Source Authors' elaboration, based on ESMAP (2015)

12.2 Annex 2: Population With Access to Electricity and Clean Cooking In African Countries

Countries	Population with access to electricity (2019) (%)	Population with access to electricity—urban areas (2019) (%)	Population with access to electricity—rural areas (2019) (%)	Population with access to clean cooking (2018) (%)
Algeria	>99	>99	96.7	91.7
Egypt	>99	>99	>99	>95
Libya	>99	>99	>99	>95
Morocco	>99	>99	>99	>95
Tunisia	>99	>99	>99	>95
Cameroon	69.8	98.3	32.2	24.7
Central African Republic	3.1	6.6	<1	<5
Chad	8.5	32.3	1.2	6.6
Congo	71.9	89.1	36.6	26.4
DR Congo	8.7	19.0	<1	<5
Equatorial Guinea	66.7	74.8	45.2	36.5
Gabon	92.4	98.5	38.5	80.2
Burundi	10.9	66.2	2.3	<5
Djibouti	42.2	54.1	<1	12.7

(continued)

(continued)

Countries	Population with access to electricity (2019) (%)	Population with access to electricity—urban areas (2019) (%)	Population with access to electricity—rural areas (2019) (%)	Population with access to clean cooking (2018) (%)
Eritrea	46.5	95.0	13.2	17.6
Ethiopia	46.7	96.0	33.5	7.2
Kenya	84.5	>99	78.6	15.0
Rwanda	52.6	76.0	47.7	<5
Somalia	17.8	34.4	3.9	5.8
South Sudan	1.1	4.4	<1	<5
Sudan	47.3	71.0	34.5	45.5
Uganda	28.9	66.0	16.9	5.9
Nigeria	61.6	91.4	30.4	9.2
Benin	32.7	58.1	9.4	5.4
Côte d'Ivoire	76.0	>99	50.8	29.5
Ghana	85.0	93.0	74.5	24.9
Senegal	70.7	93.6	49.8	29.6
Togo	43.3	76.6	19.0	7.9
Burkina Faso	21.9	68.7	1.9	14.0
Cape Verde	96.1	>99	88.6	82.9
Gambia	48.6	68.9	15.6	10.7
Guinea	45.7	83.9	23.7	<5
Guinea-Bissau	28.2	55.7	6.8	5.1
Liberia	12.0	17.9	5.7	<5
Mali	49.6	78.0	28.0	<5
Mauritania	32.2	55.8	3.8	48.4
Niger	13.6	71.4	2.2	<5
Sao Tome and Principe	70.5	86.7	25.3	16.2
Sierra Leone	25.5	52.2	5.8	<5
Angola	42.5	61.0	6.2	49.9
Botswana	58.7	71.4	28.9	65.6
Comoros	69.5	88.8	61.5	12.1
Lesotho	36.2	62.7	25.6	36.6
Madagascar	38.7	64.4	23.1	<5
Malawi	13.4	54.7	4.8	<5
Mauritius	>99	>99	>99	92.9
Mozambique	34.9	57.0	22.1	6.3
Namibia	57.4	78.1	35.8	43.3

(continued)

(continued)

Countries	Population with access to electricity (2019) (%)	Population with access to electricity—urban areas (2019) (%)	Population with access to electricity—rural areas (2019) (%)	Population with access to clean cooking (2018) (%)
Seychelles	>99	99.0	>99	90.7
Eswatini	89.5	97.6	86.9	52.4
Tanzania	39.5	70.5	23.1	5.5
Zambia	37.2	76.3	6.3	17.1
Zimbabwe	53.1	88.8	36.2	30.7

Source Authors' elaboration, based on IEA (2020)

12.3 Annex 3: Risks Associated With Investment Opportunities and Stakeholders

Solar stand-alone systems

Risk group	Risk category	Sub-category	Description	Stakeholder group
Economic and financial	Currency risk	Exchange rate	Mismatch between revenues (collected in local currency) and financing expenses (paid in hard currency)	Macro risk, public authorities, multilateral agencies
		Currency convertibility	Government's restrictions that limit or remove the exchange of a local currency into other legal tenders	Public authorities
	Inflation	–	Gap between nominal and real financial returns	Macro risk
	Interest rate	–	Unexpected changes in the value of global interest rates	Macro risk

(continued)

12.3 Annex 3: Risks Associated With Investment Opportunities ... 157

(continued)

Risk group	Risk category	Sub-category	Description	Stakeholder group
	Liquidity risk	Default/bankruptcy	Inability to pay financial liabilities due to cash-flow constraints caused by important upfront costs, long negative cash-flow periods and/or bad cash-flow management	Project developers, private investors, public authorities, multilateral agencies
		Access to affordable capital	Capital scarcity, affordability of capital and underdeveloped local financial markets. No adequate financial instruments and ticket sizes. Limited experience or little willingness to invest in the clean energy sector	Project developers, private investors, public authorities, multilateral agencies
		Refinancing risk	Incapacity to replace a financial obligation by a new capital injection	Project developers, private investors, public authorities, multilateral agencies
		Lack or little exit strategies	In the context of equity-like financing, if no or few exit options are available to investors, they cannot recoup the invested amount neither generate financial returns	Private investors, public authorities, multilateral agencies

(continued)

(continued)

Risk group	Risk category	Sub-category	Description	Stakeholder group
Overall country situation	Political, legal and regulatory risk	Policies and regulations	Changes in policies and regulations affecting off-grid companies, weak procurement laws and lack of availability of technologies from domestic and international suppliers (not available or delays due to specific policies like custom restrictions and tariffs, no tailored technologies), limited access to the market due to specific regulations linked to technical requirements	Public authorities, multilateral agencies
		Political turmoil and instability	Uncertainties related to political instability and conflicts hindering businesses to operate normally	Macro risk, public authorities, multilateral agencies
		Bad governance	Cases of corruption and poor governance preventing proper project assignments and the development of a competitive market Lack of public commitment and uncertain support for the sector development	Public authorities
		Bureaucratic hurdles	Excessive bureaucracy, time-consuming procedures	Public authorities

(continued)

12.3 Annex 3: Risks Associated With Investment Opportunities ...

(continued)

Risk group	Risk category	Sub-category	Description	Stakeholder group
		Market distortion	Public financial incentives for alternatives such as fossil fuel subsidies	Public authorities
		State of the infrastructures	In the case of stand-alone systems, the state of roads for instance can affect distribution and after-sales services	Public authorities
	Lack of investment-ready project	–	Lack of high-quality pipeline for investors	Public authorities, multilateral agencies, project developers
Business environment	Customer risk	Lack of information	Limited or no data available regarding energy access, consumption and ability to pay (for energy products or services) of targeted customers	Public authorities, multilateral agencies, project developers
		Low demand	Low consumption of targeted customers preventing the selling of sufficient quantities to achieve financial viability	Project developers
		Affordability and ability to pay	Financial constraints preventing payments related to energy consumption Lack of financial channels (consumer finance, mobile money, microfinance institutions)	Public authorities, multilateral agencies, project developers, business partners

(continued)

(continued)

Risk group	Risk category	Sub-category	Description	Stakeholder group
		Willingness to pay	Dissatisfaction leading customers not to pay for a product or a service, thereby degrading reputation, customer retention and future acquisition	Project developers, public authorities
	Operational risk	Internal operations	Bad operation management causing sub-optimal performances	Project developers
		Workforce	Lack of skilled and qualified (potential) employees leading to low productivity and/or higher costs Financial management under expectations, leading to low creditworthiness affecting the ability to secure affordable financing at scale	Public authorities, multilateral agencies, project developers
		Stakeholder management	Lack of ability to properly manage relationships with directly and indirectly involved parties (public authorities, end-users, local communities), affecting operations	Project developers

(continued)

12.3 Annex 3: Risks Associated With Investment Opportunities … 161

(continued)

Risk group	Risk category	Sub-category	Description	Stakeholder group
		Complex business model	Distribution and after-sales services can be complex for operators due to long distances and locations difficult to reach Limited product range	Project developers, business partners
		End-of-life cycle management	Management of products and assets sold once their life cycle is over	Project developers
	Counterparty risk	Breach of contract	A business partner performing under contractual expectations	Project developers, business partners
		Unreliable data	Unreliable data leading to the development of unadapted business models	Public authorities
		Delays and bad performance, technological risk	Low quality of hardware Lack of warranties for components Delays impacting the overall performance of the company	Project developers, business partners
	Competitive risk	Direct competition	Decreasing market shares due to direct competitors	Project developers
		Alternatives	Alternatives available on the market used by potential customers (diesel, kerosene, etc.)	Public authorities, multilateral agencies, project developers
		Technological evolution	Company using obsolete technologies affecting the attractiveness of the value proposition	Project developers

(continued)

(continued)

Risk group	Risk category	Sub-category	Description	Stakeholder group
Social and environmental considerations	Climate risk	Climate conditions	Environmental disasters affecting the overall performance and maintenance of stand-alone systems (storms, impracticable roads, floods, etc.)	Macro risk, public authorities, multilateral agencies
	Social acceptance risk	Lack of awareness	Targeted community is unfamiliar with stand-alone systems and not well-informed on the advantages and disadvantages of their functioning	Public authorities, multilateral agencies, project developers, civil society, end-users

Source Authors' elaboration

Mini-grids

Risk group	Risk category	Sub-category	Description	Stakeholder group
Economic and financial	Currency risk	Exchange rate	Mismatch between revenues (collected in local currency) and financing expenses (paid in hard currency)	Macro risk, public authorities, multilateral agencies
		Currency convertibility	Government's restrictions that limit or remove the exchange of a local currency into other legal tenders	Public authorities
	Inflation	–	Gap between nominal and real financial returns	Macro risk
	Interest rate	–	Unexpected changes in the value of global interest rates	Macro risk

(continued)

12.3 Annex 3: Risks Associated With Investment Opportunities ... 163

(continued)

Risk group	Risk category	Sub-category	Description	Stakeholder group
	Liquidity risk	Default/bankruptcy	Inability to pay financial liabilities due to cash-flow constraints caused by important upfront costs, long negative cash-flow periods and/or bad cash-flow management	Project developers, private investors, public authorities, multilateral agencies
		Access to affordable capital	Capital scarcity, affordability of capital and underdeveloped local financial markets No adequate financial instruments and ticket sizes Limited experience or little willingness to invest in the clean energy sector	Project developers, private investors, public authorities, multilateral agencies
		Refinancing risk	Incapacity to replace a financial obligation by a new capital injection	Project developers, private investors, public authorities, multilateral agencies
		Lack or little exit strategies	In the context of equity-like financing, if no or few exit options are available to investors, they cannot recoup the invested amount neither generate financial returns	Private investors, public authorities, multilateral agencies

(continued)

(continued)

Risk group	Risk category	Sub-category	Description	Stakeholder group
Overall country situation	Political, legal and regulatory risk	Policies and regulations	Changes in policies and regulations affecting mini-grid operators, weak procurement laws and lack of availability of technologies from domestic and international suppliers (not available or delays due to specific policies like custom restrictions and tariffs, no tailored technologies), limited access to electrification market due to specific regulations linked to technical requirements and interconnection, asset confiscation legislation	Public authorities, multilateral agencies, grid operator
		Political turmoil and conflicts	Uncertainties related to political instability and conflicts hindering businesses to operate normally	Macro risk, public authorities, multilateral agencies
		Bad governance	Cases of corruption and poor governance preventing proper project assignments and the development of a competitive market Lack of public commitment and uncertain support for mini-grid development	Public authorities

(continued)

12.3 Annex 3: Risks Associated With Investment Opportunities … 165

(continued)

Risk group	Risk category	Sub-category	Description	Stakeholder group
		Bureaucratic hurdles	Excessive bureaucracy, time-consuming procedures	Public authorities
		Market distortion	Financial incentives for alternatives such as fossil fuel subsidies	Public authorities
		State of the infrastructures	In the case of mini-grids, the state of roads for instance can affect operation management	Public authorities
		Grid arrival	Unexpected and unplanned grid arrival before a complete amortisation of the mini-grid project Unclear energy planning policies	Public authorities
	Lack of investment-ready project	–	Lack of high-quality pipeline for investors	Public authorities, multilateral agencies, project developers
Business environment	Customer risk	Lack of information	Limited or no data available regarding energy access, consumption and ability to pay (for energy products or services) of targeted customers	Public authorities, multilateral agencies, project developers
		Low demand	Low consumption of targeted customers preventing the selling of sufficient quantities to achieve financial viability	Project developers

(continued)

(continued)

Risk group	Risk category	Sub-category	Description	Stakeholder group
		Affordability and ability to pay	Financial constraints preventing payments related to energy consumption Lack of financial channels (consumer finance, mobile money, microfinance institutions)	Public authorities, multilateral agencies, project developers, business partners
		Willingness to pay	Dissatisfaction leading customers not to pay for a service, thereby degrading reputation, customer retention and future acquisition	Project developers, public authorities
	Operational risk	Internal operations	Bad operation management causing sub-optimal performances	Project developers
		Workforce	Lack of skilled and qualified (potential) employees leading to low productivity and/or higher costs Financial management under expectations, leading to low creditworthiness and affecting the ability to secure affordable financing at scale	Public authorities, multilateral agencies, project developers

(continued)

12.3 Annex 3: Risks Associated With Investment Opportunities ... 167

(continued)

Risk group	Risk category	Sub-category	Description	Stakeholder group
		Stakeholder management	Lack of ability to properly manage relationships with directly and indirectly involved parties (public authorities, end-users, local communities), affecting operations	Project developers
		Complex business model	Installation, operations and maintenance can be complicated for mini-grid operators due to long distances and locations difficult to reach	Project developers
		End-of-life cycle management	Management of products and assets sold once their life cycle is over	Project developers
	Counterparty risk	Breach of contract	A business partner performing under contractual expectations	Project developers, business partners
		Unreliable data	Unreliable data leading to the development of unadapted business models	Public authorities
		Delays and bad performance	Low quality of hardware Lack of warranties for components Delays impacting the overall performance of mini-grids (during development, construction and/or operations)	Project developers, business partners
	Competitive risk	Direct competition	Decreasing market shares due to direct competitors	Project developers

(continued)

(continued)

Risk group	Risk category	Sub-category	Description	Stakeholder group
		Alternatives	Alternatives available on the market used by potential customers (diesel, kerosene)	Public authorities, multilateral agencies, project developers
		Technological evolution	Company using obsolete technologies affecting the attractiveness of the value proposition	Project developers
Social and environmental considerations	Climate risk	Climate conditions	Environmental disasters affecting the overall performance and maintenance of mini-grids (storms, impracticable roads, floods, etc.)	Macro risk, public authorities, multilateral agencies
		Resource scarcity	Climate conditions (droughts) can decrease the water flow affecting the overall performance when using hydropower	Macro risk, public authorities, multilateral agencies
	Social acceptance risk	Lack of awareness	Targeted community is unfamiliar with mini-grids' offerings and not well-informed on the advantages and disadvantages of their functioning	Public authorities, multilateral agencies, project developers, civil society, end-users
		Resource competition	When using hydropower, mini-grids can be in competition for the use of water resources with local communities	Public authorities, project developers

(continued)

12.3 Annex 3: Risks Associated With Investment Opportunities …

(continued)

Risk group	Risk category	Sub-category	Description	Stakeholder group
		Vandalism and resistance	External players (users, local communities, competitors, etc.) hindering the development and operations of mini-grids due to negative perceptions	Public authorities, multilateral agencies, project developers, civil society, end-users
		Illegal connections	Users consuming the electricity produced without paying, thereby implying a loss of profit for mini-grid operators	Public authorities, multilateral agencies, project developers, civil society, end-users

Source Authors' elaboration

Medium- and large-scale power generation plants

Risk group	Risk category	Sub-category	Description	Stakeholder group
Economic and financial	Currency risk	Exchange rate	Mismatch between revenues (collected in local currency) and financing expenses (paid in hard currency)	Macro risk, public authorities, multilateral agencies
		Currency convertibility	Government's restrictions that limit or remove the exchange of a local currency into other legal tenders	Public authorities
	Inflation	–	Gap between nominal and real financial returns	Macro risk
	Interest rate	–	Unexpected changes in the value of global interest rates	Macro risk

(continued)

(continued)

Risk group	Risk category	Sub-category	Description	Stakeholder group
	Liquidity risk	Default/bankruptcy	Inability to pay financial liabilities due to cash-flow constraints caused by important upfront costs, long negative cash-flow periods and/or bad cash-flow management	Project developers, private investors, public authorities, multilateral agencies
		Access to capital	Capital scarcity, affordability of capital, underdeveloped local financial markets No adequate financial instruments Limited experience in investing in power generation plants	Project developers, private investors, public authorities, multilateral agencies
		Refinancing risk	Incapacity to replace a financial obligation by a new capital injection	Project developers, private investors, public authorities, multilateral agencies

(continued)

12.3 Annex 3: Risks Associated With Investment Opportunities …

(continued)

Risk group	Risk category	Sub-category	Description	Stakeholder group
Overall country situation	Political, legal and regulatory risk	Policies and regulations	Changes in policies and regulations affecting power generation plants, weak procurement laws and lack of availability of technologies from domestic and international suppliers (not available or delays due to specific policies like custom restrictions and tariffs, no tailored technologies), limited access to the market due to regulations linked to technical requirements, limited liberalisation, asset confiscation legislation	Public authorities, multilateral agencies, grid operator
		Political turmoil and conflicts	Uncertainties related to political instability and conflicts hindering businesses to operate normally	Macro risk, public authorities, multilateral agencies
		Bad governance	Cases of corruption and poor governance preventing proper project assignments and competitive tendering procedures Lack of public commitment and uncertain support	Public authorities
		Bureaucratic hurdles	Excessive bureaucracy, time-consuming procedures	Public authorities

(continued)

(continued)

Risk group	Risk category	Sub-category	Description	Stakeholder group
		Market distortion	Financial incentives for alternatives such as fossil fuel subsidies	Public authorities
		State of the infrastructures	The state of roads but more specifically the national grid (transmission and distribution infrastructures) can affect operations and management Uncertainties in T&D construction planning	Public authorities
		International disputes	International concerns linked to the development of a power generation plant, affecting more than one country	Public authorities, multilateral agencies
		Grid interconnection	Uncertainties related to interconnection with the national grid Lack of standards and new technologies for the integration renewable resources	Public authorities, multilateral agencies, grid operator
	Lack of investment-ready project	–	Lack of high-quality pipeline for investors	Public authorities, multilateral agencies, project developers
Business environment	Operational risk	Internal operations	Bad management causing sub-optimal performances	Project developers

(continued)

12.3 Annex 3: Risks Associated With Investment Opportunities … 173

(continued)

Risk group	Risk category	Sub-category	Description	Stakeholder group
		Workforce	Lack of skilled and qualified (potential) employees leading to low productivity (during planning, construction and operations) and/or higher costs Financial management under expectations leading to low creditworthiness and affecting the ability to secure affordable financing at scale	Public authorities, multilateral agencies, project developers
		Stakeholder management	Lack of ability to properly manage relationships with directly and indirectly involved parties (public authorities, power off-taker, local communities, …), affecting operations	Project developers
		System interconnection	Ability to ensure interconnection with the national grid or the power off-taker	Project developers, public authorities, grid operators
		Decommissioning	Risks linked to the management of the decommissioning phase of a power generation plant	Project developers
	Counterparty risk	Breach of contract	Low creditworthiness of power off-taker Business partner performing under contractual expectation	Project developers, business partners, public authorities, multilateral agencies

(continued)

(continued)

Risk group	Risk category	Sub-category	Description	Stakeholder group
		Unreliable data	Unreliable information regarding prefeasibility studies (sun radiation, wind speed, water flow, etc.)	Public authorities, business partners
		Delays and bad performance	Bad governance and management procedures, Low quality of hardware Lack of warranties for components Delays impacting the overall performance (during development, construction and/or operations)	Project developers, business partners
		Fuel supply risk	In the case in which natural gas is used as fuel, lack of fuel stops operations and affects the overall performance Price increase	Project developers, business partners
	Competitive risk	Direct competition	Other developers proposing high-quality project	Project developers
		Alternatives	Alternatives available on the market (coal, oil)	Public authorities, project developers
		Technological evolution	Operator using obsolete technologies affecting the attractiveness of the value proposition	Project developers

(continued)

12.3 Annex 3: Risks Associated With Investment Opportunities ...

(continued)

Risk group	Risk category	Sub-category	Description	Stakeholder group
Social and environmental considerations	Climate risk	Climate conditions	Environmental disasters affecting the overall performance and maintenance of the plant (storms, impracticable roads, floods, etc.)	Macro risk, public authorities, multilateral agencies
		Resource scarcity	Climate conditions (droughts) can decrease the water flow affecting the overall performance when using hydropower	Macro risk, public authorities, multilateral agencies
		Pollution (natural gas)	Greenhouse gases emitted during the combustion of natural gas	Project developers
	Social acceptance risk	Lack of awareness	Targeted community is unfamiliar with clean energy resources and not well-informed on the advantages and disadvantages of their utilisation	Public authorities, multilateral agencies, project developers, civil society, end-users
		Resource competition	When using hydropower, power generation plants can be in competition for the use of water resources with communities	Public authorities, project developers
		Vandalism and resistance	External players hindering the development and operations of a power generation plant due to negative perceptions, NIMBY syndrome, special interest group	Public authorities, multilateral agencies, project developers, civil society, end-users

(continued)

(continued)

Risk group	Risk category	Sub-category	Description	Stakeholder group

Source Authors' elaboration

National grid

Risk group	Risk category	Sub-category	Description	Stakeholder group
Economic and financial	Currency risk	Exchange rate	Mismatch between revenues (collected in local currency) and financing expenses (paid in hard currency)	Macro risk, public authorities, multilateral agencies
		Currency convertibility	Government's restrictions that limit or remove the exchange of a local currency into other legal tenders	Public authorities
	Inflation	–	Gap between nominal and real financial returns	Macro risk
	Interest rate	–	Unexpected changes in the value of global interest rates	Macro risk
	Liquidity risk	Default/bankruptcy	Inability to pay financial liabilities due to cash-flow constraints caused by important upfront costs, long negative cash-flow periods, bad cash-flow management and/or low financial returns	Project developers, private investors, public authorities, multilateral agencies
		Access to capital	Capital scarcity Limited experience in investing in national grid upgrade and expansion	Public authorities, multilateral agencies

(continued)

12.3 Annex 3: Risks Associated With Investment Opportunities ...

(continued)

Risk group	Risk category	Sub-category	Description	Stakeholder group
		Refinancing risk	Incapacity to replace a financial obligation by a new capital injection	Project developers, private investors, public authorities, multilateral agencies
Overall country situation	Political, legal and regulatory risk	Policies and regulations	Weak procurement laws and lack of availability of technologies from domestic and international suppliers (not available or delays due to specific policies like custom restrictions and tariffs, no tailored technologies), limited liberalisation, asset confiscation legislation	Public authorities, multilateral agencies, grid operator
		Political turmoil and conflicts	Uncertainties related to political instability hindering normal operations	Macro risk, public authorities, multilateral agencies
		Bad governance	Cases of corruption preventing proper project assignments and competitive tenders Lack of public commitment and uncertain support	Public authorities
Business environment	Customer risk	Lack of information	Limited or no data available regarding energy access, consumption and ability to pay of targeted customer	Public authorities, multilateral agencies, project developers

(continued)

(continued)

Risk group	Risk category	Sub-category	Description	Stakeholder group
		Low demand	Low consumption of targeted customers preventing the selling of sufficient quantities to achieve financial viability	Project developers
		Affordability and ability to pay	Financial constraints preventing payments related to energy consumption	Public authorities, multilateral agencies, project developers
		Willingness to pay	Dissatisfaction leading customers not to pay for a product or a service, thereby degrading reputation, customer retention and future acquisition	Project developers
	Operational risk	Internal operations	Bad management causing sub-optimal performances	Project developers, grid operator
		Workforce	Lack of skilled and qualified (potential) employees leading to low productivity and/or higher costs Financial management under expectations leading to low creditworthiness and affecting the ability to secure affordable financing at scale	Public authorities, multilateral agencies, project developers
		Stakeholder management	Lack of ability to properly manage relationships with directly and indirectly involved parties (power generators, public authorities, local communities, ...), affecting operations	Project developers, grid operator

(continued)

12.3 Annex 3: Risks Associated With Investment Opportunities ...

(continued)

Risk group	Risk category	Sub-category	Description	Stakeholder group
		System interconnection	Ability to ensure interconnection with power generators, industries and households	Project developers, public authorities, grid operators
	Counterparty risk	Delays and bad performance	Low quality of hardware Lack of warranties for components Delays impacting the overall performance (during development, construction and/or operations)	Project developers, business partners
Social and environmental considerations	Climate risk	Climate conditions	Environmental disasters affecting the overall performance and maintenance of the grid (storms, floods, etc.)	Macro risk, public authorities, multilateral agencies
	Social acceptance risk	Vandalism and resistance	External players hindering the construction and operations of the national grid due to negative perceptions	Public authorities, multilateral agencies, project developers, civil society, end-users
		Illegal connections	Users consuming the electricity sold without paying, thereby involving a loss of profit for grid operators	Public authorities, multilateral agencies, project developers, civil society, end-users, grid operator

Source Authors' elaboration

Clean cooking systems

Risk group	Risk category	Sub-category	Description	Stakeholder group
Economic and financial	Currency risk	Exchange rate	Mismatch between revenues (collected in local currency) and financing expenses (paid in hard currency)	Macro risk, public authorities, multilateral agencies
		Currency convertibility	Government's restrictions that limit or remove the exchange of a local currency into other legal tenders	Public authorities
	Inflation	–	Gap between nominal and real financial returns	Macro risk
	Interest rate	–	Unexpected changes in the value of global interest rates	Macro risk
	Liquidity risk	Default/bankruptcy	Inability to pay financial liabilities due to cash-flow constraints caused by important upfront costs, long negative cash-flow periods and/or bad cash-flow management	Project developers, private investors, public authorities, multilateral agencies
		Access to affordable capital	Capital scarcity, affordability of capital and underdeveloped local financial markets No adequate financial instruments and ticket sizes Limited experience or little willingness to invest in the sector	Project developers, private investors, public authorities, multilateral agencies

(continued)

12.3 Annex 3: Risks Associated With Investment Opportunities … 181

(continued)

Risk group	Risk category	Sub-category	Description	Stakeholder group
		Refinancing risk	Incapacity to replace a financial obligation by a new capital injection	Project developers, private investors, public authorities, multilateral agencies
		Lack or little exit strategies	In the context of equity-like financing, if no or few exit options are available to investors, they cannot recoup the invested amount neither generate financial returns	Private investors, public authorities, multilateral agencies
Overall country situation	Political, legal and regulatory risk	Policies and regulations	Changes in policies and regulations affecting clean cooking companies, weak procurement laws and lack of availability of technologies from domestic and international suppliers (not available or delays due to specific policies like custom restrictions and tariffs, no tailored technologies), limited access to the market due to regulations linked to technical requirements	Public authorities, multilateral agencies
		Political turmoil and conflicts	Uncertainties related to political instability hindering normal operations	Macro risk, public authorities, multilateral agencies

(continued)

(continued)

Risk group	Risk category	Sub-category	Description	Stakeholder group
		Bad governance	Cases of corruption poor governance preventing proper project assignments and the development of a competitive market Lack of public commitment and uncertain support	Public authorities
		Bureaucratic hurdles	Excessive bureaucracy, time-consuming procedures	Public authorities
		Market distortion	Financial incentives for alternatives such as fossil fuel subsidies	Public authorities
		State of the infrastructures	In the case of clean cooking systems, the state of roads for instance can affect distribution and after-sales services	Public authorities
	Lack of investment-ready project		Lack of high-quality pipeline for investors	Public authorities, multilateral agencies, project developers
Business environment	Customer risk	Lack of information	Limited or no data available regarding energy access, consumption and ability to pay (for energy products or services) of targeted customers	Public authorities, multilateral agencies, project developers
		Low demand	Low consumption of targeted customers preventing the selling of sufficient quantities to achieve financial viability	Project developers

(continued)

12.3 Annex 3: Risks Associated With Investment Opportunities ... 183

(continued)

Risk group	Risk category	Sub-category	Description	Stakeholder group
		Affordability and ability to pay	Financial constraints preventing payments related to energy consumption Lack of financial channels (consumer finance, mobile money, microfinance institutions)	Public authorities, multilateral agencies, project developers, business partners
		Willingness to pay	Dissatisfaction leading customers not to pay for a product or a service, thereby degrading reputation, customer retention and future acquisition	Project developers, public authorities
	Operational risk	Internal operations	Bad operation management causing sub-optimal performances	Project developers
		Workforce	Lack of skilled and qualified (potential) employees leading to low productivity and/or higher costs Financial management under expectations, leading to low creditworthiness and affecting the ability to secure affordable financing at scale	Public authorities, multilateral agencies, project developers

(continued)

(continued)

Risk group	Risk category	Sub-category	Description	Stakeholder group
		Stakeholder management	Lack of ability to properly manage relationships with directly and indirectly involved parties (public authorities, end-users, local communities), affecting operations	Project developers
		Complex business model	Distribution and after-sales services can be complex for operators due to long distances and locations difficult to reach Limited product range	Project developers, business partners
		End-of-life cycle management	Management of products and assets sold once their life cycle is over	Project developers
	Counterparty risk	Breach of contract	A business partner performing under contractual expectations	Project developers, business partners
		Unreliable data	Unreliable data leading to the development of unadapted business models	Public authorities
		Delays and bad performance	Low quality of hardware Lack of warranties for components Delays impacting the overall performance (during development and/or operations)	Project developers, business partners

(continued)

12.3 Annex 3: Risks Associated With Investment Opportunities ...

(continued)

Risk group	Risk category	Sub-category	Description	Stakeholder group
		Fuel supply risk	Lack of fuel, LPG or biomass, making operations difficult and affecting the overall performance Price increase	Project developers, business partners
	Competitive risk	Direct competition	Decreasing market shares due to direct competitors	Project developers
		Alternatives	Alternatives available on the market used by potential customers	Public authorities, multilateral agencies, project developers
		Technological evolution	Company using obsolete technologies affecting the attractiveness of the value proposition	Project developers
Social and environmental considerations	Climate risk	Climate conditions	Environmental disasters affecting the overall performance and maintenance of clean cooking systems (storms, impracticable roads, floods, etc.)	Macro risk, public authorities, multilateral agencies
		Resource scarcity	Climate conditions (droughts) can affect biomass availability	Macro risk, public authorities, multilateral agencies
	Social acceptance risk	Lack of awareness	Targeted community is unfamiliar with clean cooking systems and not well-informed on the advantages and disadvantages of their functioning	Public authorities, multilateral agencies, project developers, civil society, end-users

(continued)

(continued)

Risk group	Risk category	Sub-category	Description	Stakeholder group
		Resource competition	When using biomass, clean cooking systems can be in competition for its use with local communities	Project developers

Source Authors' elaboration

12.4 Annex 4: De-risking Matrix

12.4 Annex 4: De-risking Matrix

Part I: Economic and financial risks

	Exchange rate	Currency convertibility	Default/bankruptcy	Access to capital	Refinancing	Lack of exit strategies	Inflation	Interest rate
Governance/management practices		X						
Standardisation/streamlined regulation				X				
Pipeline facilities				X				
Technical assistance/capacity building				X				
Awareness campaigns				X				
Tariff setting			X	X				
International coop. and partnerships		X						
Fiscal incentives			X	X				
Priority sector lending	X			X	X	X		
Direct investments			X	X	X	X		
Alternative fin. instru. and schemes[a]			X	X	X	X		
Subsidies			X	X				
Credit lines/on-lending structures	X		X	X	X	X		
Guarantees and insurance (public)		X	X	X	X		X	X
Hard currency PPAs	X							

(continued)

(continued)

	Exchange rate	Currency convertibility	Default/bankruptcy	Access to capital	Refinancing	Lack of exit strategies	Inflation	Interest rate
Concessional and patient capital			X	X	X			
Structure finance	X			X	X			
Project finance				X				
Loan syndication				X				
Green bonds				X				
Carbon finance				X				
Guarantees and insurance (private)		X	X				X	X
Derivative instruments (hedging)	X							
Internal liquidity facilities			X	X				
Payment defaults management			X					
Strategic agreements, M&A and investors				X				
Good governance and staff training				X				

[a]Public and private

12.4 Annex 4: De-risking Matrix

Part II: Country risks

	Policies and regul.	Political turmoil	Bad gov.	Bureaucrat. hurdles	Market distort.	State of infra	Interna. disputes	Grid arrival	Grid access	Lack of invest.-ready projects
Energy strategy and planning	X		X					X		
Governance/management practices		X	X	X						
Market information										X
Standards of quality				X						
Standardisation/streamlined regulation	X		X	X						X
Land rights and concessions	X		X	X				X		
Pipeline facilities										X
Technical assistance/capacity building										X
Awareness campaign	X		X		X					
Rural energy agencies	X		X	X						X
Grid arrival and access provisions								X	X	
Utility reform			X			X			X	
Tariff setting	X									
International coop. and partnerships		X	X				X			
Regional power pools			X			X	X			
Subsidy reform					X					

(continued)

(continued)

	Policies and regul.	Political turmoil	Bad gov.	Bureaucrat. hurdles	Market distort.	State of infra	Interna. disputes	Grid arrival	Grid access	Lack of invest.-ready projects
Guarantees and insurance[a]	X	X								
Stakeholder engagement/market knowledge	X		X							

[a]Public and private

12.4 Annex 4: De-risking Matrix

Part III: Business environment (first part)

	Lack of info.	Low demand	Affordability	Willingness to pay	Inter. procedures	Work force	Stakeh. mgmt	Complex business	System intercon.	Decomms-sioning	End-of-life cycle mgmt
Market information	X										
Standards of quality				X					X		
Technical assistance/capacity building					X	X	X	X	X		
Rural energy agencies	X										
Utility reform			X								
Tariff setting			X								
Regional power pools		X	X								
Fiscal incentives			X								
Alternative financial instruments			X								
Subsidies			X								
Concessional finance and patient capital			X								
Flexible payment methods		X	X	X							
Stakeholder engagement and market knowledge	X			X			X				

(continued)

(continued)

	Lack of info.	Low demand	Affordability	Willingness to pay	Inter. procedures	Work force	Stakeh. mgmt	Complex business	System intercon.	Decomms-sioning	End-of-life cycle mgmt
Strategic agreements, M&A and investors					X		X	X	X	X	X
Good governance and staff training					X	X		X		X	X
External consulting/technical assistance					X	X	X	X			

12.4 Annex 4: De-risking Matrix

Part IV: Business environment (second part)

	Breach of contract	Unreliable data from a third party	Delays and techno. issues	Fuel supply	Direct competition	Alternatives	Technological evolution
Energy strategy and planning						X	X
Governance/management practices	X						
Market information		X			X		X
Standards of quality		X	X				X
Standardisation/streamlined regulations						X	
Land rights and concessions		X			X	X	
Pipeline facilities						X	
Technical assistance/capacity building					X	X	X
Awareness campaign						X	
Rural energy agencies		X					
Grid arrival and access provisions		X				X	
Utility reform	X						
Tariff setting						X	
Regional power pools	X						
Fiscal incentives						X	
Subsidy reform						X	
Priority sector lending						X	

(continued)

(continued)

	Breach of contract	Unreliable data from a third party	Delays and techno. issues	Fuel supply	Direct competition	Alternatives	Technological evolution
Direct investments/special-purpose investment vehicles						X	
Subsidies						X	
Guarantees and insurance (public)	X	X	X				
Concessional finance and patient capital						X	
Project finance	X		X	X			
Green bonds						X	
Carbon finance						X	
Guarantees and insurance (private)	X	X	X	X			
Stakeholder engagement and market knowledge		X					
Strategic agreements, M&A and investors	X	X	X	X	X		
Good governance and staff training					X		

12.4 Annex 4: De-risking Matrix

Part V: Social and environmental risks

	Climate conditions	Resource scarcity	Pollution (natural gas)	Opposition and vested interest	Social awareness	Resource competition	Vandalism and resistance	Illegal connections
Energy strategy and planning				X				
Governance/management practices				X				
Market information	X					X		
Standards of quality		X		X	X			
Land rights and concessions				X				
Awareness campaign				X	X	X	X	X
Rural energy agencies						X		
Utility reform								X
Tariff setting				X			X	X
International coop. and partnerships		X		X		X		
Regional power pools	X	X		X				
Guarantees and insurance[a]	X	X						
Stakeholder engagement and market knowledge				X	X	X	X	X
Strategic agreements, M&A and investors				X				

[a]Public and private

Source Authors' elaboration

12.5 Annex 5: Carbon Tax and Emission Trading Systems (ETS)

Carbon tax	ETS
Price setting	Quantity setting
Estimation of public revenues facilitated	Difficult to estimate public revenues as prices are determined on a secondary market
Unknown emission reduction	Emission reduction determined by public authorities (cap)
Easier implementation[a]	More difficult to implement
Less prone to be manipulated by big market players	Risk of market concentration, price escalation and illiquid markets
Difficult to apply across borders	Can be applied across borders
No countercyclical response	Countercyclical response possible

[a]It can be implemented through existing infrastructures, entities and capacities, and no secondary market is needed. However, a tax can be easily rolled back by the next government as no allowance are hold as opposed to ETS

Source Authors' elaboration

12.6 Annex 6: MSCI Market Classification Framework and Requirements

Criteria	Frontier	Emerging	Developed
Economic development • Sustainability of economic development	No requirement	No requirement	Country GNI per capita 25% above the World Bank high income threshold[a] for 3 consecutive years
Size and liquidity requirements			
• Number of companies meeting the following criteria	2	3	5
• Company size (full market cap)[b]	$776 million	$1,551 million	$3,102 million
• Security size (float market cap)[b]	$61 million	$776 million	$1,551 million
• Security liquidity	2.5% ATVR	15% ATVR	20% ATVR
Market accessibility criteria			
• Openness to foreign ownership	At least some	Significant	Very high

(continued)

(continued)

Criteria	Frontier	Emerging	Developed
• Ease of capital inflows/outflows	At least partial	Significant	Very high
• Efficiency of operational framework	Modest	Good to tested	Very high
• Availability of investment instrument	High	High	Unrestricted
• Stability of the institutional framework	Modest	Modest	Very high

[a]High income threshold for 2018: GNI per capita of $12,056
[b]Minimum in use for the May 2019 Semi-Annual Index Review, updated on a semi-annual basis
Source Authors' elaboration, based on MSCI (2019)

References

ESMAP. (2015). *Beyond connections: Energy access redefined, energy sector management assistance program.* Technical report 008/15, August, 2015.

IEA. (2020). *SDG7: Data and projections.* International Energy Agency, Paris. https://www.iea.org/reports/sdg7-data-and-projections

MSCI. (2019). *MSCI market classification framework*, June, 2019. Available at https://www.msci.com/documents/1296102/1330218/MSCI_Global_Market_Framework_2019.pdf/57f021bc-a41b-f6a6-c482-8d4881b759bf

Open Access This book is licensed under the terms of the Creative Commons Attribution 4.0 International License (http://creativecommons.org/licenses/by/4.0/), which permits use, sharing, adaptation, distribution and reproduction in any medium or format, as long as you give appropriate credit to the original author(s) and the source, provide a link to the Creative Commons license and indicate if changes were made.

The images or other third party material in this book are included in the book's Creative Commons license, unless indicated otherwise in a credit line to the material. If material is not included in the book's Creative Commons license and your intended use is not permitted by statutory regulation or exceeds the permitted use, you will need to obtain permission directly from the copyright holder.

The manufacturer's authorised representative in the EU is Springer Nature Customer Service Centre GmbH, Europaplatz 3, 69115 Heidelberg, Germany. If you have any concerns regarding our products, please contact ProductSafety@springernature.com

Printed and bound by CPI Group (UK) Ltd, Croydon, CR0 4YY

23/03/2026

02076664-0004